Culture and Development
No. 4

General Editor
Kapila Vatsyayan

The Cultural Dimension of Ecology

UNESCO Chair in the field of Cultural Development

Indira Gandhi National Centre for the Arts

The Cultural Dimension of Ecology

Edited by
Baidyanath Saraswati

Indira Gandhi National Centre for the Arts
New Delhi

D.K. Printworld (P) Ltd.
New Delhi

Cataloging in Publication Data — DK

The cultural dimension of ecology/
edited by Baidyanath Saraswati.
(Culture and development; no.4).
Includes bibliographical references.

1. Human ecology — Congresses. I. Saraswati, Baidyanath, 1932- II. Series: Culture and development; no. 4.

ISBN 81-246-0102-X

First published in India, 1998

The views expressed in this volume are those of Participants, and are not necessarily those of Editors or the Publishers.

Publishers
Indira Gandhi National Centre for the Arts
Central Vista Mess, Janapath, New Delhi - 110001

D.K. Printworld (P) Ltd.
Regd. office: *'Sri Kunj'*, F-52, Bali Nagar, New Delhi - 110015

Printed at: DP's Impressive Impressions, New Delhi - 110059

Foreword

Kapila Vatsyayan

THE Indira Gandhi National Centre for the Arts (IGNCA) has been engaged for nearly a decade in exploring all dimensions of culture understood in its widest and deepest connotations. 'Culture' here is an all-encompassing and permeating attribute of human living. It penetrates the innermost recesses of the human psyche, individual and collective, as also permeates the social structure to give shape and form to an identifiable, but not easily definable, mode of behaviour, conduct and action. The vertical and the horizontal movements intersect to contain the inner experience and give rise to outer expressions. When they are held together in balance and harmony, cultures are cohesive and creative but not static; when balances are disturbed, then turmoil takes place often resulting in disruption of the flow of movements causing stultification of some aspects and disintegration of others.

The results of many of the lifestyle studies programme of the IGNCA and the series of conferences, seminars and workshops held under the UNESCO Chair for Cultural Development have amply borne out the primary importance of considering culture as an all-encompassing and permeating phenomenon for any future modelling of societies in a post-modern or even post-post-modern world. Each of the studies, seminars and the consequent monographs viz. *Interface of Cultural Identity and Development* (Culture and Development Series No. 1) or *Integration of Endogenous Cultural Dimension into Development* (Culture and Development Series No. 2) or *The Cultural Dimension of Education* (Culture and Development Series No. 3) have repeatedly underlined the need to view the universe and, of course, our earth and the human species as a closely interrelated organic system. Each constituent is part of a whole; the whole is not a mechanical aggregation of the parts. This is as true of the macro universe and the solar system as it is of microman (and microwoman), be it the elementary biological system of his body or mind or the social and economic systems he generates. Any disturbance in the acceleration or overdue emphasis on a single constituent or an attribute within a constituent results in the phenomenon of dominance and subordination and an unbalanced growth of one aspect at the cost of the other, whether in nature or culture. Eco-balances are the norm in Nature. So are they or should be in culture and of course between the two (if we concede for a moment that the two are differentiated categories always in interaction and dialogue).

The earlier monographs highlight the nature of this interaction between Man and Nature and the integral world-view of endogenous societies which viewed and continue to view Man (woman) as one life form amongst thousands of others in Nature. Man in Nature rather than Man in domination of Nature is the recurring theme of many of these studies and essays in the monographs. Of equal significance has been the realisation that the undue importance and dominating position given to the material progress of man has resulted in creating many disruptions and imbalances in human societies. Man's dominance over Nature and his unbridled exploitation of Nature to construct his world of material progress has brought the world to a situation where the very survival of the earth as a planet is threatened. Only lately has Man realised that intervention of Man without discipline and austerity has disturbed the ecobalances and the natural rhythm of change and readjustments of these systems.

The present monograph focusses on the eco-systems of the natural world and the contrasting world-views and social organisation systems which facilitated or disturbed these systems. In the prologue to the volume, John V. Kingston unequivocally draws attention to the dangers which humanity faces on account of the momentum which some seemingly irreversible forces have gathered: "After 2000 years of almost universal belief in scientific progress we are now seeing the price of the progress." He tells us, and one can only agree with him, that "we risk planetary destruction" unless technologies developed by man are used for sustaining and not disturbing the global environment. We know that despite the initiatives taken by UNESCO in the First Bio-sphere Conference held in 1968, the subsequent global conferences on environment held in Stockholm and Rio-de-Janeiro and elsewhere, the earth and all other primal elements, water, air and fire (energy) are threatened as never before. The pollution and the over-exploitation has disturbed the eco-systems to a point where all that sustains man at an elemental level is vulnerable and fragile. Can eco-balances be restored and re-instituted and if so what is the fundamental question? It is not a matter of correcting one when it surfaces e.g. ozone layer, global warming, land use, water management and air pollution or energy crisis. These are methods of curing symptoms of the disease but not addressing ourselves to the causes of the disease which has gripped humanity — a disease caused by the avarice of Man himself.

Not without reason while global conferences and specialists of science and technology try to find solutions on the basis of the applications of appropriate technologies and political leaders advocate equitable distribution of natural resources and restraint in the use of energy (fire), there are others who are convinced that the eco-balances can only be restored by the mind of Man. His (her) innermost recesses have to re-ignite the 'consciousness' (which the modern industrial world has put to comotose state) that the human species is an infinitesimally small part of a very large and extensive universe of life-forms. The special faculties given to him which have empowered him with astounding scientific knowledge and extraordinary technical knowledge and skills must not lead to the arrogance of assuming a supremely dominant role.

Understandably this group turns to re-learn lessons from those very societies and cultures of the human species where this consciousness was ingrained as a primary article of faith. The consciousness and awareness articulated itself in a body of poetry, oral and written, the evolution of a mythical world which drew attention repeatedly to the eco-system and interrelationships. A series of festivals, customs, and rituals served as a constant reminder. Naturally the notion of sacred space and time was essential for how else could earth, water, vegetation, air, rejuvenate themselves singly or together unless left fallow or undisturbed for a time. Mangroves, rivers, waterbodies, such as lakes and tanks; tracts of land were accorded a sacred status as a most effective strategy and instrumentality of ensuring non-pollution and purity to sustain eco-balances. The agricultural practices and other lifestyle functions were designed to accommodate the cycle of inactivity and activity, the latency and potency, of both the natural and the human world. There is massive literary and archaeological evidence to convince us of Man's subscription to such a world-view as is clear from Prof. Baidyanath Saraswati's Introduction. We also know that this world-view was overtaken in some parts of the world by another where Nature was considered "Red in tooth and claw". In that era, all that the Vedic seers evoked as the waters, earth, mountains, rivers, trees, animals, air and fire was considered pagan or at best pantheistic. Defying the forces of nature was to deity the supreme power of Man. Today we are perhaps wiser. Whether in the west or the east, the hymns of these seers in India and analogous verses from other cultures are universally quoted as the highest and most sophisticated articulations of the awareness of the perennial movements of the primal elements in interrelationship and peace; another word for maintaining eco and human balances. The Vedic hymns (both of *Yajurveda* and *Atharvaveda*) of Peace on earth are the most ecological sound hymns of invoking the coexistence of the primal elements and Man's consciousness (*Shantipath*).

And yet today the small cohesive societies are the only ones who live by the deep and penetrating perceptions and knowledge systems articulated by these seers. The intellectual social world created by Man which is recognised as the civilised world of India or elsewhere is not constructed on this basis. The living evidence is instead only in those groups or small cohesive societies whether in India or elsewhere in South-East Asia, East Asia, Australia, New Zealand, Africa, Latin America and even North America or Europe who are today the minority marginalised groups whose very survival is threatened. They are the most socio-economically deprived.

The essays in this volume bear testimony to this ironical situation of our times. P.S. Ramakrishna's essay on Ecology and Traditional Wisdom echoes the experience of many who embarked on a journey of reform but soon learnt:

> Land use for agriculture, fisheries and forestry, which forms the basis for the sustainable livelihood of traditional societies, is often based on traditional knowledge and technology, developed in a given ecological, socio-economic and cultural setting. Not only is this knowledge base being threatened now, but very often we have failed to provide an alternative viable technology as a replacement for what is being eroded. The reasons for this are varied and complex. Yet, in the context of the sustainable management of land resources, there is an increasing realisation of the value of this rich heritage, and therefore a renewed interest in traditional knowledge and technology.

He remarks that the distribution of these traditional societies closely corresponds to the hot spots of bio-diversity in the country. Particularly he concludes that:

> It is therefore most appropriate to look at a new paradigm for the sustainable development and management of natural resources in the areas where the tribals live — a new paradigm based on traditional wisdom and building upon that wisdom incrementally.

The traditional wisdom articulates itself, as in the past, in a mythological system which emerges out of the environment and the perception of the ecological system. This is convincingly demonstrated by Molly Kaushal's study of Gaddis. Specific elevations, peaks and the rivers correspond to a mythic world and life on earth is governed by the myths which sanctify the physical spaces. The migrations from one order of space to another is analogous to the movement of the deities. The interplay between the mythical and the actual revalidates both. The world-view is thus not an intellectual construct; it is the *raison d'être* of living. Little wonder that the primal elements within the micro-body and without in the environment are held 'sacred': water, earth, plants, animals, air, fire — all. From a progressive evolutionary standpoint the Gaddis represent the pre-sedentary stage and are thus considered less developed, even amongst the developing. From an ecologically valid perspective their world-view, cosmology, mythology and life function are totally integrated as a single whole. Attempts at bringing them and others like them into a single pattern of sedentary nonmythologised cultural style can be ruinous for them and the environment. However, alternate paradigm and acceptance of plural models as policies and strategies of planning are yet a far cry.

B.L. Malla's essay brings to the fore another related aspect of the acute recognition of the inter-relationship of the natural and human world as crystallised in the water cosmology of many cultures. His case study although restricted to Kashmir has wider ramifications. In many cosmologies the eternal waters, and the first forms of life as the reptiles, represent primary differentiation. The *nagas* (snakes) and the lakes coalesce to give rise to the many fascinating and ecologically significant myths surrounding the primary sources of rivers (*veninagas*) and the lakes (Wuler). If Siva in the Gaddis is the mountains as celestial space (*vastospati*), he is the keeper of animals of the terrestial world as *pasupati*. In contrast, Visnu rests on the *sesa* (*Naga*) in the eternal waters. This relationship of the waters and the mountain is sanctified in thousands of myths across this country and others. As long as man was constantly conscious of the intrinsic relationship of the waters and the mountain as celestial and glacial levels, he sanctified both and was hesitant to aggressively intervene. He knew that austerity and discipline such as that of the Bhagirath in the famous *Ganga* myth was required. The loss of the sense of the sanctified and sacred lead to greed and avarice. As in myth so in life the consequences were (in myth) and will be in life disastrous.

Another facet of the traditional knowledge systems closely related to the mythical is the affirmation of the principle of bio-diversity and therefore plural methods and techniques of agro-cultivation. Agro-pastoralism is an integrated system which accommodates diversification of crops and produce. It is in essence, as R.S. Negi points out, diversification of resource utilisation which in turn promotes trans-humane and cyclic mobility. This is one of the ways of preventing exhaustion of the fertility potential of cropland and promoting regeneration.

From different spatial situations of the Oraons on the one hand and the Warlis and the Dhangars on the other, we learn that these groups too subscribe to the principle of bio-diversity and plural strategies of sustaining nature and themselves. The close man-nature relationship has resulted in their developing a remarkable sensitivity to identify eco-indicators. The Oraons, the Warlis and the Dhangars and many others in their distinctive cultural lifestyle, tell us that culture and ecological perception, if not one and the same thing, are certainly interpenetrative categories difficult to dissect as autonomous entities. This is further supported by the case study of the Nicobar and Andaman and Nepal.

Other papers deal with recent developments in projects management of water and land, protection and conservation of forests, flora and fauna. Some have had negative and others positive effects. It is clear that the recognition of the extant knowledge systems and cultural lifestyle and their validity can be or has been more successful than total replacement or uprooting.

In sum, each of the essays in this volume and the field studies carried out by the young researchers of the IGNCA (e.g., Ramakar Pant, Nita Mathur, Rakesh Khanduri, K.K. Mishra, and Richa Negi) and others in the lifestyle studies programme, all point at the need to know, learn and apply these knowledge systems to our contemporary world.

The task is challenging. It is one matter to conduct studies and to deduce principles. It is quite another matter to ensure the transformation of the mindset and the deeply entrenched system of governance, policy-making, planning and most of all ground level implementation. It is heartening to note that the work of Ramakrishnan, Sachchidananda, Madhva Gadgil, Subhash Chandra and T.N. Pandit has been recognised. At the conceptual level it has been accepted; however transformation and restoration can only take place if these investigations lead to a re-orientation of the policies, programmes and institutional structures which so far in this country and elsewhere continue to adhere (alas!) to an earlier mechanist view of linear progressive development and replication of single mono models. Uniformity is not endemic to nature and deadening in life. Both, the world-view of Man as dominant and the consequent systems and the structures for organising life as pointed out by Kingston, have brought us to tread a perilous path. Danger lies ahead in the near future if lessons are not learnt. There are numerous anachronisms and disjunctures: all cause further disturbance in eco-balances. Man (woman) if he wills can restore the natural balance if he can heed and hear the voices of these disempowered small cohesive communities who are human repertories of the other knowledge systems so vital for the future of the earth and humanity.

Prologue

John V. Kingston

We already know what the 21st century will look like: it has been mapped out for us by seemingly irreversible forces. They are not necessarily bad in themselves, but they do hold a danger because no one can control them — and their effects seems to be gathering momentum. Populations are mushrooming, state agencies and free market players are becoming interdependent, and science and technology are taking giant strides.

After 2,000 years of almost universal belief in scientific progress, we are now seeing the price of this progress. The natural environment is being destroyed by the contradiction between technical and social advancement. We risk planetary destruction through the use of new technologies by countries that are philosophically or technically incapable of handling them.

The current concern over the deterioration of the global environment, for example, is a relatively recent phenomenon. One of the first meetings on this topic was sponsored by Unesco in 1968 as the 'Biosphere Conference'. Here, for more or less the first time in history, the international scientific community collectively told the governments of the world that the environment was in bad shape and getting worse. Previous international scientific efforts had tended to accumulate data without seeking to resolve problems of land use, water, the ozone layer, urbanisation, etc. Research tended to focus on one species or to remain descriptive with little attempt to predict the impact of possible change.

But we know that living in harmony with nature has been an integral part of most cultures, including Indian culture. Tradition and ethics in nearly all countries of the world are closely interwoven with the idea of protecting nature. Why, in India we had, from very early times, cave paintings that showed the harmonious coexistence of the human and the natural worlds. Groves would be set aside for the worship of gods and goddesses, certain plants and animals would be considered sacred and would be protected.

The spectacular increase in industrial production that followed the Second World War improved living conditions around the world but also whetted appetites for material goods of all kinds. Industry provided a mass market with manufactured products at affordable prices. More and more goods were turned out at lower and lower cost, creating jobs and enabling people to buy more. Supply encouraged demand.

This situation could not last for ever. To sustain demand, products were so made as to become obsolete very rapidly. Surely this is a colossal squandering of energy and resources and creates volumes of waste that is harmful to the environment. Every American citizen, for example, throws away a ton of domestic garbage every year. In highly developed industrialised societies this refuse, which consists mainly of useless packaging, constitutes one of the most critical environmental problems today.

At least, it can be argued, the rich and industrialised world has the means to develop more 'environmentally friendly' technology if pushed to do so. The choices are far more limited and complex for developing and predominantly rural societies. Practices such as pastoral nomadism or slash-and-burn agriculture, that for centuries have had relatively little impact on the environment, are now proving to be damaging. This is due to the additional pressures on limited resources caused by rapidly growing populations. A study carried out by the Food and Agriculture Organization estimated, for example, that slash-and-burn agriculture alone was responsible for 70 per cent of the deforestation that had occurred in Africa, 50 per cent in Asia and 35 per cent in Latin America.

Factors affecting the environment can be compared to smoking — they are known to be detrimental but many people do nothing about them. In a sense this inaction is psychological. It has been found that people pay lip service to environmental protection but few participate in recycling programmes or energy conservation programmes. After an initial flurry of enthusiasm people find that they do not really want to sacrifice their time or their comfort even though they recognise the importance of making the effort. It has been noticed that if everyone exploits a share of a collective resource, there is short-term profit but the resource is gradually destroyed and ultimately all lose. An example of this can be found throughout Africa where, according to the French agronomist Rene Dumong, 'all that grows without human interference such as grass and trees belongs to everyone . . . no one worries about protecting these resources efficiently and ensuring their continuation'. Thus more than 650,000 sq km of land in Africa's Sahel region has become desert over the past fifty years, due largely to overgrazing and farming techniques that are no longer sustainable on impoverished land which is asked to produce more and more.

Clearly, survival is here the prime motivation and techniques used are based on traditional knowledge. The protection of natural resources is not consciously considered or given priority. But it is equally clear that any serious attempt to protect the environment and promote sustainable development also means an overhaul of social and cultural practices and values in both modern consumer and traditional societies.

If culture can be said to be the key which unlocks a community's creative potential, then education is the tool which shapes that potential. There is constant interaction between education and culture: if education sheds light, culture provides perspective.

Education is infused by culture; however, since cultural models and meanings are mainly transmitted through education, culture is also, in a sense, the effect of education. Education could, therefore, be regarded as possibly the most powerful agent for cultural development and change and not merely a neutral mechanism for cultural transmission. Education and culture are fundamentally allied, both are *dynamic*: culture is a form of out-of-school education and education is culture in school. The domain of culture is universal; but when several cultures coexist in a society, educators and cultural leaders have to find ways of harmonising them.

The challenge is great, and conflicts can arise. One of the great challenges of the 21st century will be the protection of minority cultures against the powerful forces of standardisation and integration. These forces — economic, linguistic, technological — tend to dilute, homogenise and regulate cultures throughout the modern world. Yet the survival and development of small cultures is important for two reasons: one, because this gives a sense of identity to their individual members; and two, because embedded in their traditions and beliefs are social, environmental, political and even spiritual solutions to some of the crises facing contemporary societies. The preservation of cultural diversity — no less than biological diversity — is crucial for the future of mankind. In the past, education has too often played a part in the destruction of minority cultures; but it can also play an important role in their survival and in sustainable development.

Inform them through example, then some of the battle — at least on the psychological front — is already won: for then we would not only be leaving a better world for our children but, I hope, a better generation for the world.

Contents

FOREWORD — *Kapila Vatsyayan* vii

PROLOGUE — *John V. Kingston* xiii

INTRODUCTION — *Baidyanath Saraswati* 1

1. ENVIRONMENT AND EDUCATION — *Sunderlal Bahuguna* 11
2. SUBSISTENCE STRATEGIES AND ENVIRONMENTAL MANAGEMENT — *R. S. Negi* 17
3. TRADITIONAL KNOWLEDGE AND MANAGEMENT OF NATURAL RESOURCES — *A. S. Mishra* 35
4. ECOLOGICAL DEGRADATION DUE TO EXPLOITATION OF NATURAL RESOURCES AND DEVELOPMENT — *Ramakar Pant* and *Rakesh Khanduri* 45
5. WATER RESOURCES AND THEIR MANAGEMENT IN KASHMIR — *B. L. Malla* 57
6. SACRED RESPONSE TO ENVIRONMENT: THE GADDI AND HIS MOUNTAIN — *Molly Kaushal* 65
7. ECOLOGY AND TRADITIONAL WISDOM — *P. S. Ramakrishnan* 73

8. THE NATURE-CENTRIC CULTURE OF THE NEPALESE 93
— *D. S. Rasaily* and *R.P. Lama*

9. THE BRAHMAPUTRA'S CHANGING RIVER ECOLOGY 97
— *A. K. Das*

10. THE WARLIS AND THE DHANGARS: THE CONTEXT OF THE COMMONS 103
— *Ajay Dandekar*

11. CULTURAL DIMENSION OF ECOLOGY: A CASE STUDY OF THE ORAONS 125
— *Virginius Xaxa*

12. ECOLOGICAL CULTIVATION IN THE KARANPURA REGION: A CASE STUDY 129
— *Sachchidananda* and *Rajiv Ranjan Jha*

13. ECOLOGY, CULTURE, HISTORY AND WORLD-VIEW THE ANDAMAN AND NICOBAR ISLANDERS 151
— *T. N. Pandit*

14. MORAL EDUCATION FOR ENVIRONMENTAL PROTECTION: THE SARVODAYA MODEL 165
— *H. M. D. R. Herath*

15. AFRICAN MODES OF TRANSMISSION OF TRADITIONAL KNOWLEDGE 177
— *Charles S. Makari*

LIST OF CONTRIBUTORS 183

PLATES 187

Introduction

Baidyanath Saraswati

THE shadowed aspects of modern civilisation are (a) urbanisation and the technocentric lifestyles associated with it; (b) industrialisation and the environmental pollution associated with it; (c) commercialisation and the degenerated consumerism associated with it; and (d) globalisation and the political violence associated with it. The positive aspect is the growing awareness of all things in the universe. Today, there remains no reasonable doubt that humankind is rushing towards an ecological disaster. Concerned people are questioning the *planners* of the nation: Where will you take us? To mega cities? We shall find no place for our spirit in that land but rather, desolation. We feel our land as if we are within a mother. Our mountains and rivers are sacred. We live in the forest with trees and birds and beasts. We honour them as our brothers. Here man and beast and plant talk together. Our life is peaceful here; we are protected by the divinities. Can the law of a nation supersede the Law of Nature? Should the rights of the people be allowed to be destructively manipulated by the rules of power? Must the wisdom tradition of our ancestors be shelved to accommodate the flagrant hypocrisies of the *planning tradition*?

As part of the Unesco Chair activities at the Indira Gandhi National Centre for the Arts, a conference on the 'Cultural Dimension of Education and Ecology' was held in New Delhi from 13 to 16 October 1995. The proceedings of this conference are published in two independent volumes. Papers related to education are published in the volume *The Cultural Dimension of Education*. The essays here collected aim at describing the cultural dimension of ecology in the mountains, forests and islands.

The Mountains

> He who thinks of Himachal is greater
> than he who performs all worship in Kashi,
> and all things that die on Himachal, and

> all beings that in dying think of
> His snows are freed from sin. . . In hundred
> ages of the Gods I could not tell thee of the
> glories of Himachal.
>
> *Skanda Purana*, Kedar Khanda

Geologically, the history of the Himalaya can be traced to the last pre-Cambrian and earliest Cambrian. There are five structural units in the Himalaya: the Siwalika, the main boundary fault, the lesser Himalaya, the Himadri (central Himalaya), the main central thrust; and the Tibetan Himalaya. Culturally, there are five *khandas* or segments, from west to east: Kashmir, Jalandhar, Kedar, Kurmachal, and Nepal Himalaya. The great Himalaya, the monarch of the mountains is endowed with sanctity by the streams of the Ganga, the snows of Kailash Mansarovar, the home of God Shiva, and the shrines of Amarnath, Kedarnath, Badrinath, Pashupatinath, and several others. In the *Bhagavad Gita*, God Krishna describes himself as *sthavarnam himalaya*, among the mountains: 'I am the Himalaya'. The *devatma* Himalaya is the abode of gods. Its fluid holiness makes a fertile land where the mother Ganga pours her life-giving waters.

Events such as the construction of the 260.5-metre-high Tehri Dam over the Bhagirathi, the main stream of the Ganga in a seismic zone, have jolted the common man into a realisation that the planners of aggressive development are threatening the very existence of life on the Himalaya. Hence people like Sunderlal Bahuguna are actively involved with the ecological movement, which is a call to bring change in the modern way of living, a call to become friends of Nature, and a call to return to the wisdom tradition. Bahuguna calls upon us to

- remember the three basic principles of Indian tradition: (i) that there is life in all creation, (ii) that one should have a worshipful attitude towards all forms of life, and (iii) that austerity is the greatest virtue;
- follow the practical way to culture from Nature, as shown by Buddha and Gandhi;
- educate children and grown-up people, specially politicians, policy-makers and technocrats, in ecology;
- use Gandhi's weapon of non-violence against wrong policies, aiming at a change of heart along with a change of mind; and
- revive the wisdom tradition of the Visnois who went to the extent of sacrificing their lives to protect trees and wild animals.

R. S. Negi's in-depth study of the ecosystem of the Garhwal Himalaya brings into light the people's wisdom tradition:

- efficient utilisation of resources in conformity with altitudinal variations and the annual cycle of seasonality;
- mixed mountain agriculture or agro-pastoralism for each ecological zone, with a well-defined and well-established mode of agricultural and pastoral activity;
- Village as an organic as well as economic unit, integrated and interdependent components having a symbiotic relationship;
- management of forests and pastures in a way in which coservation and regeneration are built into the system;
- indigenous ecological knowledge to sustain the growth of population in the mountain ecosystem and to organise women's movement against exploitation and environmental degradation.

Based on interviews with some 200 farmers, including women, A. S. Mishra's study of the Garhwal region shows that traditional technology is in tune with modern science such

- mechanical measures of terrace cultivation;
- natural resource management based on the ecologically sound system of augumenting productivity;
- watershed development concept and fixing boundaries at the common point of the drainage system between two villages;
- using tree trunks as rainwater irrigation channels, which take care of undulating topography and check seepage losses; and
- water harvesting, management of drinking water, and water-based industry without electric or any other complex machine systems.

Exploring the traditional vision as reflected in the scriptures, Ramakar Pant and Rakesh Khanduri speak about the concept of wholeness as a major influence on social ethics and values, and beliefs and attitudes that help man live in harmony with nature. Coming to what happened to that vision in the Central Himalaya, they describe the partial collapse of the traditional system:

- deforestation due to commercial exploitation of trees, developing new agricultural fields, overgrazing by animals, coming up of new habitation, replacement of natural forests by commercially profitable trees, and forest fires (both intentional and accidental);

- dissociation with the traditional concept of the forest as womb, distortion of the traditional attitude of reverence for the earth; and
- indigenous water management giving way to development programmes such as construction of dams, building of roads and tourism, causing an ecological crisis.

Following the scriptual sources, B. L. Malla refers to the water resources and their traditional management in the Kashmir valley and unfolds what lies behind the people's knowledge and creative ventures and what causes the destruction of the environment:

- religious significance of the river established by the scriptures;
- worship of springs, festivals of the first snowfall, and restrictions on fishing in the sacred springs helping to preserve the water ecology;
- self-devised inexpensive water-wheels for raising water to the higher plateaus, stone-lined dykes for guarding against inundation, drainage operations, and the traditional system of distributing water;
- the extraordinary contribution of the ancient Hindu kings to ecology and culture; and
- the neglect of the valley by the Muslim rulers during the fourteenth century, and the contemporary disturbance causing pollution of air, water and soil, and, in particular, the very presence of the military.

Contrary to the modern assumption that nomads are responsible for soil erosion and denuded forests, Molly Kaushal finds that the expressions of the ecological world-view and the lifestyles of the nomadic Gaddis inhabiting the Western Himalayas, are in complete harmony with Nature:

- identification of a geographical entity, not a mere reflection or a replica of the original kingdom but the real celestial kingdom, so that there is no place for the profane;
- acknowledgement of the fact of the bondedness of the biological being with Nature and his actions within the temporal world that sustains man in life and in death;
- the environment conceived of as being placed on a vertical axis, the horizontal axis seen as an undifferentiated mass of things and beings; and

- leading a life of austerity and restraint that follows the principle of non-pollution, minimising waste, and conserving life-sustaining elements.

The question of ecology and traditional wisdom has been examined by P. S. Ramakrishnan. Considering the consequences drawn from his comprehensive investigation in the north-east Himalayan mountains, he points out that

- through a variety of approaches, traditional knowledge, wisdom and technology, based on empirical knowledge accumulated over a long period of human evolution, traditional societies have learnt to conserve and enhance biodiversity;
- 'sacred groves' extensively maintained by traditional societies demonstrate spiritual values attached to biodiversity and;
- ecological issues in sustainable development are tied up with social, economic, anthropological and cultural dimensions.

In their short article D. S. Rasaily and R. P. Lama portray the nature-centric culture of the Nepalese of the Darjeeling hills:

- folk songs and folklore popular among the Nepali community represent deeper bond of friendship between mankind and the Earth;
- offerings to the goddess Nature form a part of every religious ceremony;
- animals and birds play significant roles in festivals and ceremonies; and
- occult art has a close link with the forest and with Nature.

In his paper on the Brahmaputra's changing river ecology due to the earthquake in the upper reaches of the Himalayas, A. K. Das provides interesting information on the indigenous method of facing floods:

- occurrence of the flood, even its magnitude and duration, are predicted by natural signs such as the movement of ants, the appearance of certain species of plants, the behaviour of an insect and the actions of birds and animals;
- natural alliance between man and the river, the Brahmaputra considered both sacred and secular; and
- facing the flood with excitement: an enjoyable method of fishing, and creating a barrier against the flow of water.

The Forests

> Those who in penance and faith dwell in the forest,
> peaceful and wise, living a mendicant's life,
> free from passion, depart through the door of the sun
> to the place of the immortal person, the imperishable Self.
>
> *Mundaka Upanishad,* I.2, 11

The sages have praised and glorified the forest as an ecological redresser. The scriptures mention five types of forests: (1) *aranya*, a place of no war; (2) *tapovana*, a place of penance; (3) *mahavana*, a dense forest spread over a vast area; (4) *srivana*, a place of prosperity; and (5) *devavana*, a god's forest. Tradition holds that the *vana*, forest, should not be within the village, but the village should be within the *vana*. In ancient times most Indian villages were located within the boundaries of *srivana*. This can be seen even today in the tribal regions. The tradition of *devavana*, sacred grove, is also preserved among the tribes people.

Ajay Dandekar's study of the Warlis and the Dhangars, hunter-gatherers and cultivators and pastoralists of Konkan and western Maharashtra, sets out to explain their traditional knowledge systems and resource use. The importance of their culture lies in:

- complete identification with the forest and the cycle of seasonality occupying an important niche in their world-view;
- developing an amazing variety of eco-indicators with the help of which the onset of the monsoon can be predicted, such as minute change in the time of sunset and the cry of the *pavasya* bird;
- observing food taboos from the first showers of rain to the threshing of the new corn, believing that the tabooed food of the season must not be partaken of unless first offered to God and the corn deity;
- celebrating festivals after sowing and the arrival of the new crops, offerings made to the rain god, to the forest and to all the living beings to the forest; and
- initiating the younger generation into the traditional knowledge of medicinal plants, methods of preservation of the varieties of paddy, and paying respect to the living beings in the forest and in the settlements.

In his paper on the cultural dimension of ecology, Virginius Xaxa presents a case study of the Oraon, one of the major tribal groups of eastern India, which shows that their culture corresponds to the reality of Nature:

- environmental features related to food habits, construction of houses, household articles, hunting implements and fishing tools, treatment of diseases, social customs, lifecycle rituals and festivals;
- harmonious interaction between the community and its environment—the attitude towards Nature is one of rational adaptation, not of mastery over the world; and
- natural order, social order and moral order integrated and maintained through prohibition or propitiation.

A case study of ecological cultivation in the tribal region of eastern India by Sachchidananda and Rajiv Ranjan Jha reveals contributory changes via non-governmental organisations, such as

- reviving traditional agriculture with low-input agricultural practices, desisting from the use of chemical fertilisers and hybrid seeds;
- making people realise that 'to protect the forest is to protect the tradition', that the diverse resources such as land, vegetation, water, animals and forest form part of the ecosystem;
- training children in ecological farming, building greater self-confidence in women; and
- leading ingeniously to integrated development and empowerment of the people at the economic and psycho-social levels.

The Islands

From blazing Ardor Cosmic order came
and Truth; from thence was born the obscure night;
from thence the Ocean with its billowing waves.

From the Ocean with its waves was born the year
which marshals the succession of nights and days,
controlling everything that blinds the eye.

Rigveda, X.190

The *Puranas* have described the Earth as the Golden Lotus which emerged from the depths of the ocean. In his cosmic form the God Vishnu includes 12 *adityas* (suns); similarly the ocean has 12 *dvipas* (islands). There are references to four, seven, twelve, and eighteen islands in the Maharnava or the Indian Ocean.

Ecologically, the Andaman and Nicobar Islands are regarded as part of the *pauranic* Jambudvipa, of which India is a major segment. T. N. Pandit has described the indigenous islanders who are among the world's most primitive communities belonging to Negrito and Mongoloid racial stock. They have faced a time of great suffering and most of them are on the verge of biological extinction. Now comes a special phenomenon called 'development planning' which complicates even further the cultural situation of the five small hunting-gathering tribes:

- ranging from 29 to 200 or so, the five indigenous groups, comprising 621 humans, are overwhelmed by 189,000 migrants;
- hunting-gathering tribes cease to be viable cultural communities due to the trauma of demographic destruction caused mainly by new diseases and upheavals resulting from contact with the colonisers;
- with a relatively large population of 21,172 the herder and horticulturist Nocabarese spread across twelve islands live in settled villages, travel from one island to another in their dugout canoes for barter, trade and social visits, keep their own calendar by reading the movements of the moon, the stars and the sun, and have deep faith in various kinds of benign and evil spirits and the souls of dead ancestors, despite large-scale conversions to Christianity; and
- ecologically fragile conditions of these islands with the influx of increasing numbers of people from the mainland ignorant of the local fauna and flora and an unwillingness to relate in any significant way to the local environment and to the indigenous tribal populations pose a serious problem to both ecology and culture.

Sri Lanka, which is India's closest neighbour to the south, presents a different story. The Veddas are possibly the earliest people of this island. With the introduction of Buddhism (247-207 BC) during the reign of Ashoka, close contact between India and Sri Lanka began. The adoption of Buddhism as the national religion was followed by major changes in Sri Lankan social and religious life. As is well known, Buddhism flourished in Sri Lanka but virtually disappeared from the place of its origin. Similarly, Gandhi's Sarvodaya movement, defined as the awakening of one and all in the society, ceases to be effective in India but has struck roots in Sri Lanka. H.M.D.R. Herath considers the significance of the Sri Lankan Sarvodaya movement which is pioneered by A. T. Ariyaratne and inspired and strengthened by Gandhian thoughts and the teachings of Lord Buddha:

- the Sarvodaya movement aims at complete human personality development, achievable within a suitable environment, which means the physical, social, emotional and mental environment in which humans live;

- moral education for environmental protection in children that helps them acquire awareness of self-protection, self-confidence and self-reliance;
- a socialisation process and implementation of a moral education programme through practical experience focusing on the integration of cultural values with environmental concerns; and
- Sarvodaya model with the Buddhist central value system.

The Wisdom Tradition

The mighty burden of the mountains' bulk
rests, Earth upon your shoulders; rich in torrents,
you germinate the seed with quickening power.

Our hymns of praise resounding now invoke you,
O far-flung Earth, the bright one.
Like a neighing steed you drive abroad your storm clouds.

You in your sturdy strength hold fast the forests,
clamping the trees all firmly to the ground,
when rains and lightning issue from your clouds.

Rigveda, V.84

Recently Jim Lovelock has pointed to the idea that the various forms of life on Earth are components of one living organism, the biosphere, or Gaia. This concept has stirred fierce debate among biologists and geologists; although it seems quite campatible with the vision and tradition of ancient cultures. Gaia is named after the ancient Greek Mother Goddess. The celebrated hymns of the *Rigveda* and the *Atharaveda* refer to the organic, superorganic and cosmic aspects of the Mother Earth. Traditional societies still hold the view that humankind and Earth have physical and spiritual dimensions that are symbolically or really reflected in each other.

Nevertheless, there are instances of unbridled exploitation of the environment. Of the large varieties of flora and fauna in the Himalayan mountains many are extinct today. Sudden change of climate has caused the disappearance of many varities of wildlife, specially elephant, white bear, flying fox and deer. Many varieties of herbal medicines, which people used to identify in the wilderness, are lost for ever; new ventures in herbal medicine are of a different order. Rivers are polluted by industries and large cities. Forests have receded. Tea gardens consume as much as 80 per cent of the total produce in the Darjeeling hills. Forest people are forced to adopt agriculture. Large parts of forests are taken away by agriculturists. The ecological balance has been shattered. Chemical fertilisers, pesticides and herbicides have caused damage to both man and earth beyond redemption. The questions thus arise: Where has the ageless wisdom gone? Do people know how to get at the source of tradition? Is the world today concerned with traditional knowledge? Is there hope for humanity?

There are three factors which make tradition operative — power, wisdom and intention. Wisdom without power is lame; intention without wisdom is blind, and tradition without all these three is orphaned. As Charles S. Makari has highlighted in his paper, the traditional African way of imparting knowledge from generation to generation persists in the Republic of Zimbabwe. He maintains that 'the African culture is full of values even richer than the modern world-view which purports to be superior to traditional world-views'. It is the power of the wisdom and the intention of the African people that make the transmission of traditional knowledge possible.

Can man destroy the Earth? Tradition does not say so. The Vedic concept of *viraj* — the Universal Cow — highlights the infinite capacity of Nature. When the Universal Cow came to men, Earth was made her milking pail, the calf was Manu and the King Prithi was her milker; he milked forth husbandry and grain for sowing. According to the *Atharvaveda*, men depend for life on tillage; he who knows this becomes the supporter and successful in the culture of his cornland. The *pauranic* tradition refers to Kamadhenu, the wish-fulfilling Cow. In the cyclic concept of time, the 'Age of Truth' follows the 'Age of the Machine'. The cycle of rise and fall is built into the cosmic design. The destiny of the Earth is not a private affair of human beings: it is a cosmic affair. What is happening today may have a higher purpose. Who knows that? Perhaps, a healthy reaction to worldwide pollution, deforestation, and dehumanisation is a sign of good hope. The hope for humanity lies with the wisdom tradition.

1

Environment and Education

Sunderlal Bahuguna

Damage to the environment is one of the three crucial problems that humankind is facing today. The other two are the threat of war and internal insecurity, and poverty and hunger. The three are interdependent. The problems of security are closely connected with the environment in the sense that the production of arms and nuclear tests create radioactivity; the atmosphere of war is created by the rich nations because they want economic domination over the poor nations, specially over those who possess natural resources — minerals, metals, water and forests — the four pillars of modern economic development. Similarly, within a nation itself the areas having these resources have become the coveted grounds for exploitation by more developed areas. The people resist. This is visible in the opposition to large dams and mining and deforestation projects in Afro-Asian countries. The national governments employ force to suppress the people agitating against these.

Poverty and hunger with plenty is the other problem which humankind is facing today. As the pace of development advances, economic inequalities increase even though economic prosperity as a whole rises. After the first decade of development in 1960 the difference between the income of the richest 20 per cent and the poorest 20 per cent was 30:1, but after three decades, by 1991, whereas it should have decreased, it doubled. It was 61:1. 20 per cent of the world's people live in industrialised countries. The only difference it has made to the so-called developing countries is that a few from the ruling elite and the business magnates join the 20 per cent of the affluent countries, whereas poverty in the poor countries increases. In India there are 40 per cent people below the poverty line. The impact of economic conditions is clearly seen. There was a saying in India that the food of the poor is *dal* (lentils) and *roti* (bread). But now *dal* — the main source of protein for the poor — has become so costly that they cannot buy it. Poverty leads to the exodus of the poor from healthy rural surroundings to filthy city slums.

I feel that whatever we are doing today to solve environmental problems is pruning the branches and not uprooting the evil. We rely too much on technology, but technology itself is ill. The root cause of environmental problems is consumerism. Consumerism has become a part of our lives since we adopted the mode of development whose indicator is economic growth. This definition of development was given by President Harry Truman, when he in his address to the American Congress after World War II said that poverty was the main problem of humankind and alleviation of poverty was possible by economic growth. To achieve economic growth man became the butcher of nature. Nature was converted into cash. We boast of a 262 per cent rise in foodgrains production during the last four decades, but to achieve this we lost 20 per cent of our forests and 20 per cent of our fertile land. Thus we put a gold ring on the nose at the cost of the nose itself. Soil and water are the basic capital of humankind. The forests, and specially the natural forests, are the factories of soil production and mothers of the rivers. These are the treasures of biodiversity. The four renewable resources, which sustain all life, grasslands, forests, croplands and oceans, have become non-renewable due to over-exploitation and pollution.

The society which we have created is a perverted one. From Nature (*prakriti*), we have moved to perversion (*vikriti*). Insecurity, pollution and poverty are the symbols of a perverted society. In such a society, the individual lives in a state of perpetual dissatisfaction. His desires (*trishna*) expand. He never enjoys real peace and happiness. We have bartered peace and happiness for temporary prosperity. For peace, one has to take pills, and for happiness, drugs.

Humankind has been aspiring to achieve the goal of culture (*sanskriti*). How to move from Nature to culture? The answer is very simple. We have to change our behaviour towards Nature. There are instances in Indian history when people, reminded of the basic principles of the Aryan culture of India, could overcome the crisis. The three basic characteristics of Indian culture are:

1. There is life in all creation.
2. We should have an worshipful attitude towards all forms of life.
3. Austerity.

One such instance is the emergence of the Vishnoi sect in the fifteenth century, when Lambhoji, a cowherd farmer, laid down 29 principles of good behaviour. Two of these were: not to kill any animal and not to cut any green tree. The Vishnois, whose number is about half a million in India, still follow these. They went to the extent of sacrificing their lives to protect trees and wild animals. The biggest sacrifice they made was in 1730, when under the leadership of Amrita Devi, 363 men, women and children laid down their lives to save acacia tress. The Vishnois are the most prosperous farmers.

The practical way to culture from Nature was shown by Lord Buddha. Buddha was a prince, brought up in the midst of prosperity; but he saw misery (*duhkha*) all around. He knew that miseries cannot be alleviated from the palace — so he left his father's palace, became a common man and subjected himself to all sorts of hardships. He undertook a forty-day fast, after which light dawned upon him. The root cause of misery was desire (*trishna*). The way to end misery was to end desire, the opposite of increasing desires as our consumer society propagates through advertisements. Buddha differentiated between need and desire. Our needs should be fulfilled, but we should not run after our desires. In order to fulfil our needs we have to sublimate Nature with the help of science and technology. Buddha also defined development. His definition of development is relevant even today. E.F. Schumacher, in his famous book *Small is Beautiful*, has devoted one full chapter to Buddhist economy. Development is a state in the life of the individual and society in which they enjoy permanent peace, happiness and fulfilment. It is in such a society that culture flourishes. Gandhi in our times reached at the same conclusion when he said, 'Nature has enough to sustain all, but nothing to satisfy the greed of anybody'.

Gandhi was a practical visionary. He had a vision of a cultural society. He showed a practical way himself by practising austerity, finding viable alternatives to energy, industry and other activities which are responsible for the pollution and wanton exploitation of Nature, and advocating afforestation, i.e. tree farming for food, fodder, fibre, etc. One of the eleven disciplines of life (*ekadasha vrata*) was non-accumulation (*asamgraha*) of things. One who accumulates more than his needs, steals the share of others. This creates differences in society — ditches of poverty and mountains of prosperity. The use of centralised energy — atomic, thermal and hydel from big dams, is creating environmental problems. Our energy priorities should be human, animal, bio, solar, wind, tidal, geothermal and hydel from the run of the river. Technology to lessen human drudgery and increase efficiency should be developed. Production of essential commodities should be decentralised, as the centralised system of production gives birth to an army of unproductive persons — managers, bankers, brokers, advertisers and transporters. They take the major share. The burden is ultimately borne by silent Nature and the consumer. The procurement of oxygen, pure and clean water, nutritious food, healthy shelter and clothing, etc., should be from the surroundings in an ideal society.

What is role of education in the creation of a cultural society? We often lay stress on the education of children, specially on the development of their minds. As a result of this we have created a society in which we have big minds, feeble hands and no hearts. Personalities are unbalanced. The best period for learning is childhood and boyhood. Today children see differences between what their parents practise at home and what they preach to them, and what they read in the books and see in real life. This is responsible for the development of a dual personality. Gandhiji's latest fad was the idea of basic education (*buniyadi shiksha*), in which education was imparted through crafts for the development of head and hands simultaneously. Service of the poor and needy as a part of daily prayers was an integral part of the way of life he advocated. He prayed:

> I do not need the Kingdom, nor a
> place in heaven or salvation,
> But O God! bless me with the service of
> those in misery!
> No system can be perfect till we provide
> for the development of heart.

Children do what they see older people and specially the parents doing. I have practical experience of this. My younger son Pradeep, when he was only six-years-old, went to prison with his mother in connection with the prohibition movement. My elder son still complains that he was not allowed by the teachers to participate in picketing the liquor shop and court arrest. Similarly in the Chipko movement the young children participated with great enthusiasm with their mothers.

There is an urgent need for educating grown-up people, specially the politicians, policy-makers and technocrats. They are the people who decide the destinies of millions. Once you give arguments in favour of your stand, immediately your opponents, who are mostly men with vast resources, will counteract these. The establishment has two strong weapons: fear and greed.

Those who revolt against the wrong policies have to devise better and more sophisticated weapons. The greatest contribution of Mahatma Gandhi is that he devised the weapons of fearlessness and selflessness. These are the weapons of non-violent struggles. The method adopted silent processions, sit-ins (*dharanas*) and fasting — all aiming at a change of heart along with a change of mind. The effect of this is more lasting. All the great teachers of humankind have tried to change hearts. They, through their preaching in simple language, supplemented with the practice of what they preached, had a permanent effect. They live in the hearts of the people even after many countries.

In the Chipko movement women, by hugging trees marked for felling, offered themselves to the axe instead. They said, 'Axe us, not the trees'. They felt the heartbeats of the trees. For this action they courted arrest and gladly accepted suffering. The message was spread through folk songs and education through stories from the scriptures (*Bhagavatkathas*). There were foot-marches, the longest of which was 4,870 km from Kashmir to Kohima. It took 300 days, but the message was taken even to remote villages.

We are engaged in a bigger struggle — the struggle to save the Himalaya, which is dying due to the onslaughts of aggressive development in the form of damming the rivers, deforestation, mining and luxury tourism. We are educating the people to press the demand for a Himalayan policy in eight countries in and around the Himalaya. The objective of this policy should be to heal the wounds of the Himalaya, keep it as a place to live for the local inhabitants and accessible to nature lovers and spiritual seekers, use natural resources in a sustainable manner to achieve regional self-sufficiency, keep the landscape intact, protect biodiversity and establish local autonomy for the advancement of culture. This will save both the nature and culture of these great mountains, a source of varied inspiration to humankind.

A practical programme for this is the agitation against the construction of the 260.5-metre high Tehri Dam over the Bhagirathi, the main stream of the Ganga, in a seismic zone. We have been camping in a hut for last four years near the dam site in non-violent protest and have been able to stop the work twice. Twice I fasted to make the government realise the need for a review of the technical, social, economic, cultural, ecological and spiritual aspects of the project. To reach hearts of the people, we popularise the hymn to Ganga:

> Ever flowing from Gaumukh Himalaya,
>   O mother Bhagirathi!
> Your name the saints ever chant.
>   At Gangotri
> From the lotus feet of Vishnu you issued
>   To disappear in the forest like the locks of Shiva
> Whereupon the gods, saints and seers prayed,
>   To let you flow on
> Through the reach of mortal beings.
>   He then released you
> To cleanse the world of its sufferings.
>   King Bhagirath had worshipped you,
> O mother goddess, and through you
>   The sons of Sagar attained their peace and deliverance.

2
Subsistence Strategies and Environmental Management

R.S. NEGI

THE Unesco programme on Man and the Biosphere (MAB) brought together an expert panel in Salzburg, Austria, in 1973 to discuss the impact of human activities on mountain ecosystems. As a part of the final report of the discussions the panel characterised mountain regions as those in which there exists an altitudinal gradient of barometric pressure, radiation, temperature and precipitation. This gradient results in vertical zonation of soils, flora, fauna and ecosystem types. Accordingly, man's way of life, his habitat and land ways and exploitation patterns, are differentiated vertically (Unesco 1973).

The Unesco project and many other initiatives such as the symposium on Himalayan, Andean and Alpine mountain ecosystems organised by the American Anthropological Association in 1973 and published in *Human Ecology*, the Munich Conference on Development Problems in Mountain Environments, 1974, IUCN'S Conference on the Management of High Mountain Resources, held in Christchurch, New Zealand, in 1976, the International Symposium on the Earth Sciences, Ecology, and Ethnology of the Himalayas at Paris (CNRS, 1977), the United Nations University Project on Highland-Lowland Interaction Systems in 1978, the inauguration of the International Centre for Integrated Mountain Development (ICIMOD) in Kathmandu in 1983 under the aegis of Unesco, and so on, were a response to the expression of great concern in the late 1950s and 1960s about progressive environmental degradation and the realisation that 'all is not well in the mountain regions of the world' (Ives 1985).

There was a spate of studies of Alpine, circum-Alpine, Andean and Himalayan mountain ecosystems during the past three decades, with growing interest in mountain environments and the human populations inhabiting them. Most of these studies were focused on the subsistence strategies employed by mountain inhabitants for survival in rugged and inhospitable regions.

Despite the strenuous and hazardous conditions, the mountains have a mystical attraction for humankind, so much so that a sizeable number, adding up to a tenth of the world's population, lives in the mountain regions. The Himalaya are the most popular and are inhabited by nearly 120 million people over a 2,500 km stretch from Afghanistan to Myanmar. Because of this demographic reality and because of the distinctive subsistence strategies of mountain populations, their comparative and analytical study became a major focus of attention (Brush *et al.* 1974; Rhoades *et al.* 1975; Hoffpauir 1978; Goldstein and Messerschmidt 1980; Guillet 1983). Most of these studies were in agreement with the vertical zonation of life support resources in mountain ecosystems as underlined by the Unesco project. However, since most studies were undertaken in the Nepal Himalaya, so far as the Himalayan ecosystem is concerned mention must be made of the pioneering study of Pant (1935) and recently that of Nitya Nand and Kumar (1989) in the Uttarakhand region of the Indian Himalaya. S.D. Pant's *Social Economy of the Himalayans* is, as a matter of fact, a path-breaking endeavour employing the ecosystem approach in analysing the subsistence strategies of the people inhabiting the Kumaon region.

It has generally been recognised that the basic characteristic of mountain life is the vertical stratification of life support resources with immense altitudinal and seasonal variations. Life sustenance therefore is totally dependent on successful adaptation to the mountain environment. Mountain populations have apparently responded with efficient utilisation of resources in conformity with altitudinal variations and the annual cycle of seasonality. The main feature of mountain life thus emerges as adaptation to the constraints of the environment, through time and space, with the application of indigenous ecological knowledge.

However, increasing awareness of the fragility of mountain ecosystems highlighted by a series of ecological disasters the world over, in which human intervention may create serious resource degeneration, have raised apprehensions about the well-being and survival of mountain populations and their immediate neighbours. In recent years serious environmental degradation of the Himalayan ecosystem and fears of impending disaster have drawn worldwide attention. In this connection two publications, Eric Eckholm's *Losing Ground* (1976) and John Lall's *The Himalaya: Aspects of Change* (1981), specially the former, have had a popular impact the world over. Eckholm, with the support of Dr Maurice Strong and World Watch, made a challenging and emotional appeal to the effect that the world's mountains, and especially the Himalaya, were facing imminent catastrophe. This, recently reinforced by Sandra Nichols' spectacular film *The Fragile Mountain*, has become standard news media fare, to such an extent that we have almost come to expect the collapse of Nepal and of much of the Himalayan system by AD 2000, with devastating consequences for the teeming millions of the Indo-Gangetic plain (Ives 1985 in Tejvir Singh and Jagdish, eds.).

There is no doubt that human intervention resulting in large-scale deforestation, leading in turn to depletion and degeneration of life support resources, is the main cause, but what is ironical is that the mountain inhabitants are the prime suspects in bringing it about. A set of pet assumptions, the chief being that uncontrolled population growth in the Himalaya induces deforestation for the procurement of fuelwood and the expansion of subsistence agricultural land, point an accusing finger towards the mountain inhabitants, completely disregarding the fact that commercial exploitation in the wake of the industrial revolution in the West is the major culprit in deforestation all over the world, including mountain ecosystems. The 'fact' that the 'growing demand for fuelwood induced by population growth' in the Himalaya 'is the cause of deforestation' is rather astonishing in view of a small observation made by Nitya Nand and Kumar (1989) that in 1976-78 timber production in Garhwal was 3.05 million cubic metres whereas fuelwood collection during the same period was 0.8 lakh cubic metres. It is to be noted that timber production (commercial activity) is from cutting fully grown trees whereas fuelwood collection (subsistence activity) is only from dead wood, branches and twigs. No tree is ever cut down just for the procurement of fuelwood.

Now the question arises, how are the altitudinally differentiated vertical life zones in mountain ecosystems integrated by mountain populations in the adaptation of alternative subsistence strategies for resource utilisation? Is there any built-in mechanism, developed over generations of living in the mountains, directed towards the regeneration and conservation of resources? An attempt is made here to address these questions by examining the subsistence strategies in a micro situation in the Garhwal Himalaya.

Garhwal: a sub-ecosystem

Garhwal signifies a land of forts. According to tradition Garhwal was under the domination of fifty-two chiefs, each with his own *garh* (fort). At present Garhwal is an administrative division of the Uttar Pradesh hills and consists of five districts, namely Dehradun, Tehri, Uttarkashi, Pauri and Chamoli, encompassing an area of 29,090 sq km and lying between 77°35.5' E to 80°60' E longitude and 29°31.9' N to 31°26.5' N latitude. According to the 1991 census of India, the total population of Garhwal was 29,82,927, of which 15,21,846 were males and 14,61,101, females. 80 per cent of the population of Garhwal resides in rural areas. There are only 35 medium and small urban centres in Garhwal and only one amongst them has a population exceeding one lakh.

The division of Garhwal into three different ecological zones from south to north is well recognised by the local population in their own classificatory terminology as *talla* (lower) Garhwal, *bichla* (middle) Garhwal and *malla* (upper) Garhwal in the context of altitudes as well as latitudes. These divisions correspond to the well recognised physiographic divisions, which are:

A. Outer Himalaya, comprising the Siwaliks and the Tarai Bhabar, ranging between 300 m and 1100 m.

B. Lesser or middle Himalaya, also known as Himachal, comprising the low and middle altitude mountain ranges and valleys between them, between 1100 m and 3300 m.

C. Great or Inner Himalaya, also known as Himadri and comprising high altitude mountain ranges, rainshed valleys and the alpine pastures locally known as *bugyals*, lying between the tree line and the perpetual snowline, ranging between 3300 m and 4200 m.

All over the Himalaya subsistence agriculture is the mainstay of life support. In Garhwal, however, there being very little level land and other conditions suitable for intensive agriculture, the people, through the experience of generations, have developed a complicated but suitable agricultural regime in adaptive response to the constraints of the mountain ecosystem. In the mountain environment altitude determines climatic conditions and temperature, which in turn influence the agricultural regime, specially the cropping pattern. Corresponding with the three broad ecological zones or sub-ecosystems mainly based on altitudinal variations, south to north, there are three clearly distinguishable production zones in Garhwal (Table 1).

Ecological zones of agriculture

A. Intensive agricultural zone in the outer Himalaya or Talla Garhwal.

B. Mixed mountain agriculture or agro-pastoral zone in the middle Himalaya or Bichla Garhwal.

C. Pastoral zone in the Inner Himalaya or Malla Garhwal.

These are not exclusively production zones but denote primacy, complemented and supplemented by other subsistence activities in varying degrees. Mountain cultivation is conditioned by environmental constraints such as nature of land, sun-facing or shady slope, temperature, rainfall, river/rivulet basin, and above all by the quantum available for

Table 1
Altitudinally determined ecological zones agriculture in Garhwal

Ecological zone	*Altitude in metres*	*Cropping pattern*
A. Outer Himalaya		
(i) Lower Doon and Tarai	300-600	Wheat, Rice, Sugarcane
(ii) Upper Doon and Lower Garhwal	600-900	Wheat, Rice, Maize, Pulses
B. Middle Garhwal	0900-1800	Wheat, Rice, Madua, Jhangora, Barley, Chua Kauri, Pulses
C. Inner Himalaya Upper Garhwal		
(i)Cool-temperate sub-zone	1800-2400	Wheat, Barley, Madua Jhangora, Cheemi, Potato
(ii)Cold/sub-alpine	2400-3600	Cropping in summer only on the sunny aspects, (the winter crops of the lower zones beoome summer crops). Wheat, Barley, Phaphra, Kauni (grown up to 3000 m) potato

Adapted from Nitya Nand and Kumar (1989).

cultivation in different ecological zones. Not all zones permit intensive cultivation nor a similar cropping pattern. The outer Himalayan zone alone permits intensive cultivation throughout, dominated by wheat, rice, specially wet rice crops, and sugarcane, which is gaining importance in the Doon and Tarai. The produce can sustain the population throughout the year and give a marketable surplus.

In the middle Himalayan zone, agro-pastoralism or the mixed mountain agriculture is the pattern of subsistence. It involves diversification and farming has to be supplemented by herding and horticultural operations. The dominant crops are wheat and *madua*, but rice also has an importance place specially in the river/rivulet basins where irrigation facilities are available. Maize is also grown in this zone.

The inner Himalayan zone does not permit intensive agriculture, and crops are restricted to barley and some mountain varieties of millets and wheat restricted to some areas. In areas such as the Dhauli valley where flat land is available and the inhabitants have constructed irrigation channels, it has been possible to grow rice during the short summer period. The main subsistence strategy in this zone is pastoralism, which takes the advantage of presence of *bugyals* (Alpine pastures). The inhabitants of this zone, the Bhotia, in the past combined trade with their transhumant pastoralism. They used to carry out trading operations in the Tibetan region during the summer months, but with the closure of the border in 1962 their trading has been disrupted. There are thus three identifiable subsistence strategies adopted by the people of Garhwal.

Land use

Garhwal has a total land area of 29,090 sq km). Of this, nearly 23,000 sq km that is, 77 per

Table 2
Land use in Garhwal
(in hectares), 1991-92

		Districts					
S.N.	*Description*	*Uttarkashi*	*Pauri*	*Chamoli*	*Tehri*	*Dehradun*	*Total*
1.	Total area for land use	801619	759562	840704	574544	315503	3291932
2.	Forest	710278	451175	520361	397201	219812	2298827
3.	Cultivable barren land	8812	45056	33734	72972	10326	170900
4.	Fallow land	3793	18258	1724	8466	6037	39278
5.	Uncultivable wasteland	19516	34756	166842	12249	1563	234926
6.	Land under other uses than agriculture	6683	17760	18305	11036	16614	70398
7.	Pasture	13495	43953	22081	2857	81	82467
8.	Orchards, gardens, other trees	7395	62501	35773	22	4296	109987
9.	Cultivated land	31647	86103	41884	69741	55774	285149

Adapted from *Yug Samvad*, January 1996.

cent, is classified as forest land, which includes the 16.5 per cent high mountainous area that lies under permanent snow cover. The forest cover as indicated by landsat imageries is only about 24.9 per cent, out of which (a) actual forest (having above 60 per cent crown cover) is only 4.1 per cent; (b) moderate forest is 11 per cent; and (c) poor forest is 4 per cent (Singh 1993). *Bugyals* and grazing lands cover about 3.7 per cent of the total land area. Besides these are areas covered by orchards and gardens and under other uses.

Agro-ecosystem

In the fragile ecosystem in which they live, the people of Garhwal over the centuries have devised a complicated but suitable agricultural regime which is acknowledged as 'unique in itself, for it is complete, self-dependent, self-contained and sustainable'. The Garhwal agro-ecosystem has also been described as a 'natural subsidized solar-powered agro-ecosystem . . .' which does not demand energy from outside as natural nutrients help to maintain the fertility of the cropland (Singh 1993). The salient features of the agricultural regime developed by the Garhwali people are:

(a) Construction of field terraces.

(b) Construction of irrigation channels known as *gul* along contours so that water flow is maintained through gravity.

(c) Manuring system with the help of natural nutrients.

(d) Mixed cropping pattern.

(e) Rotation of crops in harmony with varying environmental conditions.

(f) Diversification of produce such as cash crops, horticultural produce and fruits, etc.

However, the main characteristic of the Garhwal agricultural regime is mixed mountain agriculture or agro-pastoralism within which the above features are integrated. Mixed mountain agriculture includes cultivation and herding, one being dominant over the other depending on altitude or latitude or both. Consequently transhumance and nomadism, in varying degrees, become concomitant activities. For each ecological zone there is a well-defined and well-established mode of agricultural and pastoral activity.

Agro-pastoralism practised all over the middle altitudinal region in Garhwal is in essence diversification of resource utilisation. It is a mixed farming and herding strategy which is both supplementary and complementary: supplementary in that it makes good the shortage in the cereal produce which is not adequate to sustain the population through the year, and complementary in that the livestock level is increased, which enhances food supply for the human population and the quantum of manure for cropland. Diversification also promotes transhumance and seasonal cyclic mobility, which is one of the means of preventing exhaustion of the fertility potential of cropland and promoting regeneration.

Village as an organic unit

The subsistence strategies of a population are functions of their habitat and settlement pattern. Therefore it is important to understand the traditional Garhwal village as an organic as well as economic unit. Traditional boundaries of a village encompassed a large area including cultivated, waste and forest lands and were recognised by the rulers as well as the people. The British after their conquest of Garhwal in 1815 conducted the first land survey in 1823, that is, Vikram Samvat 1880, and entered the village boundaries in the government records without any change. These boundaries are locally known as *assi sal* (eighty years) boundaries. 'Almost the whole country, cultivated and waste, exclusive of the largest forests, came to be regarded as within the boundary of one village or another village' (Pauw 1896:36, quoted in Somanathan 1991). Earlier than Pauw, J.H. Batten, Settlement Officer for Garhwal in 1842, recorded that the areas within village boundaries were 'large portions of wasteland, including whole ranges and their vast forests. . . .' Batten further remarks that 'such a division has been found useful in giving separate tracts for pasture for the cattle of different villages . . . (Batten 1851:124, quoted in Somanathan 1991). This is indicative of the fact that in Garhwal there were vast tracts of forest, wasteland and pastures and very little cultivated land. It is therefore natural to assume that the availability of land determined the subsistence strategy of the inhabitants in the past which continues into the present with variation in degree, as indicated by the detailed study of Nitya Nand and Kumar (1989).

Traditional villages, probably the earliest settlements in Garhwal, specially in middle and upper Garhwal, still retain their characteristic feature of forest and pastures as integral components of a village economy's resource base, besides cultivated land, as their traditional boundaries remain unaltered. The forest and pasture within the village boundaries are considered the common property of the inhabitants. A Garhwal village thus is not just a human settlement but a micro-ecosystem encompassing humans, animals, physical and organic resources. Usually a village boundary rises from a river/rivulet/stream or valley bottom to hill-top spreading between two ridges which are the water divides. Human settlements as a rule are situated in the middle of hill slopes on spurs running from the middle/lower levels of the ridges, with cultivated land below and above. Above the upper cultivated land lies the grazing land and the pasture and on top the forest. With the water divide ridges on both sides, the catchment area in the shape of the forest and grazing land, and a river/rivulet flowing in the valley bottom, a village can also be considered a micro-watershed. The peculiarities of the habitat and settlement pattern in Garhwal were conducive to the agro-pastoral mode of subsistence, which may have evolved under the following circumstances:

(a) The earliest immigrants were mainly herders/pastoral nomads, who followed cyclic mobility limiting their movement, in the context of spatial realities mainly in resource (pasture/grazing land and water) availability.

(b) Population pressure, both human and animal, on resources in the middle altitudinal belt led to bringing more land in the mountain slopes under cultivation by the construction of terraces, a characteristic feature of mountain cultivation.

(c) Fresh waves of immigrating nomadic pastoralists in search of resources to maintain their herds such as the Gujar in the Siwalik and the Gaddi in the middle and high altitudinal belts.

(d) In the later period the need for generation of cash leading to diversification in raising cash crops and horticultural activities including of orchards and fruit plantations.

The complexity of the agro-pastoral economy of Garhwal can be well understood within the ecosystem framework, that is, the symbiotic relationship between the different components of the system, which are people, livestock, uncultivated land and cropland.

These components are closely integrated and interdependent. The symbiotic relationship is clear. Human beings for their subsistence depend on the produce from the cropland as well as on livestock, which in turn depend on forest and pasture. The livestock also convert leaves lopped from the forest into manure for cropland, on the one hand, and supply draught power from stored energy obtained from forest produce for ploughing and transport. Cropland continuously receives a 'subsidy' from the forest in terms of energy and nutrients through the agency of livestock, which acts as a link between uncultivated and cultivated land, building a forest-fodder-livestock-manure-cropland chain. Humans, major consumers of the produce of farmland as well as livestock, release the energy thus obtained in agricultural operations and other supporting activities such as improvement of cropland by repairing the terraces, constructing irrigation channels, etc., and raising and caring for the livestock (Singh 1993).

Land classification and cropping pattern

The mountain agricultural regime generally suffers from limitations of varying soil conditions, poor irrigation facilities and position of fields and manuring dependent on natural nutrients alone, and so on. In Garhwal, where cultivated land is only about 9 per cent of the total land area and irrigated land only about 11 per cent of the cultivated land, the Garhwali recognises a threefold classification of cultivated land from the standpoint of irrigation:

(a) *Talaon* or *sera*. Land situated near the river banks where irrigation is available is known as *talaon* and irrigated land is *sera* or *kyari*.

(b) *Panchar*. Intermittently irrigated land.

(c) *Upraon* or *ukhad*. Permanently terraced unirrigated land situated above the village settlement, on the hill slope (Pauw 1896, in Walton 1910).

(d) There is yet another type of land known as *katil* or *kheel*, situated on the highest part of the mountain slope above the *upraon* land and below the forest and grazing land. *Katil* land is unterraced and is brought under cultivation intermittently by clearing the shrubs and bushes and burning them, i.e., slash and burn, locally known as *kath kurali*.

The position of fields in terms of height and sun-facing or shady slopes is another important factor in mountain agriculture. Altitude is a determinant in the cropping pattern as it controls temperature, which places limitations on different crops in different altitudinal zones. Within the boundary of a village itself there is considerable variation in altitude, and as such a village grows different corps in different fields.

Irrigation facilities in Garhwal are meagre. It is ironical that the Garhwal Himalaya, being the richest watershed in Asia, from where originate all the major rivers of the upper Ganga system has no rivers of use as their course is through deep gorges. The Garhwali take recourse to traditional technology to construct gravitational channels along the contours of the hills to divert water from small streams and rivulets to their fields.

The Garhwal agro-ecosystem, specially in the middle and upper altitudinal belts, is 'self-supporting' and 'does not demand energy from outside' as natural nutrients maintain the fertility of the cropland. Manuring of the cropland is done in traditional manner using the indigenous ecological knowledge:

A. Recycling of natural nutrients

(a) Gathering of leaf mould from the forest floor.

(b) Gathering of cattle bedding made of dry leaves and pine needles, soaked in cattle urine and dung.

B. These gatherings are mixed with dung in compost pits locally known as *mol khud* for decomposition.

C. For outlying fields far from the homestead, manure is prepared in the fields themselves. Cattle are penned in the fields during summer under temporary sheds known as *goth*. The animal droppings and urine accumulated in the *goths* is spread over the fields. The *goths* are shifted from terrace to terrace in order to manure all.

D. Ash manuring. While harvesting the stems of crops are left uncut. Later these stems and dry grasses are burnt and the resultant ashes spread over the field as manure.

E. Green manure. Green weeds which grow in the harvested fields are ploughed back and buried in the process.

Rotation of crops

In order to maintain the fertility of cropland the Garhwali have devised a skilful rotation of crops with the application of indigenous ecological knowledge. The rotation of crops is a combination of exploitation of resource, i.e., raising of diverse crops in cultivated land and regeneration, i.e., revitalisation of cropland in order to regain fertility. There are three types, each adapted to a different type of land:

1. *Two-year rotation of four crops:* This type is prevalent in Doon and Tarai and is not very different from the usual for any land from which two harvests are gathered in the year.

Year	*Kharif*	*Rabi*
First	Rice	Wheat
Second	Maize	Mustard or Potato

In those areas where sugarcane is grown the rotation varies in that for three years continuously sugarcane is cultivated to be followed by wheat or mustard in the fourth year and again to be followed by sugarcane in the fifth year (Nitya Nand and Kumar 1989). In the *talon* land of lower and middle Garhwal also, wherever irrigation facilities are adequate this type of rotation is practised.

In the *talon* land yet another type of rotation is practised which aims at the maintenance of biodiversity in order to safeguard the yield. Different species of rice are sown by rotation every year in order to detect and eliminate the counterfeit or self-grown rice plants which could decrease productivity (Pant 1935).

2. *Two-year rotation of three crops*: This is the most typical rotation practised in the

permanently terraced and unirrigated *upraon* lands of lower and middle Garhwal. The first requisite of this type of rotation is to divide the village lands into two contiguous blocks known as *sar*. In this the village headman has a pivotal role as he indicates the division of land. In one of the *sars* rice is grown and is known as *satyara* (*sati* meaning rice), and in the other *madua kodo* is grown and is known as *kodara*. In the winter when *madua* is reaped the *kodara sar* is left fallow, while in the *satyara* after the harvest wheat is sown and the *sar* takes the name *gyunwara*; subsequently when *madua* follows wheat the *sar* is known as *kodara* while the *kodara* of the previous year is sown with rice and is known as *satyara*. This goes on in a cyclic manner. 'The system of leaving fallow a whole block of land instead of scattered fields here and there has its advantages when the cattle are turned loose to graze on the remnants of the straw and grass that can be found on the terrace walls. For this reason half or nearly half the village will be found apparently lying waste in winter. In the land which is too stony to grow rice or wheat, Jhangora is substituted for the one or Barley for the other or both; but this does not affect the system of rotation, nor the method of carrying it out' (from Pauw's 1896 report in Walton 1910).

Sar System Crop Rotation

Year	*Season*	*Crop in Sar No.1*	*Crop in Sar No.2*
First	Kharif	Rice or Jhangora	Madua
First	Rabi	Wheat or Barley	Fallow
Second	Kharif	Madua	Rice or Jhangora
Second	Rabi	Fallow	Wheat or Barley

In upper Garhwal, the cool temperate zone, lower temperatures and shorter growing periods necessitate a change in the patterns of crop rotation. 'Another two-crop rotation is that of chuwa and barley. This is much practised in northern villages, in fields near the homestead which are regularly enriched with manure. In the south there is similar rotation with ugal or buckwheat (*Tagophrum esculentum*) substituted for chuwa; but confined to outlying land. In the higher villages of the north where barley does not ripen till May or June the double crop becomes impossible and the rotation then practised is chuwa (April-September) followed by barley (October-June), followed by mustard (August-December). The land then remains fallow till April, when chuwa is again sown. But the people of these villages are shepherds rather than agriculturists by profession, and the rotation is not always practised' (from Pauw's report of 1896, in Walton 1910).

Year	*Summer Months*	*Crops*	*Winter Months*	*Crops*
First	April to September	Marsa(Chuwa) or Ogal or Phaphra or Kauni	October to June	Wheat or Barley
Second	August to December	Potato, Mustard or Chheemi (Beans)	December to April	Fallow

3. *Six- to nine-year rotation on katil land*: This type of rotation is practically confined to unterraced *katil* land above the terraced *upraon* lands and below the forest. The land is outlying and far away from human settlements, at a higher altitude.

Year	*Summer*	*Winter*
First	Madua or Phaphura	Wheat or Barley
Second	Madua or Phaphura	Fallow
Third	Gahat or Ogal or Phaphura	Fallow continuously for three to six years

The whole rotation occupies five years and is known as *tisali*, since the land is left fallow for three years. However, sometimes the fallow period is prolonged to six years, thus extending the rotation to nine years.

The rotation of crops practised in Garhwal seems to have been developed by experience gained through generations of living in the particular ecosystem. It was already well developed when the British conquered Garhwal (Traill 1828; Pauw 1896; Walton 1910) and continues to be practised almost unchanged to the present (Nitya Nand and Kumar 1989).

Rotation of different species of grains in different years aims at the preservation of biodiversity in environmental conditions where one single species may fail. S.D. Pant (1935) has aptly highlighted this type of rotation in the case of rice cultivation. But unfortunately with the propagation of so-called modern scientific agriculture, promoting high-yielding species, in the wake of the green revolution, without taking into consideration the environmental conditions and without regard to indigenous ecological knowledge, that valuable genetic diversity has been allowed to disappear. The sturdier species of rice that used to be cultivated in the Himalaya some 50 years ago no longer exist. Perhaps the germplasm of those species are preserved in the laboratories of the International Rice Research Centre, but they are no longer available to the Himalayan farmer.

Agro-pastoralism, which is practised all over the middle and higher altitudinal regions, is in essence diversification of resource utilisation. It is mixed farming in the sense that the farmer is also a herder as almost each family raises cattle, sheep and goats depending upon the existence of grazing ground and forest within the village boundary.

Diversification

Diversification and seasonal cyclic mobility are interrelated and effectively utilise the village resources. During the summer months and the rainy season the farmer takes up the role of herder and drives his livestock to the uncultivated land on the fringe of the forest, often known as *danda*. *Danda* is under the ownership of the entire village where almost every family is allocated a plot which is used to raise millet crops and horticultural produce, specially potato. In recent years the process of diversification has resulted in farmers taking to raising sweet peas and tomatoes and planting orchards of apple and plum as a supplementary mode for the generation of cash.

In the *danda* region, which is actually forest land, sheep, goats and cattle get ample and nutritious grass which is rather scarce in the lower regions, specially in the summer months. This way there is an augmentation of productivity. Towards the end of September the farmers and their herds trek back to the village settlement in the lower region. The cyclic mobility thus far has proved to be a successful adaptive strategy for food production and generation of cash on the one hand and regeneration of resources on the other.

Pastoralism and transhumance

Diversification in the mode of food production also promotes transhumance on a large scale. While intra-village cyclic mobility is limited to the spatial limits of a village, transhumance involves mobility, also cyclic, in a larger circuit. Transhumance encompasses (a) winter migration to lower regions in Tarai and Bhabar and (b) summer migration to high-altitude *bugyals*.

It is observed that several types of pastoral practices are followed in Garhwal. On the one hand there are agro-pastoral communities practising transhumance, both vertical and horizontal, limited to small distances, and on the other there are communities like the Bhotia and the Gujar, who are transhumant in the classical sense, where long journeys and vertical traverses are involved. Transhumance is a highly developed form of pastoralism and has varying forms in different parts of the world. In the Himalaya transhumance is almost universal in the form of seasonal movement of people and livestock between previously earmarked sites, which become permanent seasonal encampments or bases. These cyclic movements allow time for the regeneration of resources, which alone can sustain this kind of lifestyle. The seasonal cyclic movements and the utilisation of resources in a rotational manner has placed the transhumant people in a situation where they are nomadic on the one hand, and transitionally or marginally sedentary on the other.

The Garhwal Himalaya supports a number of such transhumant populations. Chief among whom are the Bhotia, the Khadwal, the Kharkiya, the Jaunpuri and the new immigrant Gujar, who unlike others, base their transhumant pastoralism on buffalo herding. These communities move along the availability of vegetative growth at various altitudes, though this adaptive measure is gradually losing sustainability with the growth of population, both human and animal, and the degradation of the resource base.

Forest and resource and management

The forest is the most important renewable resource in the Garhwal Himalaya. It plays a vital role in the lives of the people as there is near total dependence on the forest for life support in the forms of 'food, fuel, fodder, fibre and fertiliser'. Degradation of their forest wealth is detrimental to their survival as their agro-pastoral production system is totally dependent on the forest.

However, in the present century and in the post-Independence era specially, the forests have undergone severe degeneration due to variety of reasons, but chiefly due to commercial exploitation, illicit felling and mismanagement in which the people have almost no role. On the other hand, their subsistence strategy is oriented towards efficient resource utilisation concomitant with environmental management. Since the forest and pasture/grazing land havc been within the traditional village boundaries, under community ownership and control, their efficient management was always a sensitive issue. The village communities did manage their forests and pastures in a way in which conservation and regeneration was built into the system while the forests were under their control. The Van Panchayat and Joint Forest Management in actuality draw heavily on the tradition of community forest management operating in Garhwal and Kumaon (Somanathan 1991). The Chipko movement which today is acknowledged all over the world as an environmental movement is not the product of modern ecological awareness but that of the traditional and indigenous ecological knowledge of the Garhwali farmer, especially women, who are most affected by environmental degradation.

Char system: management of grazing land

Management of pasture and grazing land is undertaken under the *char* system. The grazing land commonly owned by the village is divided into blocks which are alternately closed for grazing or sharing under the common authority of the village community, for designated periods. The practice prevents overgrazing and allows regeneration and conservation of resources, both the grazing land and the produce, that is, the grass. The *char* system as a matter of fact is a traditional roster system, where periodic grazing and sharing is allowed in the interest of protection and management.

Concluding remarks

The foregoing account of the subsistence strategies of the people of Garhwal underlines a series of operations which have been developed through the experience of generations and undertaken as the application of indigenous ecological knowledge to sustain the population in the mountain ecosystem through the efficient utilisation of resources simultaneously with action taken for regeneration and conservation. There are, of course, limiting factors such as the growth of population and the general depletion of resources. Whether optimality has been reached or not will need further probing.

References

Brush, S.B., 1976, 'Introduction to cultural adaptations to mountain ecosystems'. *Human Ecology*, 4, 2, pp.125-33.

———, R.McC. Netting and D.A. Messerschmidt, 1974, 'Cultural adaptations to mountain ecosystems'. *Human Ecology*, 4, 2, pp.123-85.

Goldstein, Melvyn C. and D.A. Messerschmidt, 1980, 'The significance of latitudinality in Himalayan mountain ecosystem'. *Human Ecology*, 8, 3:117-34.

Guillet, David, 1983, 'Towards a cultural ecology of mountains: the central Andes and Himalayas compared'. *Current Anthropology*, 24, 5, pp.561-74.

Hoffpauir, R., 1978, 'Subsistence strategy and its ecological consequences in the Nepal Himalaya'. *Anthropos*, 73, 1-2, pp.214-52.

Ives, Jack D., 1985, 'The mountain malaise: quest for an integrated development'. In Tejvir Singh and Jagdish Kaur, eds., *Integrated mountain development*, New Delhi.

Negi S.S., 1994, *Garhwal. The land and people*, New Delhi.

Nitya Nand and Kamlesh Kumar, 1989, *The holy Himalaya: a geographic interpretation of Garhwal*, Delhi.

Pant, S.D., 1935, *Social Economy of the Himalayans*. George Allen and Unwin, London.

Pauw, E.K., 1896, *Report on the tenth settlement of the Garhwal District.* Allahabad.

Rhoades, R.E and S.I. Thompson, 1975, 'Adaptive strategies in Alpine environment beyond ecological particularism'. *American Ethnologist*, 2, 3, pp.535-51.

Shailat, 1996, 'Uttarakhand: parivesh aur vikas'. *Yug Samvad*, 1, pp.5-8.

Singh, V., 1993, 'Ecological farming system for Garhwal'. *Uttarakhand*, 7, pp.117-28.

Somanathan, E., 1991, 'Deforestation, property rights and incentives in central Himalaya'. *Wasteland News*, August-October, pp.14-27.

Walton, H.G., 1910, *British Garhwal: a gazetteer*, Vol. XXXVI of the District Gazetteers of the United Provinces of Agra and Oudh. Allahabad.

Yug-Samvad, 1993, 1,pp.23-24. Dehradun.

3

Traditional Knowledge and Management of Natural Resources

A.S. Mishra

Soil, water and vegetation are three basic natural resources. The survival of God's creation depends upon them and nature has provided them as assets to human beings. The management of natural resources to meet people's requirements has been practised since the pre-Vedic era. Farmers were ranked high in the social system and village management was in their hands. In order to manage land, water and vegetation, technical knowledge suitable to the specific conditions of a region was required. They gained this knowledge and developed skill through experience and learning by doing.

Over-exploitation of natural resources by growing population resulted in various severe problems. Destruction of vegetation has resulted in land degradation, denudation, soil erosion, landslides, floods, drought and unbalanced ecosystems. A balanced ecosystem is an urgent need.

The Central Soil and Water Conservation Research and Training Institute, Dehradun, has activities in the rural areas of Garhwal for the management of resources with people's participation. The present investigation was the outcome of experience gained in the villages of Outer Himalaya and the Doon Valley. The Institute began extending its technology in 1954 and has achieved grand success through watershed management and lab to land activities. In contact with the farmers, traditional wisdom was documented. A wealth of traditional knowledge could be harnessed through their cooperation. Their experiences are required to be shared and discussed to promote modern technology for development.

Methodology

The investigation was carried out in villages of Dehradun district and Narendra Nagar (Tehri

Garhwal). These villages were selected from the Doon Valley and the Outer Himalaya hill range with a view to obtaining comprehensive information on traditional knowledge of natural resource management in both foothills and mountainous regions. Eight villages from Sahaspur block of Doon Valley and eight from Narendra Nagar block in the hills were selected. Farmers were interviewed to obtain information on traditional knowledge. Individual contacts were made and questions were asked about traditional systems in the villages. Representation of women among the farmers was also ensured. By means of informal interviews and interaction with old and young farmers and farm women, responses were recorded for critical analysis. It was also observed how traditional knowledge is transmitted from one generation to another. In order to educate young farmers, elders communicate innovation through proverbs, short stories and examples.

Information was collected with respect to the social and historical perspective of the Garhwal region, zoning system, depletion of natural resources, methods of conservation, concept of watershed management, prediction and beliefs, and cultural education. A total of 200 farmers including women were interviewed.

Historical, Cultural and Social Perspectives

The Himalayan hill range of Uttar Pradesh is known as Uttarakhand. The region comprises two hill zones, Garhwal and Kumaon. The Garhwal Himalaya covers an area of 14,565 square miles and has 4,724 villages. After the British occupation the region was divided into British Garhwal and Tehri Garhwal. References to Garhwal are found in the *Skanda Purana* (*Kedarkhanda*) and the *Vanaparva* in the *Mahabharata*. The *Skanda Purana* defines the boundary of this holy land, Kedarkhand, 50 *yojana* long and 30 *yojana* wide. It extends from Haridwar in the south to perpetual snow (Himalaya) in the north. To its west is the river Tamsa (Tons) and in the east it is flanked by Baindhachal. Badhan is not only a *paragana* but a mountain range too, which demarcates Garhwal from Kumaon. In the *Vanaparva*, where Dhaumya is telling Yudhisthira about the *tirthas* of India, Gangadwar, i.e., Haridwar and Kankhal, have been referred to. The hill tract of Garhwal in those days was known as 'Himvat'.

In the Garhwal region the Ganga, Yamuna, and many rivers and rivulets are seen in their blissful infancy. Garhwal is a constant source of spiritual attainment where people come to visit ancient holy places for realising their *moksha*. It is the expression of divinity, meditation, penance and attainment. Garhwal has a galaxy of peaks and glaciers, a vastness of meadows and valleys, and a wealth of colourful dales which have no parallel in the world. Mountain peaks are visible everywhere and because of altitude, complexities and physiographic features and geological structure, the region has several classifications. But the major divisions are Outer Himalaya, Middle Himalaya and Higher Himalaya.

HIMALAYAN ZONES: ANCIENT CLASSIFICATIONS

The Doon Valley has its own significance in view of its culture and traditions. It has a historical background from the period of Dronacharya. Dehradun is formed from the name of Guru Drone (Dera + Drone). The valley occupies an area of 1,500 sq km (20 km by 76 km) between the Outer Himalaya, the Ganga, the Yamuna and the Shivalik hill range. The valley is known as Dronakshetra.

The Himalaya of northern India was divided into five zones: Nepal Khand, Kurmanchal, Jalandhar, Kedarkhand and Kashmir Khand.

In the Himalaya there were vast resources of forest, scenic beauty, agriculture, horticulture, minerals and, above all, hardy and painstaking people with their rich cultural heritage.

The Kole were the first historically recorded people of Garhwal, descended from the Munda ethnic group. Subsequently the Kirats, Khasas and the Shakas settled in the region. Many other lineages also came and intermixed with those who had already settled. In the ancient period and even in modern days powerful races or castes dominated politics and the economy. In present-day Garhwal three main castes are found: Brahmans, Rajputs and Shilpkars. Shilpkars are descendants of Koles and are supposed to be the autochthonous of Garhwal.

Depletion of Natural Resources

During the ancient period Garhwal was full of dense forest and lush green vegetation. The Himalaya is the perennial source of water for rivers, streams and reservoirs. Undoubtedly, nature takes care of its resources through natural process over a period of time and maintains them. But ever-increasing population, developmental activities and technological modernisation have over-exploited available resources without taking into consideration the damage and consequences for coming generations. Vegetation plays an important role in protecting land and water. These resources are being depleted at an alarming rate because of human intervention. Degradation and destruction of forest cover in the Himalaya is directly responsible for the denudation of watersheds. In the absence of vegetative ground cover, during the monsoon rainwater comes down to the plains unchecked. Sudden swelling of streams, flash floods in the hills and severe floods in the plains and drought in upstream areas are the consequences.

The downward rush of water has tremendous erosive force and moves millions of tonnes of fertile soil during the rainy season. It causes all types of erosion as well as devastating landslides in the Himalaya. Developmental activities, construction of roads, extraction of building material and mining, etc., are a constant threat.

Denuded hills and other wastelands pose serious problems which adversely affect agriculture and human life in the region. Landslides and landslips block hill roads and charge streams with heavy sediment loads. The soil erosion taking place crosses the permissible limit of 4.5 to 11.5 tonnes/ha many times (Narayana and Ram Babu 1983).

Management of Natural Resources

Broadly, farmers have indicated three ways to protect resources by means of traditional technology. They are mechanical, agricultural and vegetative.

MECHANICAL MEASURES

The main occupation of the hill farmers is agriculture. They usually construct terraces for cultivation known as *nala* with risers known as *pusata*. These terraces are small but there are many of them. In one acre of landholding a farmer possesses 50 *nalas*. In these it is possible to manage to rainwater. Construction of terraces depends upon space and grades of land. The farmers, with their expertise, are able to prepare fields for crop production.

According to scientific recommendations cultivation is allowed to 33 per cent of land slope. But in the hills, farmers are able to make terraces from top to bottom of the mountain terrain without taking into account the land slope. With terraces they construct loose boulder retention walls (risers) by putting grass over them. These grasses keep both stones and the land intact.

Cement and sand are scarce materials in the hills. In making risers farmers simply arrange boulders of the proper size along the terrace wall. It retains the soil perfectly and gradually gets stabilised.

Farmers make the slopes of the terraces inwards to check soil erosion and enhance *in situ* moisture conservation. Soils are gravelly and have a high rate of percolation. Due to rainwater retention enough moisture becomes available to the crops.

On mild slopes farmers construct shoulder bunds to protect their lands from soil erosion and grow vegetation over the bunds, particularly grasses for binding the soil.

Farmers of the hill region used to make brushwood or longwood check dams across the drainage channels for controlling soil loss by means of local materials. They are economical. Gabion walls and stone check dams are by and large cost intensive and beyond not affordable to hill farmers.

Farmers in the Doon Valley in order to train torrents use *Ipomea carnea* and *Arando donex* plants sps. as vegetative spurs, and they are found to be very successful.

TRADITIONAL KNOWLEDGE FOR NATURAL RESOURCE MANAGEMENT

In order to achieve the objective of development in villages, people's participation is essential. It is required to involve them actively in project activities by respecting their traditional knowledge and experimental ethics. Traditional knowledge has a sound base as it has been tested and practised over the years. It is appropriate technology in particular climatic conditions and in the living conditions of people.

Projects to develop ecology should start with traditional knowledge as they are proven technology for natural resources management. In a real sense, every culture of a social system, traditionally, is the result of people's action to survive and their attempts to optimise the use of available resources, i.e., soil, water and vegetation.

The science of natural resource management is based on the ecologically sound traditional wisdom of farmers and its contribution in augmenting productivity. Traditional values which are sustainable in nature need to be compared with values of modern systems. It is obvious that traditional practices of agriculture may disappear unless their values are promoted.

The wisdom of farmers with respect to watershed development, agricultural management, and conservation of soil, water for sustained production are documented in the present investigation.

WATERSHED DEVELOPMENT CONCEPT AND VILLAGE BOUNDARIES

Farmers pointed out that watershed management had been introduced for the integrated management of a particular area that includes agriculture, natural resources, forest management, village development and above all the ecosystem. Virtually, a watershed was defined as a unit of development in which there is a highest point and a lowest point with common outlet. The Government of India has given special attention to watershed development to manage natural resources and schemes like NWDPRA, a watershed project with foreign collaboration, are being implemented.

During the ancient period, village boundaries were decided upon on a watershed basis by the expert farmers in the villages. Such boundaries were socially acceptable to all the members of the system. Such age-old village boundaries are fixed at the common point of the drainage system in between two villages. It is still in vogue and people do not go beyond the limits of their hydrological boundaries.

IRRIGATION

Farmers used to carry water to their fields through small irrigation channels known as *gulas*. These go from the source of water along the slopes to the fields. In order to avoid seepage losses farmers use pipes. By means of gravitational force they transport irrigation water from its source. In hills it is difficult to construct *gulas* for all the terraces, and pipes are convenient in transporting water to every field. In order to make judicious use of water, they use a sprinkler system through gravitational force and economical utilisation of water.

In the Garhwal Himalaya farmers use tree trunks as rainwater irrigation channels by taking care of undulating topography and checking seepage losses (Sharma and Sinha 1993).

WATER HARVESTING

The region of Garhwal comes in the high rainfall area and in the lack of proper management system most of the rainwater goes waste as runoff. Farmers of the hill region have their traditional technology for making small dug-out ponds to harvest rainwater. They construct such ponds at several places and use the water for survival or for supplemental irrigation. Improvement over the traditional practices are that at the bottom LDPE sheets are placed to check seepage losses. Lined tanks are cost-intensive and beyond the reach of the farmers.

MANAGEMENT OF DRINKING WATER

Streams are the source of water in the Himalaya. Farmers pay regard to these water resources. They use the water for drinking and make efforts to keep streams clean and unpolluted. They maintain vegetation on the banks to have a clean flow without sediment for human consumption. They do not permit their cattle at the places from which they collect drinking water. They have their own traditional system for the management of drinking water. They do not allow anyone to throw garbage in its current to avoid pollution and infection.

WATER-BASED INDUSTRY

In the hills flour mills are not available. Farmers have their indigenous technology to run flour mill by means of water fall. They use home-made wooden wheels as turbines to run the mills. These mills are locally known as *gharat* or *panchaki*. It is a local response to needs of the people without electric or any other complex machine systems.

WOMEN'S KNOWLEDGE IN MANAGEMENT OF RESOURCES

For centuries, nature's various products and women's knowledge of their properties have provided the basis for making water safe for drinking in every home and village of India. The seeds of the *nirmali* tree are used to clear muddy water by rubbing them on the insides of vessels. The drumstick tree also produces seeds which are used for water purification.

Moringa seeds inhibit the growth of bacteria and fungi. *Tulasi* is a water purifier with antibacterial an insecticidal properties. Copper or brass pots are what Indian women use to carry and store water; and unlike plastic, they do not breed bacteria. The technologies women have used for water purification are based on locally available natural products and locally and commonly available knowledge (Shiva 1988).

Practically each terraced field has a row of fodder trees along its edge. The household women manage these carefully for procuring maximum leaf fodder yields through lopping. They know when and how to lop without damaging the main tree (Sarin and Khanna 1991).

Older women train the younger ones in the art of lopping. When women lop trees they enhance the productivity of the oak forest under stable conditions. Groups of women and old people go together to lop fodder and develop expertise by learning by doing (Shiva 1988).

Farm women know the nutritional needs of their families. That is why women in Garhwal continue to cultivate *mandua*. They say that without their *mandua* and *jhingora* they could not labour as they do. These grains are their source of health and strength (Shiva 1988).

Women in the Garhwal hills are architects of the rural economy. They are devoted to agriculture, animal husbandry, dairying, child-rearing, cooking, fodder and fuel management, etc. They work harder from morning to evening than their male counterparts for the welfare of the family. Girl children share the work of their mothers and get training in home management.

AGRICULTURE

Farmers' traditional knowledge of agriculture includes tested technologies in the field.

- They use a special type of traditional plough. Other types of 'improved' ploughs do not work in the hills as the soil is gravelly and not deep.

- Under rainfed conditions farmers in hill regions plough their land several times before the onset of rain to conserve water and increase water retention capacity.
- Farmers plough their land straight instead of in circles and open parallel furrows for rainwater harvesting and retaining moisture. However, there is a recommendation to plough the land across the slope to check erosion.
- Farmers of hill regions prefer mixed cropping for minimising risks under rainfed conditions and creating ground cover for checking runoff and soil loss. They grow legumes with maize and ginger or turmeric with maize.
- After sowing ginger, colocasia and turmeric, farmers use paddy straw, wheat straw or leaf litters as mulch to ensure proper germination.
- Farmers do not practise weeding and interculturing in the maize crop because of soil conditions and the requirement of fodder in the rainy season.
- Farmers of the Garhwal hills store seeds by selection for different plots with special identification and use them in those particular plot.
- In the outer Himalaya farmers were reluctant to grow maize because of wild animals such as bears, wild boars and monkeys. In *khadar* (lowland) areas they grow paddy and irrigated wheat and in uplands they take rainfed rabi crops.
- In the hills farmers grow mainly *mandua*, *jhingora* and *guar*. Because of recent developments they have been attracted towards off-season vegetables, e.g., peas, tomatoes, etc.

MANURE AND MANURING

In view of the soil's condition and texture the farmers of the Doon Valley and the hill region use farmyard manure in the fields before sowing. In lowland areas, for paddy they do green manuring also. Use of chemical fertilisers has increased but people retain their belief in traditional methods.

Farmers do not dig compost pits for the collection of cowdung, residues and garbage. Instead of pits they accumulate the matter in heaps in the open for decomposition. The reason behind it is that decomposition is slow due to low temperature and little sunshine. In pits compost would not get ready in time. In the open rapid decomposition takes place. This practice is traditional but has a scientific basis.

VEGETATIVE MEASURES FOR NATURAL RESOURCES MANAGEMENT

Hill farmers grow trees of economic value and suited to their requirements. In order to have conserve soil and water they grow grasses for ground cover such as *Eulaliopsis binnata*, *Chrysopogun fulvus* and agave sps. Shrubs like *Ipomea icarnea*, *Arando donex*, *Dendrocalamus strictus*, napier grass, *Vitex negundu*, *Morus alba* and *bagrera* are grown, and in wild form are available *bhang*, lantana, sweet *neem*, etc. Among trees they grow *Grewia pitiva*, *Bauhinia* sps., *Albezia labek*, *Timla*, *Gainthietic*, to meet fuel and fodder requirements.

For the development of horticulture in the Doon Valley the trees grown are citrus, mango, jackfruit, guava, pomegranate, pear, peach and plum. In the hills of Mussoorie and Narendranagar areas peach, pear, *khumani* and apple are grown at higher elevations. There is tremendous potential to develop horticulture in the hill ranges because of undulating topography and climatic conditions. Farmers are well aware of the potential of their lands, but due to poor economic conditions and infrastructure it is not possible for them to go ahead with alternative and more profitable land use.

Hill farmers are hard-working that even in adverse topographic conditions they are devoted to agriculture for grain production. Hill farmers do not like to work as labourers or beg in villages for their livelihood; instead, they prefer to go to cities to earn. Many hill farmers migrate for jobs to the cities or join army service. The women and children look after the village property, while the men send them money to run their homes.

References

Narayana, V.V and Rambabu, 1982, 'Estimation of soil erosion in India'. *Journal of irrigation and drainage engineering.*

Sarin, Madhu and Renu Khanna, 1991, *Wasteland development by a women's group: a case study*. New Delhi: ILO.

Sharma J.P. and B.P. Sinha, 1993, 'Traditional wisdom of hill farmers of Uttarkashi'. National Seminar on Indigenous Technology for Sustainable Agriculture.

Shiva, Vandana, 1988, *Women and environment: case studies from selected villages of Orissa*. New Delhi: Council of Professional Social Workers.

4

Ecological Degradation Due to Exploitation of Natural Resources and Development

Ramakar Pant and Rakesh Khanduri

THERE is a story related to the environment, in which a boy who was a very good painter made a big painting of a scene. There were big mountains covered with trees, except a few in the far background which looked snow-covered. From one of the mountains flowed a beautiful river. Down in the valley could be seen a few cosy cottages surrounded by gardens, a few butterflies, some birds soaring high in the air and little children playing happily in the open fields. Indeed it was a beautiful painting.

The boy had a little brother. He also wanted to try his hand at painting. As soon as he got the chance, he picked up the brush and painted the mountain all black. The sparkling blue-white water of the river became brown, and with just one stroke of his brush, the flowers and trees and butterflies disappeared. His older brother was heartbroken. The only consolation was that the child who destroyed the painting was so small that he had done it in ignorance. Though it would require a lot of time and effort, the painter could paint another picture.

Something very similar is happening in our lives. How many of us have looked at nature's beauty, a thousand times more beautiful than any painting can ever be, and realised how fragile it is? Just like the child's stroke of the brush, one action of ours can destroy this beauty — be it the mountains with their forest cover or the sparkling streams and rivers of life-giving water, be it the immense sand deserts or our oceans which are teeming with life; be it our lush green rain forests or the stark beauty of our cold deserts. But, and this is an important but, there is a major difference. While the painting was spoiled by an ignorant child, our earth and its environment are being spoiled by adult humans. Even more significant is the possibility that if nature's system or what we call the environment is destroyed, the effect may be fatal for many species.

Environmentalist and social activist Shri Sunderlal Bahuguna once pointed out that the agony of the present-day world is the offshoot of an illogical and indiscriminate spoliation of the sources of the earth and nature by man for his meaningless material development that is leading him fast towards destruction.

Environment: A Concept of Wholeness

The environment is a concept of wholeness (nature), with non-living and living components interdependent among themselves. It is aptly defined as 'the sum total of all conditions and influences that affect the development and life of organisms'. This comprehensive definition stresses totality, and every living organism from the lowest to the highest, including human being, has it own environment. The word 'nature' in the *Gita* also conveys the idea that it does not belong to anyone but everyone belongs to it, like a family does not belong to anyone but everyone belongs to the family. Like in a family, in the environment also interactions between its different constituents are expected, and these interactions sometimes might lead to hazardous situations. Interaction is leading to the faster deterioration of the environment.

Traditionally, our understanding of the environment was holistic. A *shloka* from the *Isha Upanishad* goes, 'the whole universe together with its creatures belongs to the Lord (nature). One can enjoy the bounties of nature by giving up all greed'. Implicit in this thought is that no creature is superior to any other, and human beings should not have absolute power over nature. Let no one species encroach on the rights and privileges of nature. The element of sustainability is ingrained in this, because the emphasis is on using nature without greed. Once the element of greed enters, exploitation starts and we cease to utilise nature for the good of all human beings.

Traditional cultures have always lived in harmony with their natural environments. Nature and humankind (*prakriti* and *purusha*) form inseparable parts of the life support system. This system has five elements: air, water, land, flora and fauna, which are interconnected, interrelated and interdependent. Deterioration in one element affects the others.

Traditional social ethics placed great emphasis on the values, beliefs and attitudes that helped man to live in harmony with nature. The *Bhumi Suktam* in the *Atharvaveda* is said to be the most impressive and eloquent testament of ecological values that can be found anywhere in world literature. These and similar texts from diverse cultural traditions throughout the earth express a world-view which is informed by the spirituality inherent in nature and stress the holistic and harmonious relationship between humanity and nature.

In the *Manusmriti* (5.45) it is written that 'he who injures innoxious beings from a wish to give himself pleasure, never finds happiness, whether living or dead'. Reference to ecological concerns is also found in *Charaka Samhita, Vimansthan*, 3.2. 'The destruction of forests is most dangerous for the nation and human beings. *Vanaspati* has a direct relation with the well-being of society. Due to the pollution of the natural environment and the destruction of forests, many diseases crop up to ruin the nation'.

During Ashoka's time (272-232 BC), perhaps for the first time in the history of the world ecological concerns became state concerns. His imperial edicts laid down rules of conduct that had to be obeyed with respect to the environment. Non-compliance was met with punishment.

T.N. Khoshoo writes, quoting Gandhiji in *Mahatma Gandhi: An apostle of applied human ecology*, that 'it is an arrogant assumption to say that human beings are lords and masters of the lower creatures. On the contrary, being endowed with greater things in life, they are the trustees of the lower animal kingdom'. The delicate and holistic balance that exists in nature has to be respected and maintained.

The Himalayas, the proverbial 'Third Pole', have always remained a source of fascination and inspiration for different people and have been deemed to be the cradle of civilisation in the subcontinent. There seems to be general agreement that the ecology of the Himalayas has been endangered. The Himalayas have exercised a great influence on the environmental conditions of northern India and the people living in the Indo-Gangetic plain. They have prevented the monsoon winds from crossing over Tibet and forced them to precipitate most of their moisture on the Indian side in the form of rain and snow. This unique ecology of the Himalayas, which has such an extensive and pervasive influence on the life of our people, needs to be preserved, conserved and qualitatively upgraded.

The developmental activities of man such as the construction of high dams, roads, exploration for minerals and mining activity and the quest for arable land have to face the challenge of intensified dynamic process, commonly referred to as geographical hazards. Natural resources are being exploited in the name of economic development. Indira Gandhi's interpretation is that the real conflict is not between environment and development but between the environment and reckless exploitation by man in the name of efficiency. We have to live a life according to the rhythm of nature. Human inference in natural environmental conditions often gives these dynamic processes catastrophic proportions, leading to disasters and irreparable damage to the natural balance of the ecosystem.

It is not just concern about the extinction of the big cats, but concern for all inhabitants and non-living resources. We have to stop this undeclared war against nature. Human beings are at the crossroads. Careless application of technology is leading to eco-degradation and pollution. Gandhiji emphasised, 'The earth provides enough for every man's need but not for every man's greed'.

Sustainable development is, therefore, a concept of good and sound economic growth that can be maintained indefinitely with damage to the environment. Good environment generally begets good economics.

The words 'economics' and 'ecology' have the same root, *oikos*, which refers to a house. While economics deals with financial housekeeping, ecology deals with environmental housekeeping.

Studies have shown that the perspectives of ecology are different from those of economics in that the former stresses limits rather than continuous growth, stability rather than continuous 'development'. The ecosystem is the basic unit which has biotic and abiotic components that form an interrelated, interconnected and interdependent system. The most important characteristic of an ecosystem is that it is dynamic, evolving and auto-sustainable as long as it remains reasonably undisturbed and there is incoming sunlight. The equilibrium of an ecosystem is disturbed by external stimuli such as natural cataclysmic changes and ever-increasing human activities dictated by socio-economic growth. The basic difference is that the socio-economic system, in contrast, is hitched only to one species, human beings. In an ecosystem, different species of plants and animals including human beings and micro-organisms form an interacting system. Thus, the economic process is unidirectional and human beings can only progress forwards. Conflict between the ecosystem and the socio-economic system arises from unidirectional and unlimited human wants to meet genuine needs as also greed. This has caused ecological crisis, which in other words means human exploitation of resources at a greater rate than can be normally regenerated under natural conditions.

Central Himalayas

The central Himalayas comprise eight hill districts of Uttar Pradesh, namely Chamoli, Pauri, Tehri, Uttarkashi, Dehradoon, Almora, Nainital and Pithoragarh, spread over an area of about 52,000 sq km. The people of the region are poor, ignorant and backward but the environment has made them simple, honest, hard- working, cheerful and courageous. The region is quite rich in religious and cultural heritage. The Hindu shrines of Badrinath, Kedarnath, Gangotri, Yamunotri and the Sikh gurudwara at Hemkund near the famous valley of flowers attracts pilgrims every year. People come not only on pilgrimage but also to escape the stresses and strains of urban life, to relax and to enjoy the beauties of nature.

Forest: a Womb

The term 'forest' applies not only to trees but also to scrub vegetation and grassland. It is aptly defined as 'a peculiar organism of unlimited kindness and extends generously the products of its life activity; it affords protection to all beings, offering shade even to the axeman, who destroys it'. Trees and forests are also important for deep psychological reasons. In returning to the forest, we are returning to the womb, not in psychoanalytical terms but in cosmological terms. We are returning to our origins.

For centuries forests and the people living around have complemented each other, the latter deriving their livelihood from the farmer, who in turn maintained the ecological balance and environmental quality together with conservation of soil and water. The hill people utilise their traditional knowledge to use forest resources without destroying them. From the forest they get fuel for cooking, fodder for their cattle, fruit, timber for building their houses and medicinal herbs for curing diseases. The forest helps in maintaining the flow of perennial springs, in bringing rain, in keeping the soil and water conserved, in preventing landslides, thereby giving protection from this natural calamity. It helps regulate watershed management so as to maintain the fertility of the soil, control droughts and floods, and preserve wildlife.

Massive deforestation in the Himalayan region is the important factor in ecological degradation. Non-availability of certain species, decline of fodder and wood resources, loss of the habitat of wildlife, soil erosion, recurrent floods and drying-up springs and seasonal streams and climatic changes are the consequences of man's activity. It is obvious that there is something wrong with the management of these vital resources.

The deforestation which has taken place due to commercial exploitation of trees for timber, resin, medicinal herbs, etc., the developing of new agricultural fields, over-grazing by animals, the coming up of new habitation (e.g. because of the construction of the Tehri dam), the building of roads mainly after the China invasion of 1962, tourism development and other development activities, increase in the population (men as well as animals), all have had an adverse affect on the environment and have brought about ecological imbalance.

The forest has gone away from the villages. It is reported that there is a scarcity of fuel, fodder and fruit. Medicinal herbs are going to be extinct. The adverse affects noticed by us were that due to deforestation in the villages of Garhwal there is watershed failure, which has resulted in both drought and flood conditions, soil erosion, landslides, changes in the microclimate, increase in the silting rate which has caused a rise of the river beds, loss of wildlife, drying up of natural springs on which the villagers depend for drinking water.

The Chipko movement took place in April 1973 in Mandal near Gopeshwar of Chamoli district. It is a grassroots non-violent and non-political movement. It is purely an ecological movement which has brought the women of the region in the mainstream of public life, and it is guided by common rural folk and not by professional leaders. 'Chipko' means to cling to the trees to save them from being cut. It awakened among the people the need for the protection of the forests.

One aspect of the deteriorating forest ecology is the large-scale replacement of natural forests by the plantation of only commercially profitable trees. These man-made forests are not capable of working in the same way as the natural forests for maintaining the ecological balance. In some instances they may do positive harm. For example, in the Himalayan forest, the oak tree is regarded as the farmer's best friend because it absorbs water for a long time and releases it slowly. This gives rise to springs around which hill villages have been established. Its leaves are used as fodder, it has a leafy canopy and a rich undergrowth of grasses which protect the soil from being directly struck by rain, and its wood is used for making agricultural implements.

Now it is being replaced by pine trees because of their commercial use. The pine tree has not the capacity to retain water, which has resulted in the drying up of springs, creating a scarcity of drinking water. It has no canopy and no undergrowth, thus leaving the mountain slopes fully exposed to erosion by rain and wind. Its leaves are not used as fodder, and they are inflammable and acidic, which makes the land infertile. But in order to extract resin from the trees the planting of pines is going on.

Forest Fires

Forest fires are another cause of the destruction of trees, vegetation, thick layer of humus and animals. The two major causes of forest fire are:

(a) *Intentional fire*: The forest is often set on fire by the villagers during the summer season to get a good growth of grass following the rains. The fire burns the debris that is lying on the forest floor and hence the grass is able to grow well in the rainy season. Sometimes it spreads and destroys vast tracts of valuable trees. The forest is also set a fire by the forest department to clear it of dry vegetation in order to avoid the risk of a huge fire. Firing is done from top to bottom by cutting fire-lines at regular intervals to control the fire. Villagers also set fire to pine leaves falling on the surface as they inhibit the undergrowth.

(b) *Accidental fire*: Fire is also caused by man's carelessness. Unextinguished campfires of trekkers and picnickers, forest labourers throwing away burning cigarettes, bidis and matchsticks, villagers burning the unwanted material on their fields during summer, throwing away of torches used by travellers to see their way in the forest at night, and acid applied to increase the yield of resin. This acid may be spilled on the dry needles of a pine forest, thereby leading to forest fires.

The flow of air in the hills is upwards, which is responsible for huge fires, and a fire may go beyond control if it spreads from the bottom of a hill. It is easily controlled if it is from top to bottom. Too much dryness also helps in spreading fires.

There are several traditional methods of controlling fires: by beating the branches of trees on the fire, by throwing soil and water on it, and by cutting a fire-line to prevent its further spread.

Removal of leaf litter by the villagers to spread under their cattle and for use as fuel is responsible for soil erosion, disturbances in the hydrological cycle in the hill areas and of organic manure in the soil. But at the same time too much accumulation of dry leaf litter increases the risk of forest fires.

Soil: an Anchorage for All

Soil is the receptacle of all that lives. The hymn dedicated to the earth in the *Atharvaveda* (12.1.12) sums up the traditional attitude of reverence:

> Impart to us those vitalizing forces
> that come, O Earth, from deep within your body,
> Your central point, your navel; purify us wholly.
> The Earth is mother; I am son of Earth,
> The rain-giver is my father; may he shower
> on us blessings!

Soil is our most valuable material heritage, the basis of all terrestrial life. As an ecological factor, soil is of great significance, for it affords a medium for the anchorage of plants and a depot for minerals and water.

Normally, soil is constantly generated and enriched when an ecosystem is left undisturbed or minimally disturbed. However, due to loss of vegetal cover, there is a progressive loss of soil due to erosion, together with attendant consequences like landslides and siltation.

Water: Flow of Life

Water is yet another important element of the life support system. Water is also the home of aquatic life. The presence of aquatic life is an indication of the well-being of water. The personification of water is integral to the Indian ethos. All rivers are feminine and so associated with fertility (except the Brahmaputra, which is male). Most important of all rivers is the Ganga, and her sacredness is enshrined in the myth of *gangavatarana* or the descent of the Ganges.

According to Indian mythology the Ganges was brought down to the earth and the nether world by the penances of Bhagirath, descendant of Sagara, king of Ayodhya, to atone for the sins of his ancestors and to bring them once more to life. Lord Shiva's matted locks acted as a breakwater to gentle the rush of water which would otherwise have split the world asunder. The ecological message of this myth is as apparent as the physical reality of the course of the Ganga. The rich Deodara forests are associated with the breakwaters of Shiva's matted locks, through which it meanders.

The region receives plenty of rain, but due to deforestation there is a failure of watershed which results in the unchecked flow of water during the monsoon to cause a sudden swelling of streams in rivers so that there are floods in the foothills and even in the plains, and droughts in the villages located on the slope of the mountain. A watershed is a natural drainage area draining off water to a common point which ultimately meets with a river. Integrated development of watersheds thus takes care of water, crops, fuel, fodder and livestock with a view to develop the overall economy. Several NGOs with people's participation are trying to reset watershed management by planting trees on the top of the slope to retain the water, building tanks of cement and alkathene to save rainwater, building check dams on the streams to break the velocity of gushing water which brings silt along with it.

The region has a number of rivers, streams and springs, but the people are unable to use the water since it flows in deep channels.

Thus the people used springs for drinking water and *gulas* for irrigation and other daily needs. The skill of the people is reflected in the canals (*gulas*), the gravitational channels which they make to divert stream water to various levels in the difficult hilly terrain. They also run small water mills, using the power of the falling water. The water mill is locally known as *gharrat*, which grinds cereals and spices.

Impact of Development

Development in the region is the other major feature of the ecological crisis, which takes different forms such as the coming up of dams, building of roads, tourism development, etc. Quarrying, mining and blasting operations also give rise to landslides, which not only block traffic on the roads but sometimes form lakes by the temporary blockade of rivers. When the water exerts pressure these burst, causing devastating floods, sweeping away roads, bridges, agricultural land, etc. For example, the Alaknanda flood of 1970 was of a similar type. Such floods are a constant threat to highways, villages, streams, dams, agricultural land and tourists.

The limestone industry in the Doon valley has caused severe damage to the environment — loss of topsoil, lowering of the water table, deposition of dust on plant surfaces, emission of gases from the kilns. Processing of limestone in the kilns leads to the emission of CO_2, CO and SO_2 gases. Plants show defoliation, chlorosis, necrosis, etc.

The coming up of big dams like the Tehri dam, which submerge large fertile areas which are so scarce in the region, and standing on a seismically active zone having many thrust and faults, may also be responsible for an ecological crisis.

The traffic of vehicles alters the composition of vegetation. Building of roadways in the mountain system creates disturbances. This does not mean that roads in the hills are not important, but they need to be constructed in consonance with the nature of geological formation. The construction of a hill road involves felling of existing protective vegetation, cutting and blasting otherwise stable hill slopes, and the rolling down of the resultant debris which in turn destroys vegetation and causes severe erosion resulting in extensive slope failures. These are often termed as landslides. The phenomenon of landslides is not linked with road making alone but also with land use in general.

Tourism

The Himalayan region is considered to be abundantly suited for tourism since it offers all kinds of attractions to tourists. A paradise for anglers and a challenge to hikers. The lush green valleys, emerald meadows, vast icefields have now started showing abrasion due to increasing human activity. Tourism brings a large number of people together, which leads to marked changes that are detrimental to the ecosystem as a whole. Tourism is found in the form of pilgrim tourism and for pleasure and adventure. To accommodate the large tourist influx, hundreds of new buildings are being constructed every year. The tourist activity has to be in consonance with the principles of conservation of nature and with the protection of associated resources. Unplanned development in the Himalayas is causing irreparable damage. The problems of litter, noise, erosion, destruction of fauna and flora have become acute. The garbage problem is another Himalayan task to solve. Litter and garbage piles are all around, as we have noticed during our visit to Gangotri.

Thus tourism development is another big problem in the region. *Dhabas* (roadside hotels) are coming up frequently right from Gangotri to Gomukh, which is responsible for the rise in temperature; grassy trails have started in Rudranath, Madhmaheshwar and Tungnath due to trekkers and mountaineers. A number of people visited the hill stations every year mainly in the months of May, June and October.

Observations

Suggestions which may help in maintaining the ecological balance in the Himalayas are: afforestation should be encouraged by planting mixed trees, both conifers and broad-leaved. Monoculture of trees should be avoided; on the higher slopes cultivation of agricultural crops should be stopped. Instead of agriculture, crop trees should be planted. To stop the over-exploitation of the forest by government contractors for resin, medicinal herbs, timber, etc., there should be a total ban on cutting of trees on mountain slopes and in catchment areas. Instead of big dams, small dams and hydro-electric power stations can be constructed. For a very small village a hydro-electric generator can be installed in the water mill. The region has plenty of water, which can promote the growth of fisheries. Promote horticulture and small-scale industry in the region, which will provide job opportunities to the local people. Promote *sulabh sauchalaya* and bio-gas plants for recycling biodegradable material. To reduce the pressure of the growing population on natural resources, they should be provided LPG gas, kerosene oil, solar cookers. Preventive measures have to be taken to avoid the chances of forest fires. In the summer of 1995 the fire in the central Himalayas has made the air polluted and caused a rise in the temperature, loss of vegetation, animals, etc.

There should be a check on quarrying, mining and blasting operations. Efforts should be made to develop more hill stations as tourist centres in the region to avoid the overcrowding of tourists in the well-known hill stations. Kilns with filter devices and higher chimneys should be constructed to minimise the effect on the environment. Any sort of development should be in harmony with the environment, and renewable resources like ground water and forests should be used at a rate at which they are being replenished by nature.

References

Chadha, S.K., (ed.), 1988, *Himalayas: ecology and environment*. Delhi: Mittal Publications.

Chaube, S.K., (ed.), 1985, *The Himalayas: profiles of modernisation and adaptation*, New Delhi: Sterling Publishers.

Dewan, M.L., 1990, *People's participation in Himalayan eco-system development*. New Delhi: Concept Publishing Company.

——— and B.D. Joshi, (eds.), 1993, *Vedic philosophy for Himalayan eco-system development*. New Delhi: Concept Publishing Company.

Dhar, T.N. and P.N. Sharma, (eds.), 1987, *Himalayan energy systems*. Nainital: Gyanodaya Prakashan.

Gupta, Krishna Murti, (ed.), 1990, *Himalaya: man and nature*. New Delhi: Lancers Books.

Jayal, N.D. and Motwari Mohan, (eds.), 1986, *Conservation, tourism and mountaineering in the Himalayas*. Dehradun: Natraj Publishers.

Khoshoo, T.N., 1988, *Environmental concerns and strategies*. New Delhi: Ashish Publishing House.

———, 1995, *Mahatma Gandhi: and apostle of applied human ecology*. New Delhi: Tata Applied Research Institute.

Negi, S.S., 1990, *Himalayan forest and forestry*. New Delhi: Indus Publishing Company.

Nitya Nand and Kamlesh Kumar, 1989, *The holy Himalaya: a geographical interpretation of Garhwal*. New Delhi: Daya Publishing House.

Pokhriyal, H.C., 1994, *Human environment and socio-economic development in the Himalayas*. Delhi: B.R. Publishing Corporation.

Prakriti, 1993, Information brochure on an exhibition on man in harmony with the elements. New Delhi: Indira Gandhi National Centre for the Arts.

Qasim, S.Z., 1993, *National policy for integrated development in the Himalayas*. New Delhi: Planning Commission.

Raha, M.K., (ed), 1987, *The Himalayan heritage*. Delhi: Gian Publishing House.

Rajan, Madhu, 1993, ' Man against nature? *The Tribune*, New Delhi, 20 June.

Rustomji, N.K. and C. Ramble, (eds.), 1990, *Himalayas: Environment and Culture*. Shimla: Indian Institute of Advanced Study; New Delhi: Indus Publishing Company.

Shah, S.D. Bhatt and R.K. Pande, R.K., (eds.), 1990, *Himalaya: environmeent, resources and development*. Almora: Shree Almora Book Depot.

5

Water Resources and their Management in Kashmir

B.L. Malla

THE valley of Kashmir has been a great seat of learning and erudition from its hoary past. Its beauty and verdure, snow-capped peaks, sparkling waters, rustling leaves of dense forests, lakes and springs, have charmed poets and creative minds to sing its praises, calling it 'a paradise on earth'. Inspired and motivated by the pristine beauty of the landscape, the genius of Kashmir has contributed to almost all segments of human knowledge and creative ventures.

Among the earlier settlers in Kashmir are believed to be Nagas. There are geological and mythological reasons to believe that the valley was once a vast span of water, similar to a huge dam, walled in by high mountains. The *Nilamatapurana* records how the valley was elevated out of water and left under the care of the Nagas, of whom Nila, the son of Kashyapa, was the chief. Although legends are legends and do not provide hard evidence in most cases, the present description regarding the drawing of water is reconcilable with the geological scenario of violent earthquakes accompanied by darkness and cloudburst.

It is said that the valley is named 'Kashmir' after Kashyapa. The term 'naga' stands for spring, *chesmah*, and *negin* for small spring. Springs are the main source of water in Kashmir. The five primordial elements (earth, fire, water, air and sky) are, in fact, complementary to the people's rituals, cognitive system, religious beliefs and sacrificial practices. Interestingly, the auspicious and famous river of Kashmir, the Vitasta (Jhelum) originates from a spring near Verinag and is responsible for the water supply to most parts of the valley. The religious significance of the river is established by the *Nilamatapurana* when it records the entire land of Kashmir as the material manifestation of Uma and describes her as the divine form of the Vitasta.[1]

Apart from meaning a spring, the term *naga* had tremendous theo-cultural relevance for the lives of the people of Kashmir. As the sacredness of water gets echoed in the worship of *nagas*, the Naga as spring is the source of life. Some scholars have identified the *nagas* as personified forces of nature.

Naga Worship

A large number of temples were built near springs and were dedicated to the worship of *nagas*. The *Nilamatapurana* admits that *nagas* reside in lakes and springs. These places have become great centres of religious pilgrimage. The place names of certain areas, e.g. Verinag, Anantnag and Seshanag even today remind one of the intimate relations between the valley and the popularity of the Naga cult. The *Rajatarangini* of Kalhana mentions Sushravas and Padma Nagas, who were tutelary deities connected with the Wular lake. The Dikpalas of Kashmir are believed to be four *nagas*, viz. Bindusara in the east, Srimadaka in the south, Elapatra in the west and Uttarmansa in the north.

There are many festivals in Kashmir which have a bearing on the worship of Nagas, for example during the first snowfall, Nila, the Lord of Nagas, is worshipped. The Nagas are also propitiated in April and are related to *Iramanjari Puja* and to *Varuna Panchmi*, which is organised in July-August. Kashmir spoke highly of the festival in the darker half of the month of Jyeshtha, when a big festival is organised to propitiate the king Taksakyatra. The *Nilamatapurana* listed 527 Nagas that were worshipped in Kashmir. In the account of Abul Fazal, the court historian of Akbar, there are references to seven hundred places sacred to serpents.

The *Nilamatapurana* also draws attention to the close association of the cult of Nagas and that of Shiva. In the *Mahabharata* and *Harivamsa* texts, Sesha was considered the son of Shiva. Such an attempt at compromise was also attempted between the cult of Vaishnava and the cult of Nagas. The Nagas became Vishnu in the *seshashayi* form, which belongs to water cosmology, and his images were made accordingly. Balarama, the elder brother of Krishna, is the personification of the snake and he is Ananta incarnated in human form. Names like Vishnasar and Krishnasar carry Vaishnavite import. Interestingly, the word *sar* stands for reservoir. The goddess Lakshmi is said to have taken the form of the river Visoka (now known as the Vishov) to purify the people of Kashmir. Most probably, treating springs and rivers with great reverence wittingly or unwittingly resulted in the ecological balance necessary for a healthy and natural interaction between the environment and man.

In Muslim-dominated contemporary Kashmir the spring is understood as *naga* and enjoys the respect of every religion. It is generally believed that every *naga* has a snake as its guardian deity. Fishing is prohibited in these springs, though the fish which come out of the main *garbha* of a *naga* can be caught. Restrictions on fishing have definitely helped to some extent to preserve water ecology. Hindus still propitiate these *nagas*. At Martanda Naga even *srada* is performed. Water is offered by Hindus to the Sun God and to their ancestors (*purvaj*). Before having *darshan* of the snow *linga* at Amarnatha a holy dip is essential in the Seshanaga. A person suffering from a skin disease is said to be cured after having a bath in Gandhakanaga (sulphur spring) at Naghbal, Anantnag.

Muslims show their respect for these *nagas* in many ways. They offer sacrifices and organise fairs on many festivals such as *Id*. Even they do not catch fish in these *nagas*. Their faith in *nagas* can further be established by an example from Anantnag district, where during days of water scarcity or extra rainfall, people offer sacrifices to the Vasuk Naga (the water of which remains in the valley during summer only and disappears in winter). They have full faith that offerings to Vasuk will bring rain or stop it as desired.

Besides, spring water is considered pure for drinking. The Public Health Engineering Department of the state supplies spring water to most urban and semi-urban areas. In most of the rural areas there is at least one *negin*[2] (small spring) within the boundary or nearby. The people also prefer to take baths in spring water because it remains hot in winter and cold in summer.

Water Management

With the vast majority of Kashmiri people living in villages and their income coming mainly out of land, the importance of irrigation is considerable. Being a hilly state, the problem of irrigation is complicated in many areas. At higher altitudes the main source of water is *naga* or lift irrigation. The first claim on the water of a spring is of the village near it. Paddy, the staple food, is generally grown on the fertile lands adjoining the river Vitasta, although it is produced on some higher plateaus also.

The autumn or *kharif* crops consist of maize, pulses (*moong*, *mash* and *motha*), etc. The spring or *rabi* crops include wheat, peas, beans and mustard. Thanks to the formation of the valley, irrigation is easy and in ordinary years abundant. If there is normal snowfall in the winter and the great mountains are well covered, the water supply for rice is sufficient. On both sides of the Vitasta, the valley rises in bold terraces, and water passes quickly from one village to another in years of good snow. In earlier times, at convenient points on the mountain, weirs or protecting snags were erected, and the water was taken into main channels which pass into small networks of ducts and eventually empty themselves in the

Jhelum. Lower down in the valley, where the streams flow gently, dams were erected. On every main channel there was a *mirab*—one of the villagers—whose duty it was to maintain the system.

In earlier days, in alluvial plateaus water was scarce. Many kings of Kashmir, therefore, tried to extend irrigation facilities there. The first known work of this kind was a canal called Suvarnamani (modern Suman Kul) constructed by king Suvarna in the pre-Ashokan age. It irrigated a part of the Advin Pargana, situated on the alluvial plateau to the south of the Rembyar river.

In the eighth century a great ruler of Kashmir, King Lalitaditya, is credited with having introduced a new device called the water wheel for raising water to the higher plateaus. In this device a peasant used a long pole at the top of which was a bucket to be with water, balancing it with his feet to draw the water from a well or channel. At present this inexpensive method is used in many parts of the valley, especially for the irrigation of house gardens, and the device is now called *tol* or dip-well. With the advance of technology diesel or electric pumps are preferred for the lift irrigation of agricultural lands. For this purpose the Government of Jammu and Kashmir has a department of irrigation which looks after the lift irrigation schemes.

In Kashmir the problem of recurring floods, especially in the Vitasta, was often caused by heavy summer rains and melting of snow which flooded the arable land around. To protect cultivable lands from floods, attempts were made from early times. According to Kalhana, King Damodara built stone-lined dykes in order to guard against inundations. The minister of King Baladitya erected an embankment. The construction of embankments was meant to protect cultivable land from floods, and the surplus water thus obtained could be passed into several channels to irrigate other fields. An important attempt in this direction was made by King Lalitaditya, who arranged for distributing the waters of the Vitasta at Cakradhara (modern Tsakadar) to various villages. These drainage operations made the valley productive to some extent. But the work of irrigation started by the monarch was neglected by his incompetent successors. However, an attempt was made by Suyya, the irrigation minister of King Avantivarman in the ninth century to regulate the waters of the Vitasta and to drain the whole valley. Near Yaksadara (modern Dyargul), large rocks which had rolled down from the mountain, lining both banks, obstructed the Vitasta. Suyya dragged out the rocks and the level of the river was lowered. He thus regulated the water of the Jhelum, constructed protective works and arranged for the supply of water to each village on a permanent basis. He dammed the lake, which by its depth and well-defined boundaries was naturally designed as a great reservoir to receive the surplus waters of the dangerous floods. The endeavours of Suyya met with unique success.

Due to lawlessness and insecure conditions, agriculture steadily declined. With the advent of Islam in the valley, Hindu rule came to an end in the fourteenth century. The Muslim rulers did not give any attention to the development of the valley. Sultan Zain-ul-abidin (fifteenth century) was perhaps the only Muslim ruler who was keen to cure the miseries of the cultivators and promote their welfare. Agriculture occupied his special attention. One important measure was the construction of canals in the valley. To quote Srivara, 'There was not a piece of land, not a region and not a forest where the king did not excavate a canal. Some of these were the Kakapur canal, the Karla canal, the Chakdar canal, the Avantipur canal, the Shahkul canal (of Safapur), Lachham Kul or Zainaganga, Lall Kul or Pohri canal, Shah Kul on the Martanda canal and the Mar Canal. The Shah Kul was taken out on the left bank of the Lidder river and ran along the face of the limestone cliffs above Martanda. Here it split into four distributing channels, and finally fell over the edge of the plateau into the Jhelum valley at Anantnag. Some of these canals are still important sources of irrigation, but in most cases they have narrowed down. Before the Mar Canal was constructed, the surplus waters of the Dal Lake used to flow into the Jhelum river at Habba Kadal. This junction was closed, forcing the outflow of the lake's water into the Mar Canal, which then extended up to Shadipura. Several other earlier canals were revived and repaired, and some of them supplied water to otherwise dry Karewa lands. At present the Vitasta has narrowed,[3] which is the main cause of floods in the valley over last many years. The river needs a fresh drainage programme, and the traditional knowledge system can play an important role in its management. As tourism is an important industry in Kashmir and the Jhelum one of the main attractions, it is necessary to take up the task of drainage on a priority basis. Tourists also like to stay in the houseboats, which are either in the Jhelum or in Dal Lake.[4]

The net result of the above irrigation projects was the draining of marshes and the reclamation of large areas for cultivation, which is essential while looking to the growth of the population.

Besides irrigation, water was used in many ways in the valley. The tradition of *pana-chaki* (*greta*) still continues in many rural areas.

We should keep in mind that the state of the environment of any place is an indication of its spiritual health, in which the deeper issues of culture, values, politics and the economic and social outlook of a community are involved. Besides, no eco-system is altogether self-contained; it is further linked to another system and so on. The scarcity of snowfall in the winter can lead to a famine. Although nature has endowed the valley with beautiful gifts, the inner forces of matter and mind are stamping these gifts out of existence at a rapid pace. The priorities and patterns of development, coupled with whimsical decision-making, have greatly contributed to the brutalisation of the landscape,[5] the silting of the great lakes and rivers, the pollution of air, water and soil. Not long ago, the high mountains of Kashmir supported one of the densest and richest subtropical and temperate forests of the world, covering more than 60 per cent of the total land area. But after the mid-1970s there has been a licensed massacre of green trees. Currently the jungles of Kashmir are destroyed in search of *kuth*, a highly priced medicinal plant. The smuggling of wood for building, etc., has been high for many years.[6] As per a recent study about 91 thousand hectares of forest land were lost to various development projects during the period 1952 to 1976. The deforestation in the valley has unfortunately disturbed the ecological balance and has lessened the average snowfall. Because of it there is scarcity of irrigation and drinking water in the summer season. At many places drinking water is supplied by the Public Health Engineering Department in tanks, and irrigation is mostly dependent on rainwater. If all this is not controlled at this stage the economy will be shattered. The dream of industrialisation which we people also see in Kashmir will come to a stop, as most industries are dependent on electricity, which is produced by hydel projects in the valley. It will not be wrong to say that the economic progress of the place is largely dependent on water and its proper management.

Similarly, the problems arising from the pollution of air, water and soil caused by cement factories, stone crushers, brick kilns, smelting industries and the unchecked use of chemicals have become very serious. It seems that ecological consciousness is confined to words only. Even after 49 years of freedom there is not scientific sewerage system in the summer capital (Srinagar) of the Jammu and Kashmir state. The night-soil, which is carried on the head or in poorly maintained vehicles, spreads a foul smell all along.

The inhabitants of houseboats and the boatmen living in *dongas* dispose of their refuse in the Dal Lake or the Jhelum, thereby polluting the water. It has been shown that the drinking water supplied to some parts of Srinagar city was worse than the polluted water of the Jhelum. This polluted water does pose a serious threat, not only to human life only but also to wildlife, particularly in the Dachigam National Park.

Militancy has added fuel to the fire. It has disturbed entire eco-system and the law of the jungle prevails these days. If this situation is not brought under control quickly the entire past of Kashmir will come to a sad end. From its seminal stages to the present state of civilisation, Kashmir has been famous for tolerance, mutual goodwill and humanism. The spirit of synthesis and assimilation is the key to Kashmiri culture. Kashmir has carved a niche for itself in the fabric of Indian culture. The present-day attempts to insulate her from humanism and synthetical modes of thinking cannot be overlooked as a mere aberration as these are aimed at destroying the essential genius of Kashmir.

Notes

1. In fact, the Vitasta is the lifeline of all Kashmiris. With the advent of spring, *vyth truvah* was celebrated by all the Hindus of the valley (at least until the beginning of militancy and the mass migration of Kashmiri Pandits from the valley in 1989) as the birthday of the river in March-April (*Chaitra*). On this day prayers were held on either side of the river and milk and flowers were offered to her. After sunset earthen lamps were lit and offered to the river after placing these on *shali* (paddy) grass rings. The day was commonly celebrated as *Durga Puja* or Kashmiri *sounth*.
2. Most probably *negin* is a corrupt form of the word Nagin, the snake goddess. Interestingly, the worship of the snake goddess was prevalent in the west. In this connection, a reference may be made to a charming statue of the snake goddess in ivory and gold dated sixteenth century BC from Minoa, the island of Crete in the eastern Mediterranean (Shali 1993:105).
3. The river is getting silted at an alarming speed. The liquid and solid wastes of the entire valley also go into it.
4. The famous Dal Lake, which was described by Abul Fazal as thee 'delight of the world', has shrunk from 24 sq km to 10 sq km. The fate of the other lakes such as the Wular and the Mansbal is no different. The Anchor and the Gilsar lakes are now gone.
5. The City Forest Project at Srinagar introduced by Jagmohan in his first term as governor of the Jammu and Kashmir state became the talk of the valley. He developed a vast area of about 907 ha of land lying near Pari Mahal, Shankaracharya hill and Zeethyar hill into a sort of natural woodland within the metropolis of Srinagar. The entire complex became a haven for nature lovers, being restored to its pristine simplicity and charm. But all this was sacrificed for a sprawling artificial golf course which is being laid at the phenomenal cost of over Rs.10 crore. It seems that development is for the elites by the elites and there is not any attempt to enhance the quality of the common man's life.

   The Gulmarg Cable Car Project is yet another example of inappropriate development. In the execution of the project many fully grown trees have already been cut and more are expected to be butchered. Although the estimated cost of the project is placed at more than Rs.40 crore, there is hardly any chance of economic and financial advantage from it. An individual is supposed to pay Rs.100 and a family of five Rs.500 for the gondola trip. But how many families in India can afford this in addition to other expenditure on a trip to the state? I think it would be wiser to follow an independent and creative path, in harmony with the social conditions and the cultural heritage of the state, for its development schemes.
6. Besides, the current consumption of firewood in the state is believed to be 100 lakh quintals.

References

Bamzai, P.N.K., 1987, *Socio-cultural history of Kashmir*. New Delhi.

Jagmohan, 1991, *My frozen turbulence in Kashmir*. New Delhi.

Kapur, M.L., 1976, *History and culture of Kashmir*. Jammu.

———, 1983, *Kingdom of Kashmir*. Jammu.

Kumari, Ved, 1968, *The Nilmata Purana* (Vol. I). Jammu.

———, 1973, *The Nilmata Purana* (Vol. II). Srinagar.

Malla, B.L., 1990, *Sculptures of Kashmir*. New Delhi.

———, 1996, *Vaisnava art and iconography of Kashmir*. New Delhi.

Ray, S.C., 1957, *Early history and culture of Kashmir*. Calcutta.

Shali, S.L., 1993, *Kashmir: history and archaeology through the ages*, New Delhi.

6

Sacred Response to Environment
The Gaddi and His Mountain

Molly Kaushal

The Himalayan ecological crisis is today a major concern among policy-makers, environmental activists and academicians. The Gujars and the Gaddis, two Himalayan nomadic groups, and their grazing cattle are seen as the main cause of soil erosion and denuded forests. These two groups are being urged to give up their nomadic way of life and accept a more developed and supposedly eco-friendly sedentary mode of life. Many development programmes are being launched to 'rehabilitate' these wandering nomads.

In this presentation I seek to explore the ecological world-view of the Gaddis and show how this world-view as well as the life-style based on it are in complete harmony with nature and have for centuries helped preserve the eco-socio-cultural nerve centre of their existence, namely the Dholadhar range of the Himalayas.

The Gaddis are a semi-nomadic pastoral group whose economic activity revolves around sheep rearing and agriculture. The Bharmaur sub-tehsil of the Chamba district, Himachal Pradesh, is the homeland of the Gaddis and is called Gadiyar or Gaderan after its inhabitants.

Gaderan, situated on the Dholadhar range of the Himalayas, is not just a physico-geographical entity but possesses a symbolic multi-level identity. The Gaderan land contains within itself the Brahmalok — Bharmaur. Brahmalok belongs to Brahma Mata or Bharmani, the original deity and ruler of Bharmaur. Chaurasi, the main temple complex at Bharmaur, which according to popular belief contains 84 *shivalingas*, represents the celestial kingdom both at the micro and the macro levels. What appears to the naked eye is at the micro level; and to the wise or to those with deep inner vision the real and pure celestial kingdom is perceivable. Thus Chaurasi is not a mere reflection or a replica of the original kingdom, but in fact is the real celestial kingdom. Chaurasi is immortal. Situated at the *yoni* basin of Shiva, it remains intact during the cosmic dissolution. Chaurasi also represents the meso-space, the middle space mediating between the individual microcosm and the macrocosm of eternal space — the Mani-Mahesh Kailash. It is not just Chaurasi, but the entire hill terrain inhabited by the Gaddis, that is held sacred. There is no place for the profane here, as the entire land is the *Shiv Bhumi* or Shiva's *jalhairi*.

The *Shiv Bhumi* or the *yoni* basin (*jalhairi*) stretches from Kharamukh (15 km west of Bharmaur village), the meeting point of the river Ravi and its tributary the Buddhal Nallah, to Mani-Mahesh (36 km east of Bharmaur). Mani-Mahesh represents eternal space, which has neither an end nor a beginning. The soil from Kharamukh to Sundrasi (a spot en route to Mani-Mahesh) is made of copper, and that from Sundrasi to Mani-Mahesh, of gold. The Dal lake, located at the feet of Mani-Mahesh, has a spot, Kali-kund, the endless pit leading to Piyalpuri, the nether land. The peaks of Mani-Mahesh represent Shiva's Vaikunth, and Bharmaur is Bharmani's Vaikunth. Lord Vishnu's Vaikunth is located deep inside the Ksheer-Sagar, which is situated under the waterfalls at Dhanchcho (one of the stopovers en route to Mani-Mahesh).

The temporal world consists of four paths, and they all lead to Chaurasi, where the river Vaitarani flows. The 2½ steps the soul climbs to reach the court of Dharamraja are also located at Chaurasi. After death, the soul crosses 16 bridges and then by one of the four paths reaches Dharamraja's court located at the Dharameshwara temple in Chaurasi. The gates of the celestial space of Chaurasi are guarded by Bhe or Bidh Mata, who is also known as Lakhna Mata.

As in life, so in death man is seen as closely related to cosmic elements. If during his lifetime man's survival is conditioned by his response to the environment, whether social or natural or biological, his fate after death is decided by 14 witnesses who accompany the soul on its journey to Dharamraja's court. These witnesses are day, night, morning, afternoon, evening, moon, sun, stars, air, water, fire, earth, *akasha*. The shrine of the fourteenth witness, Chitra Gupta (who in a sense encapsulates the deeds of the soul in the temporal world), is situated in front of the entrance to the Dharameshwara temple. In my view this is an ultimate statement about man's total dependence on nature as well as an acknowledgement of its supreme power. This is also an acknowledgement of the fact that it is indeed the bondedness of the biological being with nature and his actions within the temporal world (both physical and social) that sustain a Gaddi in life and death.

The ultimate destination of the soul is the Mani-Mahesh Kailash, beyond the boundaries of mundane space and time. The ultimate goal is to become one with the cosmic realm of

Shiva, the lord of the Dholadhars. Mani-Mahesh represents eternal celestial bliss — for here Shiva at his benevolent best lives with Mata Gorja, whose *man ka mahesh* (beloved) he is. Shiva created Mani-Mahesh as his abode after his marriage to Parvati.

Shiva resides at Mani-Mahesh for a period of six months and migrates to Piyalpuri, the nether land, during the winter months. The migratory period of the Gaddis coincides with the migratory pattern of their main deity, Lord Shiva. It will not be off the mark to state that the Gaddis' notions of space and time as well as their eco-socio-cultural configurations are conceptually derived from this upward-downward movement of Lord Shiva. The Gaddi annual calendar of activities is accordingly divided into two halves and represents two distinct modes of life during the summer months at Bharmaur and the high passes of the Dholadhar, and winter months in the valley of Kangra.

The Gaddi universe is spatially conceived of as being on a vertical axis.[1] On the one end of the axis is Shiva's Kailasa and on the other is the nether land. The up and down movement on this vertical axis is cyclical and follows nature's rhythm. When Shiva migrates to Piyalpuri, he takes away with him all the living creatures, so the Gaddi too migrates. This upward-downward movement is so important to the Gaddi that it is reflected in his more sedentary existence as well, namely in the construction of his houses, which stand as if on a vertical pole and the life within the house, which also follows this movement.[2] The vertical axis is so important that the horizontal axis in fact is seen as an undifferentiated mass of things and beings.[3]

Nothing would be more off the mark than to view Gaddi migration as a mere economic pursuit. Ironically, all development programmes launched in the Dholadhar mountain range are aimed at making the Gaddis move towards a sedentary way of life. Their migration pattern is seen as a clever attempt at grabbing land on both sides of the Dholadhar on the one hand, and retaining their scheduled tribe status on the other. The relationship between the Gaddi and his flock is again understood in purely materialistic terms, so he is urged through various administrative means to give up sheep rearing. High taxes on sheep and goats, the closing of traditional pastures and routes, the planting of trees in traditional grazing grounds, the introduction of horticulture and offers of clerical jobs at local C.P.W.D and electricity departments are some such means, which according to the Gaddis have done more harm than good.

What must be understood is that to a Gaddi his way of life is not dispensable. His mountains, his sheep and his pastures are not dispensable either. He derives his socio-cultural, religious and territorial identity from these. They not only sustain him but are also sustained through him. The protection of sheep is the reason why Shiva created the Gaddi in the first place. He is a nomad because his lord himself is a nomad. He roams from pasture to pasture, from hill to hill, because his lord has ordered him to do so. In his nomadism and pastoralism he is doing what the lord of the Dholadhar himself does. The boon of sheep rearing was not granted to the Gaddi easily. A Gaddi became a Gaddi by Shiva's blessings, who first tested his integrity as a shepherd.

Shiva tested the Gaddi. He gave him a flock of sheep to tend. The Gaddi saved the flock from the attacking bear, risking his own life. He saved it from the attacks of the wild dog. At last, when he sat to eat, Shiva drove his flock away. The Gaddi forgot his meal and ran after the flock and brought it back. At night, when he was about to sleep, Shiva led his flock astray. The Gaddi ran after the flock and spent the whole night bringing it together. Shiva was convinced at last. He gave the Gaddi his flock and his garb and made him a Gaddi.

The *chola* and the *dora* (the Gaddi dress) are indeed an extension of Shiva's own self in the same way, as sheep rearing and nomadism are. The Gaddi body is created with the *mitti* (earth) taken from Shiva's body, and this act of creation takes place while Shiva is seated on his royal seat (*gaddi*). The area where the Gaddi lives and tends his flock is the majestic Dholadhar (the grey pasture land, grey because of the clouds). This pasture land rests in Parvati's lap or in the *yoni* basin of Shiva. Space thus is seen here as a Shiva-Parvati continuum or as a *purusha-prakriti* continuum. The Gaddi is an extension of this space. The Gaddi body, created with *mitti* (earth) from Shiva's body, the Gaddi garb a symbolic extension of Shiva's own self, the Gaddi cap, whose top represents Shiva's Kailasa, and the flaps of the cap that represent the inner chambers of Parvati's abode, repeat the *purusha-prakriti* continuum. The Shiv Bhumi or the *jalhairi* that protects and nurtures the Gaddi has the central axis of its existence in Lord Shiva, who himself is embedded in this *bhumi*.

Thus the Gaddi space is both immediate and physical on the one hand and eternal, metaphysical and transcendent on the other. The five primeval elements that fill the ecological space also fill the biological space of the Gaddi body. Thus water is what flows in the form of blood. Air constitutes breath. Earth makes flesh and bone. It may be pointed out here that it is only he who is created from *mitti* is blessed with life (motion), *prana* (air).[4] Fire gives strength, vigour and vitality. *Akasha* is consciousness. *Akasha* as sun are the eyes. The soul resides in the innermost chamber of the heart.

This world-view of the Gaddi does not just remain discussed or referred to discourse but is actively practised. The life of the Gaddi shepherd is a life of discipline, austerity, and acknowledgement of the interdependence and bondedness of man with the great forces of nature and its eternal rhythm. Nature and its forces are revered, and the most sacred act is the act of maintaining their purity. This is done through the moral and ethical order. As body and mind are kept away from pollution through moral conduct, so is the environment.

Each stone, each *dhar*, each slope and each spring is sacred. Each has a deity or represents a deity. Obeisance is paid to each. Each *nallah*, each stream, has appeared as a result of some sacrificial act by ancestors. The *sui* fair at Chamba annually pays homage to Rani Naina Devi, who sacrificed her life in order to release the flow of waters. Bharmani Mata is the most revered deity, from whose feet flow the waters of the Bharmani Nallah. She, according to one of the legends, stole the waters from the *naglok* in a *bibri* (a long vessel made of dry pumpkin) and provided them to Bharmaur. *Minjar ka mela* worships rain, sun and Varuna.

The village *panihar* (place for washing, bathing and drawing water) is a sacred place. Each newly-wed daughter-in-law is taken there to offer prayers. After the bath the bather cleans the *panihar*, removes the dirt and offers *dhupa* (incense), *sindur* (vermilion) and flowers. *Panihars* are beautifully carved places where figures of gods and ancestors are prominently displayed and worshipped. The great reverence for water comes in the form of an acknowledgement of mother earth as *jalhairi* (water reservoir). Along with the worship of water, the sun is worshipped too. Water is offered to the sun. There is some archaeological evidence that the Gaddis were sun worshippers at one stage. It is noteworthy that the Gaddi calendar of fairs and festivals is solar in nature. The festival of Patroru is associated with the worship of fire and Shiva. It is also a festival of flowers and green leaves. Domestic fire is revered too. *Halva* is offered to the fire god at the time of lighting a new oven.

The Gaddi shepherd on the mountain passes interacts with his resource base in a responsible manner. He not only reveres the mountains but leads a life that follows the principle of non-pollution, minimising waste and conserving self, flock and land. The Gaddi refrains from taking liquor as a mark of respect to the deity of a given pass. He does not spit or litter the place in any manner. Where and when the shepherd can relieve himself are specified. The Gaddi shepherd is well aware of noise pollution. Up in the mountain passes, he is prohibited from talking aloud, making loud sounds or laughing aloud. If he does so, stones will start rolling down the mountains and snowstorms will destroy him and his flock. The Gaddi shepherd at the passes eats only once in a day and that too at a specific time. Nobody is allowed to eat or light a fire after that. The Gaddi shepherd, while up in the high pastures, does not erect tents. No matter how cold it may be, he sleeps in the open along with his flock and receives warmth from his sheep. Rock projections serve as his shelter from rain. Rock spirits are offered three coloured grains of rice, five sweet cakes, a loaf, a flour-lamp with a red wick, three kinds of flowers, three pieces of *dhupa* and a she-goat. The deities of the *dhars* (mountain summits) are offered a he-goat. Permission is taken from the deity of the pass at the time of entering and leaving his area. This life of austerity and restraint is oriented towards the preservation and the conservation of life-sustaining elements, which we very often dismiss as the superstitions of primitive minds.

Gaddi pastoralism or transhumance also helps conserve the ecology of the Himalayas. Studies of transhumance show that "it maintains an equilibrium among men, animals and pastures in the mountain regions that are unsuitable for conventional agriculture. The animals are important sources of primary products such as milk, meat, wool, hides and skins. The system calls for a judicious use of the available resources — herds and pastures . . . . The ecological aspect of transhumance is as important as its economic significance. In high altitude areas movement of cattle helps afforestation. While traversing over mountains they exert pressure on seeds and spawns deposited on leaves of plants, thereby fixing these in the soil to regenerate. . . . Also, the process of rotation grazing and weeding out of necessary shrubs and grass helps tree and plant growth in these regions" (Sud 1992:4; Khatana 1992).

And one last word about the Mani-Mahesh *jatar*. Shiva is supposed to have come to Bharmaur from Kashmir with 84 *siddhas*. They lit a fire and filled the area with smoke. The ruling deity, Mata Bharmani, was furious. She turned the 84 *siddhas* into stone *lingas* and ordered Shiva to leave and move to his Kailasa. Shiva in veneration to this deity decreed that all persons intending to go on a pilgrimage to Mani-Mahesh must have a dip in the Bharmani pool and offer prayers at the Bharmani temple. Failing this, the pilgrimage would not be acceptable to him. So even the lord himself was not allowed to desecrate the socio-ecological order. The annual pilgrimage to Mani-Mahesh is a Gaddi's way of paying tribute to this order. The Mani Mahesh *jatar* not only reinforces the Gaddi's moral and socio-cultural order, it also makes him an integral part of the cosmic-ecological rhythm of the lord of the Dholadhars.

Notes

1. Even the creation of the world is conceived of as having taken place on a vertical pole. The world according to the Gaddis originated from the *mulvriksha* (the *arbour mundi*). In the beginning there were only deep waters. First a *kumbha* (pot) appeared in them, from which emerged a banyan tree. The upper portion of the tree got transformed into the three faces of Brahma, Vishnu and Mahesh, the lower part of the tree became *prithvi* (earth), on which later appeared *rishis* and *gurus*. The primal image of the emerging world gets translated into the symbolic representation of the Gaddi land, where the *arbour mundi* and the pot appear in the forms of the *axis mundi* (Mani-Mahesh) and the water reservoir (*jalhairi*).
2. A Gaddi house, made of pine logs, planks, mud, cowdung and slate slabs, generally consists of three storeys. The ground floor is called *obra* and is used for keeping cattle. A staircase called *manjh* leads to the first floor, called *mandeh*. The *mandeh* serves as the living room during the winter months. The second floor is called *chhapar* and is used as family quarters in the summer. This is the most auspicious space in the house and family idols and icons are usually kept here in a cavity called *thola*,

in which also rests the central beam of the roof. Life within the house symbolically replicates the seasonal migratory pattern of the Gaddis. The entire household along with the hearth moves up to the second storey in the summer and comes down to the first floor during the winter.

3. Horizontally viewed, Mani-Mahesh stands in the centre of the earth, and on either side of it stretches the temporal world, which is the homeland of humans, animals, deities, spirits and demons. It is *devaloka* (land of deities), *mrityuloka* (land of mortal creatures) and *rakshasa bhumi* (land of demons) all at once.

4. In one of the Gaddi myths of creation Brahma first created a man of gold, but he wouldn't breathe, no matter how much Brahma blew into his mouth. The same fate was met with men made of silver and copper. Brahma then took a small piece of *mitti*, created a human form out of it and blew into its mouth; and the form became alive.

References

Khatana, R.P., 1992, *Tribal migration in the Himalayan frontiers: a study of Gujjar Bakarwal transhumance economy*. Gurgaon: Vintage Books.

Sud, K.N., 1992, 'Labour of love'. New Delhi: The *Hindustan Times*, 4 June.

7

Ecology and Traditional Wisdom

P.S. Ramakrishnan

INDIA is a land of diversity, varied cultural and ecological landscapes being embedded in rich traditional wisdom. Caught up in the process of modernisation, much of the traditional rural-based empirical knowledge base developed over a long period through trial and error, is being depleted very rapidly. Traditional societies, including tribals, living in the forested uplands, however, have so far been able to conserve their traditional wisdom in the face of the onslaught of the modernisation process.

Land use for agriculture, fisheries and forestry, which forms the basis for the sustainable livelihood of traditional societies, is often based on traditional knowledge and technology, developed in a given ecological, socio-economic and cultural setting. Not only is this knowledge base being threatened now, but very often we have failed to provide an alternative viable technology as a replacement for what is being eroded. The reasons for this are varied and complex. Yet, in the context of the sustainable management of land resources, there is an increasing realisation of the value of this rich heritage, and therefore a renewed interest in traditional knowledge and technology. It is in this context that this paper examines a variety of situations in which the linkage between ecology and culture is crucial for the sustainable development of our upland regions in general and for the sustainable livelihood of traditional societies in particular.

Managing Complex Landscapes Through Traditional Wisdom:

TRADITIONAL SOCIETIES OF INDIA

Over 400 tribal communities are distributed throughout the country, forming about 8 per cent of India's total population (Anonymous 1981). However, it should be noted that not all tribal groups are recognised by the government for special treatment and benefits, and those that are, belong to the 'scheduled tribes' category under the Indian constitution. Indeed, many traditional societies inhabiting upland areas (e.g. traditional Himalayan societies) may not be tribal in their characteristics and yet may form ecologically distinct groups, sharing similar developmental problems with tribals elsewhere. Therefore, social groups that could be considered traditional/indigenous are many more than are recognised. The distribution of these traditional societies closely corresponds to the distribution of the 'hot spots' of biodiversity in the country.

A number of development programmes have been taken up during the last few decades in order to improve the socio-economic conditions of tribals and other weaker sections of society. These programmes suffer from many deficiencies. Highly heterogeneous tribal groups, each with distinct ecological, social and economic characteristics, are often treated as a homogeneous whole. This has resulted in the funds for development often being allocated without due consideration for the felt needs of individual tribal groups. Even within the same tribe, access to benefits was often restricted to limited sections. Consequently (a) some tribes are more advanced than others, and (b) economic stratification within a tribe is often very pronounced, leading to the emergence of an elite class within it.

From the marginalised primitive existence of the pre-Independence period, the tribals now have become acutely conscious of their rights and privileges, largely due to the protection afforded through constitutional safeguards. In spite of the deficiencies associated with developmental planning, the smaller impact made through conventional development has raised the expectations of the tribal people. It is therefore most appropriate to look at a new paradigm for the sustainable development and management of natural resources in the areas where the tribals live — a new paradigm based on traditional wisdom and building upon that wisdom incrementally. The following case study elegantly exemplifies these concerns.

SHIFTING AGRICULTURE AND THE SUSTAINABLE DEVELOPMENT OF THE NORTH-EASTERN HILL REGION

In the north-eastern hill region of India live more than a hundred tribes with their own languages and cultural characteristics, but with shifting agriculture (locally called *jhum*) as a major land use (Ramakrishnan 1992). Other land use systems available in the region are valley land wet rice cultivation and home gardens (Box 1). Each one of these land use systems shows large variations in cropping patterns, economic yields and ecological efficiency, depending upon ecological and social settings.

During the last 20 or 30 years, the shifting agricultural cycle (the length of the fallow period between two successive croppings on the same site) has drastically come down from a favourable 20 years or more to about 5 years or even less. This is partly because of large-scale timber extraction from the region, leading to the invasion of the landscape by exotic and native weeds, resulting in the replacement of forests by an arrested succession of weeds or large-scale desertification. Increasing population pressure on the land has also contributed to the shortened shifting agriculture cycle. A 5-year-cycle obviously is not tenable because it exacerbates environmental problems in a variety of ways, apart from low crop productivity and social disruptions (Appendix-I).

Governmental agencies, over the past 50 years or more, have tried in vain to replace shifting agriculture with sedentary terrace farming, which demands high energy inputs in the form of fertilisers, weedicides and pesticides. As the soil cover is thin and infertile and the nutrient losses from the system are very heavy, more and more fertiliser may be required to sustain the system over a period, but with very low efficiency. As the weed problem gets exaggerated under sedentary farming, weed control assumes alarming proportions. For these ecological reasons and for a variety of social and cultural reasons related to land tenure and cultural and religious practices centred around shifting agriculture, the farmer rejects the alternatives to shifting agriculture as a permanent solution to the problem.

It is in this context that we stepped into the region to look at the whole issue of sustainable development with people's participation. On the basis of extensive studies on agroecosystem and forest ecosystem function in a variety of situations and human ecology-based analysis of village ecosystem function, short-term and long-term possibilities for sustainable development were identified (Ramakrishnan 1992). A holistic approach for sustainable development that would link agriculture, animal husbandry, and domestic sub-systems of the village ecosystem in the overall context of the forest ecosystem function and management was identified (AppendixI-II).

The short-term (5-10 year) strategy considered the transfer of technology from one tribe to another as one of the pathways. Strengthening the agroforestry component of the shifting agriculture system, using locally acceptable species such as the Nepalese alder (*Alnus nepalensis*), and the improvement of valley agriculture and home gardens with appropriately identified scientific inputs (linking traditional and modern technology) was considered as part of the short-term strategy. On the other hand, a shift towards a plantation economy based upon the home garden concept and the organisation of families in a cooperative production/marketing system along with forestry-based activities was considered to be a possible long-term (50-100 year) objective for the sustainable development of the region.

The whole approach was to build upon traditional wisdom, technology and knowledge base through modern scientific inputs, based upon a value system with which the people could identify and therefore participate effectively in the developmental process.

CONCLUSIONS RELEVANT TO SUSTAINABILITY

Specially designed packages have to be developed for each cluster of villages, taking into account micro-climatic conditions, socio-economic levels, and the socio-cultural backgrounds of the people. The aspirations of the tribal people are unique (Ramakrishnan 1992) because of their close integration with the forest environment. This dependence on nature is reflected in the undisturbed 'sacred forest' which was often maintained as part of the village system (Box 3). These village ecosystem-rain forest-ecosystem linkages should be adequately protected when planning for development. Embedded within these interlinked economic-ecologic systems are traditional ways of enhancing and protecting biodiversity, and indeed their sustainable use.

Scientists, planners and administrators have often tried to impose development plans that they consider good, without trying to understand the social processes that operate in traditional societies and the linkages with ecosystem level processes. Planning should try to link ecological processes within a landscape (a set of interacting ecosystem types) with the social processes operating within the system. Such a planning philosophy would take care of the traditional value systems, and therefore would not only find ready acceptance by tribal societies but would also ensure their participation in the developmental process.

The village headman is the key person in each tribal settlement. Village level institutions linked with the District Council infrastructure could provide the necessary institutional framework for development planning. The planning approach should incorporate a review period so that appropriate adjustments may be made based on experience. Village Development Boards (VDB) constituted by the Nagaland Government (Anonymous 1980) appropriately linking the existing Village Councils for the purpose of managing developmental funds allocated for rural development, form a model that is headed in the right direction for ensuring people's initiatives and participation. A few specific conclusions are:

1. Sustainable development has to be considered in the context of the ecological framework within which the system operates. In the north-eastern Indian context the short-term strategy for agriculture redevelopment is best formed by strengthening the agroforestry component, using traditional technology, for building up soil fertility, which otherwise is built up through natural processes of forest succession where trees play a key role. Modern agricultural technology, through external subsidies of fertiliser, has not been able to effectively replace the traditional way of

recovering soil fertility through forest regrowth under shifting agriculture in the humid tropics.

2. Social constraints such as a land tenure pattern that is based on community ownership, and the present level of economic development of the society, do not permit drastic departures from traditional land use practices. Therefore, sustainable development has to consider a short-term strategy based on traditional technology that would avoid social disruptions. A better long-term strategy, appropriately designed, should be based on a gradual shift in land use through community participation. Thus, a shift to cash crop plantation economy could be a long-term strategy in the north-east Indian context, but by basing it on the concept of home gardens and organising the whole on a cooperative basis. This would permit exploiting to the maximum the integrity of the family as a unit for development (tribals can be fiercely independent) and yet capitalising upon the cooperative spirit of the tribals (even in *jhum* operations, all labour-intensive activities are done on a cooperative basis).

3. Traditionally, different communities deal with decline in soil fertility in different ways. This is evident from the variety of agroecosystems that have developed in similar ecological conditions. The transition from shifting to sedentary agriculture requires a detailed understanding of the farmer's preferences and the inputs required to maintain the natural resource base. In the same site, a given community may change the cropping pattern to cope with decline in soil fertility. The shift towards nutrient use and the growing of efficient tuber and rhizomatous crops under shortened cycles of shifting agriculture in Meghalaya are indicative of community response to declining soil fertility. Crop placement on a given slope with more nutrient use, efficient species being placed at the top of the slope, under the *jhum* system, represents a fine level of appreciation of plant-soil interaction by farmers. The release of nutrients from organic matter, synchronised with their uptake by the crop species, is refined through the sequential harvesting and management of crop and weed biomass in the *jhum* farmer's plots. Nutrients released from the organic matter of the earlier crop biomass are made available to the next crop at the peak of its growth in the mixed cropping *jhum* system. In the transition from shifting to permanent agriculture, the earliest sedentary land use is the traditional home garden systems. The success of these systems is based on the effective use of nutrients by strengthening internal nutrient recycling processes. Use of different rice cultivars by the Apatanis of Arunachal Pradesh, depending upon soil fertility levels, implies the farmer's understanding of changes in soil

fertility. Ecologically important species (referred to as keystone species) such as bamboo (*Dendrocalamus hamiltonii*) for conserving potassium and the Nepalese alder (*Alnus nepalensis*) for nitrogen economy in the *jhum* system in north-eastern India are also species that are traditionally valued and conserved by the *jhum* farmer.

The linking of traditional knowledge with soil biological process studies would, in the ultimate analysis, provide the framework for basing soil management practices on a value system that farmers can appreciate.

4. In the rehabilitation of degraded lands in north-east India, keystone species such as the Nepalese alder and others are important. Bamboo, which often has a key nutrient conservation role for nitrogen, phosphorus and potassium, is also traditionally valued by the tribals of north-eastern India. Such parallelism between ecologically valuable keystone species and socially valued key species often trigger people's participation.

5. Biodiversity concerns in agriculture and sustainable agroecosystem development are linked with each other in a variety of ways. Yet, talking of agriculture, one often visualises a monotonous monocropping system totally devoid of biodiversity. This perception is largely due to the energy-intensive modern agriculture that we see all around us. However, there exists in the tropics a wide range of complex agroecosystem types with biodiversity comparable to that of natural ecosystems and indeed occasionally exceeding it. This biodiversity contributes in a variety of ways towards agroecosystem ecosystem function such as production, decomposition and nutrient cycling dynamics, and thus towards stability and resilience. The traditional agroecosystem types available in north-eastern India have a variety of agroecosystems ranging from casually managed through low-intensity management to middle-intensity management systems. Shifting agriculture, home gardens, valley land wet rice cultivation, rotational fallow and the traditional horticulture and cash crop farming systems, with all their variants, contribute to rich crop biodiversity where a variety of species and cultivars are handled and conserved by the tribes of the region.

6. It is generally acknowledged that biodiversity decreases as habitats change from forest to traditional agriculture, and then to modern agriculture. While a variety of models for loss in biodiversity under varied intensities of management regimes for agriculture are proposed, it seems obvious that biodiversity decline is sharp somewhere in the area close to the middle intensity of management. If that be so,

it is crucial to have a level of management that is closer to this critical area for sustaining biodiversity in agriculture (Swift, *et al.* 1994). The sustainable development of agriculture suggested for north-east India being in the middle-intensity management range, harmonizes with biodiversity concerns.

7. There could be three different pathways for sustainable agriculture: (a) evolution by incremental change; (b) restoration through the contour pathway; and (c) development through the auto-route (Appendix-III) (Swift, *et al.* 1994). Realising that biodiversity does contribute in a variety of ways to ecosystem functions (Ramakrishnan 1992) and that agroecosystems do harbour a great deal of biodiversity valuable for human welfare, it is reasonable that we go in for a mosaic of natural ecosystems coexisting with a wide variety of agroecosystem models derived through all three pathways. Such a highly diversified landscape unit is likely to have a wide range of ecological niches conducive to enhancing biodiversity and at the same time will ensure sustainability of the managed landscape.

   Arising out of this discussion, and relating this to the north-east Indian context, it seems that for the tribals in the region, following an incremental pathway seems to be the most obvious choice, at least as a short-term strategy for sustainable development. While the auto-route seems to be out of question in view of the fragile mountain soil conditions in this humid tropical region, the contour pathway offers possibilities for sustainable agriculture, at least as a long-term strategy, provided people's participation is ensured right from the planning phase.

8. The linkage between ecological and social dimensions in evaluating a landscape system may often lead to identifying one or two critical driving factors that can trigger the developmental process with people's participation. In the Himalayan region, the present author, in collaboration with scientists from the G.B. Pant Institute of Himalayan Environment and Development, identified water as the key limiting resource for land use development in the rural areas. Even meeting drinking water needs, particularly during the drier 8-9 months outside the monsoon season, was critical. Right across the Himalayas, over more than 2000 sq km, communities consistently identified water as the key resource in short supply. By harvesting surface runoff water and by diverting sub-surface seepage water through cheap rainwater harvesting tanks (Kothyari *et al.* 1991) we were able to link it with a variety of ecosystem rehabilitation work — mixed plantation forestry, agroecosystem redevelopment, *ringal* bamboo regeneration, and watershed redevelopment as a whole — in different parts of the Himalayan region. Indeed, the successful redevelopment of shifting agriculture in Nagaland based upon traditional

Nepalese alder technology is one of the outcomes of this programme that is relevant to our discussion here.

9. An important indicator of sustainable development is related to the development of local institutional frameworks, considering the following aspects: (a) identification and strengthening of local level institutions that are already available, such as those existing in the north-eastern region; (b) the representative nature of these bodies and the extent to which individual family interests are taken care of; (c) their role in decision-making right from project formulation through different levels of implementation; (d) flexibility in function so as to take care of the interests of all sections of the society; (e) the education and human resource development that these institutions have been able to trigger, particularly for the weaker and vulnerable sections; (f) the ability of these institutions to stand on their own through empowerment in terms of capability building.

10. Sustainable development with people's participation demands closer interaction between ecologists and social scientists, who have traditionally worked in isolation, using different paradigms for development. It also calls for interaction between developmental planners and the local communities that could trigger people's participation. In order to achieve this, developmental strategies have to be based on a value system that the target people can understand and appreciate.

In the ultimate analysis, through a variety of approaches, traditional knowledge, wisdom and technology, based on empirical knowledge accumulated over a long period of human evolution, these and other traditional societies have learnt to conserve and enhance biodiversity. They have done it in the agroecosystem types and in the natural ecosystems — indeed, in the landscape as a whole. The forest dwellers of the south-east Asian uplands have done it, the Mayans of Mexico have done it, the natives of Amazonia have done it. Indeed, they managed biodiversity reasonably well until the advent of 'modern civilisation'. The concept of the 'sacred grove', extensively maintained by traditional societies in different parts of the world and in north-east India, is suggestive of the traditional value attached to biodiversity by them (Appendix-IV). Having distorted their life-styles through over-exploitation of their natural resources induced from outside, having tried, often unsuccessfully, to impose a value system that we consider is important for them, it is high time that we share the benefits of biodiversity that we industrialized humans are exploiting now.

THE CONCEPT OF THE SACRED LANDSCAPE AND ITS ECOLOGICAL VALUE

While we have much general information on sacred species and sacred groves, the concept of the sacred landscape adds a new dimension to our understanding of ecology and culture. One of the best examples of a sacred landscape that I can visualise is that represented all along the course of the river Ganga, originating from the higher reaches of the Garhwal Himalayas, and tracing through the plains of Uttar Pradesh, Bihar and West Bengal, before draining into the Bay of Bengal. The sacred land all along the course of the river, the human habitation and land-based activity, the temples dating back to antiquity, the sacred cities such as Badrinath, Kedarnath, Rishikesh and Haridwar in the Himalayan and sub-Himalayan tracts, Allahabad and Varanasi in the Gangetic alluvial plains, all represent a set of interconnected ecosystem types bound together by the sacred river. The variety of natural ecosystem types ranging from the alpine vegetation above the timberline, through the temperate oak and pine forests down below, the sub-tropical moist-deciduous to dry-deciduous forests in the plains, and a variety of human-altered ecosystems — terraced agriculture and valley land agriculture — all are tightly linked together and controlled by the sacred river and its tributaries in a variety of ways through flooding and silt deposition. The sacred groves of the Bishnois in Rajasthan, viewed as units around each Bishnoi village (Appendix-V), could indeed be enlarged to encompass a cluster of villages forming a landscape unit to include interacting ecosystem types such as agriculture, animal husbandry and domestic units of the village ecosystem, natural water bodies, and the protected natural ecosystem. In a conceptual sense, this is an area which needs further exploration for its value as a conservation tool.

The concept of the sacred landscape found further holistic expression in the Buddhist philosophy of non-violence and kindness to all living beings. Whilst the concept of the sacred grove is now well recognised through many studies from Asia and Africa, I am not aware of any documentation of the 'sacred landscape' concept. It is in this context that the example detailed below assumes significance.

Demojong in West Sikkim District: a Unique Example of a Sacred Landscape

Sikkim has a long tradition of Buddhism. It is practised by about 25 per cent of the population while the majority religion is Hinduism (70 per cent). Since the time the first Chogyal (king) of Sikkim was crowned in 1642 in Norbugang in Yuksom, Buddhist traditions have been deeply ingrained in the psyche of the Sikkimese people. This is evident in all walks of life — a rich tapestry woven with Buddhist symbolisms, legends, myths, rituals and festivals, the typical Sikkimese architecture, and the large number of monasteries and *stupas* dotting the state. It is important to note that these traditions are shared by all three communities: the unique culture so developed is a blend of the Buddhism of the Lepchas and the Bhutias and the Hinduism of the majority Nepalis.

Of the four Buddhist sects, the Nyngmepa, Kagupa, Gelugpa and Sakyapa, in the state, the Nyngmepa sect, initiated by the Buddha incarnate, Maha-guru Padmasambhava, is the most significant. Whilst Sikkim as a whole is considered to be sacred by Sikkimese Buddhists, according to the sacred text *Nay Sol* the area below Mount Khangchendzonga in west Sikkim, referred to as Demojong, is the most sacred of all, being the abode of Sikkim's deities. Interestingly the air, soil, water and the biota are all sacred to the people because of the interconnections that they perceive to exist. Any human-induced perturbation is considered by Sikkimese Buddhists to spell disaster for Sikkim as a whole, because of the disturbance caused to the ruling deities and the treasures (*ters*) placed in the landscape (Box 5). Interestingly, it is believed that there is no way of knowing where the *ters* are hidden, as they will be revealed only to the right person when the right time comes.

This region has a number of glacial lakes in the higher reaches. These are sacred lakes. The Rathong Chu, itself a sacred river, is said to have its source in nine holy lakes at the higher elevations, close to the mountain peaks. Besides, the river in the Yoksum region itself is considered to have 109 hidden lakes. These visible and less obvious notional lakes identified by religious visionaries are said to have presiding deities, representing both good and evil. Propitiating these deities through various religious ceremonies is considered important for the welfare of the Sikkimese people.

It is no wonder that Rathong Chu is the focus of religious rituals. During the *bum chu* ritual, considered holiest of all festivals, held annually at Tashiding, the Rathong Chu is said to turn white and start singing, and this is the water to be collected at the point where the Rathong Chu meets the Ringnya Chu. Attracting thousands of devotees from the state and the neighbouring region, the *bom chu* ritual is predictive in nature, in that it is suggested to be indicative of coming events—possible calamities or prosperity for the people of Sikkim. The water kept in vases, if it overflows, is indicative of prosperity. Decline in water level is indicative of bad events such as drought, disease, etc. Turbid water is indicative of unrest and conflicts.

More generalised rituals, such as the one done throughout Sikkim by the Buddhists during *pang-lhabsol* to propitiate the various ruling deities of the mountain peak of the Khangchendzonga, the midlands represented by the Yoksum region, and the lowlands down below, are indicative of the widespread respect with which this sacred region is worshipped by the people.

Of the total catchment area of 328,000 ha of the Rathang Khola, 28,510 ha is under snow cover. The vegetation is varied, ranging from alpine scrub at the higher reaches to sub-tropical moist evergreen forests down below. Afforestation is essential over 4,290 ha of the catchment area of the Rothang Chu. This task is crucial for the conservation of the sacred landscape and for its ecological integrity. Implementing this activity is crucial for controlling erosion and flash floods. According to the data collated by the Himalayan Nature and Adventure Foundation, Siliguri, Ouglthang and Rathong glaciers are retreating rapidly, with a reduction in size. Retreating glaciers create several moraine dams containing sizeable quantities of water. Increased snow melting and exceptionally high rainfall in a given year could result in dam bursts and flash floods in the lower regions. The 1988 dam burst is an example that could recur if adequate catchment treatment measures are not initiated immediately.

The Sikkim Himalayas are richly endowed with biological resources spread over a variety of ecosystem types over a range of altitudes, from the alpine *Rhododendron* dominated scrub forest through conifer forests with *Abies densa* and *Tsuga demosa* getting down to mixed evergreen forests dominated by species such as *Castanopsis spp.*, *Quercus lamellosa, Lithocarpus spicatus, Elaeocarpus lanceaefolius, Michilus edulis, Michelis spp.*, etc. The region under consideration here has all these types over a very short tract running down from the alpine to the sub-tropical zone. Orchids are abundant. With rich wildlife represented by the Himalayan black bear, musk deer, fishing cat, leopard cat, black capped *langur* and a rich bird life, this unique landscape unit should be protected.

The region is rich in medicinal plants of value to the traditional Tibetan pharmacopoeia, nurtured in Sikkim by the Buddhist monasteries. Conserving these plants and their cultivation would ensure the survival of one of the oldest systems of medicine stretching back more than 2,500 years. With recent attempts to revive traditional medicine, the possibility of providing a sustainable livelihood to local communities through cultivation of medicinal plants is immense.

Yoksum is an area which the Sikkimese perceive as the very basis of present Sikkimese culture. The entire region, right from the Khangchendzonga to the Yoksum lowlands, is most appropriate to be declared a National Heritage Site, with all its people, ecological and cultural heritage, the land and the land use systems (the traditional terraced agricultural system included), all the water bodies (the obvious and notional lakes), the Yoksumchu, the monasteries, the historical sites and the rich biodiversity, for conservation in a truly holistic spirit.

CONSERVATION AND SUSTAINABLE DEVELOPMENT OF 'SACRED LANDSCAPES'

Conserving 'sacred landscapes' is highly complex because of the interconnected ecosystem types in which humans are integrated. We need to have a sustainable development strategy, complex by definition and involving enormous cost. The Sikkimese sacred landscape, for example, is a unique case where ecological considerations cannot be separated from historical, social, cultural and religious dimensions. Here is a sacred landscape where the people are truly integrated within the landscape unit itself, in a socio-economic sense. Therefore, one has to consider sustainable development of the region as an integrated issue with vernacular conservation. Declaring the sacred landscapes as National Heritage Sites and their eventual recognition as World Heritage Sites of Unesco would be a step in the right direction, not only for conservation but also for evolving and implementing a meaningful sustainable development action plan, with people's participation.

The Concept of Sustainable Development

At this point it is appropriate to briefly consider the concept of sustainable development. Sustainable development and the effective management of natural resources and indeed, the rehabilitation of degraded ecosystems, are all closely interlinked. Ecological issues are tied up with social, economic, anthropological and cultural dimensions, since the guiding principles of sustainable development (Appendix-VI) cut across these very disciplinary realms, with obvious trade-offs.

This implies that we have to make a series of compromises to achieve sustainable development in such a way that we do not lose track of the ultimate objective, namely, rehabilitation and management of natural resources in a manner that satisfies current needs, at the same time allowing for a variety of options for the future (Ramakrishnan 1993; Ramakrishnan *et al.* 1994). Though an ecosystem type (man-made ecosystems such as agriculture, a fish pond in a village or a village itself visualized as an ecosystem; or natural ecosystems such as grazing land, forests or rivers) may be the appropriate unit for the convenient handling of rehabilitation, a cluster of interacting ecosystem types (a 'landscape') may be the most effective for holistic treatment. A watershed is one such landscape unit. Further, from a sustainable developmental point of view, while one may bear in mind a long-term ideal objective to be achieved, ecological, social economic or cultural constraints may necessitate designing short-term strategies for enabling people's participation in the developmental process. To quote one example, while forest-based economic activities and cash crop plantation programmes may be the most appropriate as a long-term alternative to shifting agriculture in north-east India, there is no option other than a redeveloped agroecosystem package for the region, using traditional knowledge and technology as the starting point for a short-term strategy (Ramakrishnan 1992). Thus, sustainable development has spatial and temporal dimensions that need to be reconciled.

Indicators of sustainable development are varied; therefore, here again, compromises are called for. Monitoring and evaluation have to be done using a number of diverse currencies that may be (a) ecological (land use changes, biomass quality and quantity, water quality and quantity, soil fertility, and energy efficiency), (b) economic (monetary output/input analysis, capital savings or asset accumulation, and dependency ratio), social (quality of life with easily measurable indicators such as health and hygiene, nutrition, food security, morbidity symptoms; and difficult to quantify measures such as societal empowerment, and the less tangible ones in the area of social and cultural values). Further, institutional arrangements have to ensure people's participation through a bottom-up approach for their organisation, ensuring that each household takes part in the decision-making process from the lowest level in the hierarchy, and with special dispensations for the weaker and vulnerable sections of a society. In this effort to involve people in sustainable development, the role of traditional knowledge and wisdom cannot be overemphasised, because then the people will be able to identify with a value system that they understand and appreciate.

Appendices

I

Shifting Agriculture (*jhum*) in North-Eastern India and Social Disruption*

North-eastern India has over 100 different tribals, linguistically and culturally distinct from one another; the tribes often change over very short distances, a few kilometres in some cases. Shifting agriculture or *jhum* is the major economic activity. This highly organised agroecosystem was based on empirical knowledge accumulated through centuries and was in harmony with the environment as long as the *jhum* cycle (the fallow length intervening between two successive croppings) was long enough to allow the forest and the soil fertility lost during the cropping phase to recover.

Supplementing the *jhum* system is the valley system of wet rice cultivation and home gardens. The valley system is sustainable on a regular basis year after year because the wash-out from the hill slopes provides the needed soil fertility for rice cropping without any external inputs. The home gardens extensively found in the region have economically valuable trees, shrubs, herbs and vines and form a compact multi-storeyed system of fruit crops, vegetables, medicinal plants and many cash crops; the system in its structure and function imitates a natural forest ecosystem. The number of species in a small area of less than a hectare may be 30 or 40. It represents a highly intensive system of farming in harmony with the environment. Linked to this land use are the animal husbandry systems centred traditionally around pigs and poultry. The advantage here is primarily that they are

---

* from Ramakrishnan 1992

detritus-based or based on the recycling of food from the agroecosystem unfit for human consumption.

Increased human population pressure and decline in land area resulting from extensive deforestation for timber for use for industrial man and *jhum* have brought down the *jhum* cycle to 4 or 5 years or less. Where population densities are high, as around urban centres, burning of slash is dispensed with, leading to a rotational/sedentary system of agriculture. These are often below subsistence level, though the attempt is to maximise output in rapidly depleting soil fertility. Inappropriate animal husbandry practices introduced in the area, such as goat or cattle husbandry, could lead to rapid site deterioration through indiscriminate grazing/browsing and fodder removal, as has happened elsewhere in the Himalayas. The serious social disruption caused demands an integrated approach to managing the forest-human interface.

II

Shifting Agriculture (*Jhum*) and Sustainable Development for North-Eastern India

For improving the system of land use and resource management in north-eastern India, the following strategies suggested by Ramakrishnan and his co-workers are based on a multidisciplinary analysis. Many of these proposals have already been put into practice.

- With wide variations in cropping and yield patterns under *jhum* practised in diverse ecological situations, the transfer of technology from one area to another alone could improve *jhum*, valley land and home garden ecosystems. Thus, for example, emphasis on potato at higher elevations compared to rice at lower elevations has led to a manifold increase in economic yield despite the low fertility of the more acid soils at higher elevations.
- Maintain a *jhum* cycle of at least 10 years (this cycle length was found critical for sustainability when *jhum* was evaluated using money, energy, soil fertility, biomass productivity, biodiversity, and water quality as currencies) by greater emphasis on other land use systems such as traditional valley cultivation and home gardens.
- Where *jhum* cycle length cannot be increased beyond the five-year period that is prevalent in the region, redesign and strengthen this agroforestry system by incorporating ecological insights on tree architecture (e.g. the canopy form of tree should be compatible with crop species at ground level so as to permit sufficient light penetration and provide fast recycling of nutrients through rapid leaf turnover rates).
- Improve the nitrogen economy of *jhum* in the cropping and fallow phases by the introduction of nitrogen-fixing legumes and non-legumes. A species such as the Nepalese alder is readily taken in because it is based on the principle of adaptation of traditional knowledge to meet modern needs. Another such example is the less known food crop legume *Flemingia vestita*.

- Some important bamboo species, highly valued by the tribals, can concentrate and conserve important nutrient elements such as N, P and K. They could also be used as windbreaks to check the loss of ash and nutrient losses in water.
- Speed up fallow regeneration after *jhum* by introducing fast-growing native shrubs and trees.
- Condense the time span of forest succession and accelerate restoration of degraded lands based on an understanding of tree growth strategies and architecture, by adjusting the species mix in time and space.
- Improve animal husbandry through improved breeds of swine and poultry.
- Redevelop village ecosystems through the introduction of appropriate technology to relieve drudgery and improve energy efficiency (cooking stoves, agricultural implements, biogas generation, small hydroelectric projects, etc.).
- Promote crafts such as smithying and products based on leather, bamboo and other woods.
- Strengthen conservation measures based upon the traditional knowledge and value system with which the tribal communities can identify, e.g. the revival of the sacred grove concept based on cultural tradition, which enabled each village to have a protected forest. Only a few are now left.

III

Pathways of Agricultural Development*

THE 'AUTO-ROUTE' TO MAXIMAL PRODUCTIVITY

Modern agriculture as a production system is based upon heavy external energy subsidies and in that sense is different from natural ecosystems that are regulated by internal controls. An appropriate metaphor would be the engineer who plans an auto-route by drawing a straight line on a map and proceeds to build a straight and level road regardless of physical impediments. Such an agroecosystem type would stand apart as an artificial entity from the rest of the landscape — an attempt to convert the natural ecosystem into one that contains only those biological and chemical elements that the planner desires, almost irrespective of the background ecological conditions, e.g. the 'Green Revolution' model.

RESTORATION: THE 'CONTOUR PATHWAY' TO SUSTAINABILITY

The 'contour pathway' seeks to acknowledge and work with the ecological forces that provide the base on which the system must be built, while acknowledging the social, economic and cultural requirements of farming communities. Working with nature rather than dominating it, this approach would involve active planning with the nature of the background ecosystem

* after Swift et. *al.* 1994

fully in mind, e.g. the Sloping Agricultural Land Technology (SALT) developed in the Philippines is one such system that comes close to this approach, though the initial reaction to the extension of SALT has not been very encouraging for reasons related to (a) land tenure difficulties, and (b) heavy labour investment. Many agroecosystem types in the 'low' and 'middle' intensity management categories will come under this pathway.

EVOLUTION BY 'INCREMENTAL CHANGE'

Many traditional agricultural systems need to be redeveloped through incremental rather than quantum change; anything drastic may not find acceptance by the local communities. In this incremental change towards sustainable development, one may have to consider a short-term strategy that may be constrained because of ecological, economic, social or cultural reasons, apart from a more desirable long-term strategy. The possible ways in which a forest farmer practising shifting agriculture and other land uses such as valley wet rice cultivation or home gardens include picking up an appropriate variant from the local types that may be available, or else incremental change could be brought about by strengthening the agroforestry component of the distorted shifting agriculture under a short cycle of 5 years or less through the introduction of the Nepalese alder. These options are illustrative of this pathway to sustainable development.

LANDSCAPE MOSAIC

Compared with a landscape model that is often seen now, where pristine unmanaged ecosystems are set in a sea of intensive large-scale agroecosystems, it may be desirable to have a mosaic of agroecosystem types derived through all three pathways coexisting with natural ecosystem types, managed or unmanaged. Maintenance of the overall sustainability of the system requires a mosaic that may be the best plan for biodiversity conservation in general.

IV

The Sacred Groves of Meghalaya

In Meghalaya in the north-eastern hill region, many sacred groves are still well protected, in spite of a rapid decline in the traditional value system with the advent of Christianity (Boojh and Ramakrishnan 1983; Khiewtam and Ramakrishnan 1989). The traditional religious belief is that the gods and the spirits of the ancestors live in these groves. The Mawphlang grove close to Shillong town is one of the best preserved, set in a degraded landscape all around. Indeed, the Mawsmai grove in Cherrapunji of about 6 km^2 of protected mixed broad-leaved rain forest, though subject to some disturbance along the peripheral region, is an island in a bleak desertified landscape. Though ceremonies used to be performed regularly in this grove and others to propitiate the ruling deity, they have been stopped in many of them for the last few years. Removal of plants or plant parts is considered to offend the ruling deity, leading to local calamities. We have recorded, in the Cherrapunji region, 21 sacred groves with varied degrees of human disturbance.

V

The Concept of 'Sacred Landscape'

THE BISHNOI VILLAGE CLUSTER

There is the story of a sect, the Bishnois, founded about 500 years ago in the Rajasthan desert, that led to absolute protection not only to the *khejadi* tree (*Prosopiscinerares*), a multi-purpose legume tree valued by the villagers, but also to the promotion of plant and animal biodiversity within their village ecosystem boundary. These trees are valued by the local people for pods for food, leaves for fodder and manure and branches as construction material. It is said that some 350 years ago, many Bishnois even laid down their lives when the prince of Jodhpur tried to fell *khejadi* trees for his lime kilns.

DEMOJONG: THE LAND OF THE HIDDEN TREASURES

Padmasambhava, who is highly revered and worshipped by the Sikkimese Buddhists, is believed to have blessed Yoksum and the surrounding landscape represented by Demojong in the West Sikkim District, placing a large number of hidden treasures (*ter*). Many of these sacred treasures were hidden by Lhabstsun Namkha Jigme in the Yoksum region. It is believed that these treasures are being discovered slowly and will be revealed only to enlightened lamas at appropriate times. Conserving these treasures and protecting them from polluting influences is considered important for human welfare.

The area below Mount Khangchendzonga in West Sikkim, referred to as Demojong, is the core of the sacred land of Sikkim. Yoksum is considered to be a *lhakhang* (altar) and *mandala*, where offerings are made to protective deities. No meaningful performance of Buddhist rituals is possible if this land and water is desecrated. Any large-scale human-induced perturbation in the land of the holy Yoksum region would destroy the hidden treasures in such a manner that the chances of recovering them in the future by a visionary will diminish (it is said that the last such discovery was made by Terton Padma Lingpa, 540 years ago). Any major perturbation to the river system would disturb the ruling deities of the 109 hidden lakes of the river, thus leading to serious calamities (here they quote the example of the Khecho-Palri lake that is said to have moved away from the river during a period of bloodshed.

Indeed, the very cultural fabric of Sikkimese society is obviously dependent upon the conservation of the whole sacred landscape of interacting ecosystems, as was evident during discussions this author had with respected religious leaders and a cross-section of Sikkimese society, cutting across religious, cultural and professional backgrounds. The issue here is not merely one of protecting a few physical structures or ruins. The uniqueness of this heritage site is that the value system here is interpreted in a more holistic sense -- soil, water, biota, visible water bodies, river and the less obvious notional lakes, all are to be taken together with the physical monuments.

VI

The Guiding Principles of Ecologically Sustainable Resource Management*

- Inter-generational equity: providing for today while retaining resources and options for tomorrow.
- Conservation of cultural and biological diversity and ecological integrity.
- Constant natural capital and 'sustainable income'.
- Anticipatory and precautionary policy approach to resource use, erring on the side of caution.
- Resource use in a manner that contributes to equity and social justice while avoiding social disruptions.
- Limits on natural resource use within the capacity of the environment to supply renewable resources and assimilate wastes.
- Qualitative rather than quantitative development of human well-being.
- Pricing of environmental values and natural resources to cover environmental and social costs.
- Global rather than regional or national perspective on environmental issues.
- Efficiency of resource use by all societies.
- Strong community participation in policy and practice in the process of transition to an ecologically sustainable society.

References

Anonymous, 1980, *Village Development Boards — Model Rules.* (Revised). New Delhi: Government of Nagaland.

Anonymous, 1981, *Census of India: 1981 Series 1: Primary Census, Abstract — Scheduled Tribes.* Government of India.

Hare, W.L., J.P. Morlowe, M.L. Rae, F. Gray, R. Humphries and R. Ledgar, 1990, *Ecologically sustainable development.* Fitzroy: Australian Conservation Foundation.

Kothyari, B.P., S. Rao, K.G. Saxena, T. Kumar and P.S. Ramakrishnan, 1991, 'Institutional approaches in development and transfer of water harvest technology in the Himalaya'. In G. Tskiris, (ed.), *Proceedings of the European Conference on advances in water resources technology.* Rotterdam: A.A. Balkema.

Ramakrishnan, P.S. 1992, *Shifting agriculture and sustainable development of north-eastern India.* Unesco MAB Series. Paris: Parthenon; New Delhi: Oxford University Press.

* adapted from Hare *et al.* 1990

———, P.S., 1993, 'Evaluating sustainable development with peoples' participation'. In F. Moser, (ed.), *Sustainability: where do we stand?* Graz: Technische Universitat.

Ramakrishnan, P.S., J. Campbell, L. Demierre, A Gyi, K.C. Malhotra, S. Mehndiratta, S.N. Rai and E.M. Sashidharan, 1994, *Ecosystem Rehabilitation of the Rural Landscape in South and Central Asia: An Analysis of Issues*. ed. by M. Hadley, special publication. New Delhi: Unesco (ROSTCA).

Swift, M.J., J. Vandermeer, P.S. Ramakrishnan, J.M. Anderson, C.K. Ong and B. Hawkins, 1994, 'Biodiversity and agroecosystem function'. In H.A. Mooney *et al.*, (eds.), *Biodiversity and ecosystem properties: a global perspective*. SCOPE Series. Chichester: John Wiley.

8

The Nature-centric Culture of the Nepalese

D.S. Rasaily and R.P. Lama

DARJEELING, known as the queen of hill stations, was gifted to the East India Company by the Maharaja of Sikkim in 1835. History reveals that during the 160 years of its lifetime, the Darjeeling hill area, though ethnically and culturally varied, its people both tribals and non-tribals, has contributed to a large extent to the progress and promotion of a sense of coexistence and assimilation.

The panoramic scenario of the lofty Himalayas, its guardian deities, beautiful landscapes, lush green valleys and soothing climatic conditions have always been the source of inspiration to the hard-working but ever-smiling people of these hills. Numerous traditional dances, folk songs, much folklore, folk music and folk forms of theatres and oral tradition of the Nepalese and other tribals residing in different regions, mostly in the north and the north-eastern parts, have made significant contributions to the enrichment of the cultural heritage of our country. In fact these simple folk dances and joyful, rhythmic and lilting folk songs and music have helped cement deeper bonds of emotional understanding, feeling and goodwill and have strengthened the mainstream of our national life.

However, with the passage of time and changing needs and circumstances, sizeable populations of Nepalese have spread all over the plains, from Kashmir to Kanyakumari and Arunachal Pradesh to Saurashtra. In these areas Nepalese are found engaged in different occupations and professions ranging from agriculture to army service and from factories to forestry. The Nepalese are also known all over the world as one of the best military forces. Loyalty, devotion to duty, honesty, amiable disposition and hard work are some of the inborn qualities of the Nepalese.

Once the Darjeeling hills, the nerve centre of Nepali social and cultural life were famous for three T's — tea, tourism and timber. Although tea and tourism are still the main sources of livelihood of the local people, timber has been relegated to the background. The massive deforestation and indiscriminate felling of rich forest wealth in the hills over the last few decades are the main factors for the degeneration of the environment and ecological degradation of the hills. The massive tree felling by the West Bengal Forest Development Corporation and the local timber merchants have depleted the local forest wealth to a large extent.

Nature, mother earth and the environment have also had an influence on our literature and culture from the ancient period. Nepali language and culture drew their inspiration from the Vedas, *Gita* and other sacred Hindu books. The famous English poet Wordsworth once said that the world was poisoned at the root. Design with nature must replace design against nature.

Similarly, the famous Nepali poet Laxmi Prasad Devkota, in his epic *Sakuntal*, said: '*sad jnan chhan prakritika hariya kunama*', i.e., real wisdom lies or exists with the greenery of Nature.

Man can make and unmake, man can create and destroy. This selfish motive of man on earth has been depicted by another famous Nepali poet, Lekhnath Paudyal:

> *mai khawoon, mai lawoon*
> *mai matra sukh sayal garoon.*
> (Let me alone eat, let me alone wear dress
> Let me alone enjoy all pleasures of the world.)

The Nepali population is made up of different races professing various religions, castes, creeds and culture. The majority are Hindus whose language and literature have their roots in Sanskrit in the Devanagari script. Their sacred scriptures are the *Mahabharata*, *Ramayana*, Vedas and *Gita*. These sacred books were translated into Nepali long back. The translation of the *Ramayana* into Nepali was done by the poet Bhanubhakta Acharya, who is considered the architect of the modern Nepali language. The *Mahabharata* was translated around 1901, and the *Gita* in 1935 by Pandit Dharnidhar Sharma and published by the Nepali Sahitya Sammelan, Darjeeling. Nepali culture is a treasure house of varied and colourful folk dances, folk songs and folklore. Most of the songs, dances and folklore are linked with the nature and its gods. Epics and other sacred scriptures have a deep impact on the hill culture and social life which has flowed in the history of mankind from generation to generation, mostly in the form of oral tradition. Only recently have the folk songs, folklore and other musical forms been made available in printed form. Folk instruments, costumes, ornaments and household materials have been sidetracked because of the onslaught of modern musical trends. Decadent culture has infiltrated social and cultural life. But in spite of this, the folk culture in its traditional style has survived.

In support of the above, a few examples are given here. Beliefs and behaviour in social life have been amply reflected in folk songs and folklore. The Nepali Tamang's folklore based on the episode of Himalayan *munal* (tragopan pheasant) of the hills and the *mayur* (peacock) of the plains represents deeper bonds of friendship and brotherhood between mankind and the earth. This folklore, very popular among the Nepali community, is an outstanding example of cultural links with the wildlife and its protector, nature. Similarly, the flora and fauna of the hills have equally found their place in the love songs of Nepali Tamangs. The English rendering of the song, in which the boy says to his beloved, is:

> If our love is true,
> let us meet in rebirth.
> You become a blossoming flower and
> wait for me in Brindaban.
> I will come to you as a butterfly and
> we will go together to heaven riding on a flower.

No religious ceremony is complete without invocation and offerings to the goddess nature. After a harvest, the first grain is offered to the gods and goddesses of nature, and in some cases to the souls of dead forefathers.

Animals and birds have a very significant role in festivals and ceremonies. During *Diwali*, the festival of light, every family in Nepali society offers *puja* and worships cows, dogs and crows. Garlands are offered to these animals on particular days and sumptuous food is made available to them.

Kirats, who form formidable soldiers in the army, are also nature's worshippers similar to other tribes in Nepali society. Their culture, specially rituals and ways of worshipping nature, are quite different.

Nepalese occult art in the form of *jhankris* (witch doctors or ghost-busters) also have a close link with the forest and nature. The ghost-busters, popularly known as *jhankris*, are used in most cases to ward off evil spirits from the house. These *jhankris* owe their spiritual strength to *Ban Devis* like Lati Bureni and Chamki Bureni. The strange feature of the occult art in the Nepali community is the existence and belief in the cult of *ban jhankris* (witch doctors of the forest). In spite of the fruits of science and technology penetrating deep into society and the day-to-day life of the people, this cult has thrived and forms a part of religious. *Ban jhankris*, dwarves with long hair and reversed footsteps, roam about in the thick forest by the side of pure natural streams. But due to environmental degradation and the cutting down of the thick forests in the countryside, they have started disappearing from the forests. But the village folk still believe that in a dark and lonely night, the drumming and jingling of the bells of *ban jhankris* are heard.

The traditions and customs of the Newars in the Nepali community are more interesting, rarely to be found in other Indian societies. Daughters of teen age are married to the *bel* (*Aegle marmelos*), a fruit found in the plains, with customary rituals. Even after the death of her real husband, a woman is not considered a widow so long as the *bel* is not broken or destroyed.

Women are regarded with high esteem and respect in Nepali society. No dowry system exists. In fact the father of the daughter dictates the terms of marriage to the other side. *Buhari jhhaar* (*Minosa pudica*), a small bushy plant found in the hills, is symbolic of the social traditions of the Nepali community. The plant when touched closes its leaves and bows down as if in veneration to the elders of the society, which is reciprocated with blessings from the elders.

For ages, tribal groups such as Bhotias, Lepchas, Sherpas and Yolmos have had a close relation with the Nepalese; in fact, the assimilation of these tribal cultures and traditions has taken place. Among the tribals, the Lepchas are considered rich in cultural heritage. Lilting folk songs, dances, folklore and colourful costumes form parts of their traditional style of living. Although the tribal groups have their own scripts and languages, Nepali is the *lingua franca* for all of them. Tribal boys and girls are given education with the Nepali language as the medium of instruction not only in schools and colleges but also at the University level.

It may be mentioned here that with the recognition of the Nepali language in the 8th Schedule of our Constitution, it has gathered momentum and importance in our national life. The recognition has offered an opportunity to the Nepali-speaking people in India to be a part of the mainstream of our national life.

9

The Brahmaputra's Changing River Ecology

A.K. Das

THE great earthquake of 1950 created havoc, specially in the upper reaches of the Himalayas in and around the Siang and the Diboug river courses as well as in the upper Assam plains. There was considerable impact on the topography on both sides of the Brahmaputra Valley. This natural calamity was mainly responsible for the abrupt changes in the river ecology. The river Brahmaputra and its many tributaries in upper Assam badly suffered due to blockage caused by uprooted trees, boulders and soil erosion.

The first casualty was the small township of Sadiya on the north bank (and virtually the headquarters of the erstwhile NEFA) due to change of the course of the Digaru river, which eroded the entire township in a very short time. This was followed by the constant soil erosion of the Brahmaputra in and around Dibrugarh town on the South bank in upper Assam. About one-third of the total area of the township was eroded, cutting across the horseshoe-shaped bank of the river. A considerable population had to be shifted to safer places.

This was the major ecological disturbance faced by the people of Dibrugarh and the neighbouring areas. There were, however, quick responses to the situation using traditional means without having to depend on outside relief measures. In spite of dislocation and losses there was no let-up in indigenous efforts either in the mountains or in the plains.

Prior to this great earthquake, Dibrugarh town and the neighbouring areas experienced floods a couple of times in the rainy season. On many occasion the low-lying areas adjacent to the river were under waist-deep water, sometimes even more. Water usually entered the town from two sides: from the Brahmaputra itself from the north and from the Dibaru, a small channel, from the south-east. The south-eastern part of the town was a little higher. These were the outskirts of the town surrounded by tea gardens and paddy field, while the north-west of the township was at a lower elevation so that flood water regularly inundates the houses in the area. As a long-time measure several houses in this area were built on platform, even the official residence of the district administration. Such houses were traditionally called *changbangla* or *changghar*. A few such houses still exist in the town as an epitaph of the past.

Dibrugarh was a very green town with lots of big trees. *Kathal, lichi, pipal, simalu, bargad, nahar*, mango, *ajar*, and many other valuable timbers grew luxuriantly in and around the town. Wherever there was fallow land, herbs, shrubs and bushes of wild foliage were a common sight.

Prior to the introduction of the tube-well there were traditional wells, both *kechanad* (without a brick lining) and *patanad* (with a lining). The water was good. There were several ponds in the town privately owned, as well as marshy land full of *meteka* (water hyacinth) and other aquatic vegetation, some of which was edible. These ponds were used for fishing in the lean season and never created any major health hazard. Malaria occurred occasionally but there was no epidemic as has been reported in recent time. Probably because of the fish and other aquatic creatures the ponds remained clean and because of the floods they were regularly flushed.

The floods which occurred regularly in suburban Dibrugarh due to the Brahmaputra were not considered a threat to the people living in the 'water ecology'. Because of their recurrence, people with their traditional wisdom know when they would occur, even their magnitude and duration. Sometimes certain natural signs were taken into consideration such as the movement of ants, the appearance of certain species of plant, the behaviour of an insect called *gagini* (a species of locust), some actions of birds and animals, etc. Well before the floods people were ready to tackle them with age-old means. If necessary they moved to an elevated place. Otherwise country boats were used or quickly assembled rafts called *bhoor* made of the trunk of plantain and split bamboo. The use of boats and plantain rafts was a sort of pastime for the children of the town during the floods. Many young children enjoyed swimming in the flood-water in the courtyards of their houses.

Another pastime connected with the floods was fishing. The most important and enjoyable was the method called *dewapata*. Generally a barrier is created against the flow of water in with a bamboo *dewa* (a sort of loose bamboo matting), or occasionally by placing boulders across the water channel. Normally a fish swimming in with flowing water jumps over the barrier and falls on a net or a piece of cloth which is kept hanging just below the *dewa*. Sometimes fish jump over and fall to one side of the barrier on a dry patch. During floods plenty of fish were caught with traditional devices such as *porangijal* (a lever-operated deep net), *jakoi, polo* (basket traps), etc. On many occasions people would catch fish overnight and bake them.

As soon as the flood was over everything went back to normal. There was no panic because of an epidemic, no worry about the paddy transplantation or about the kitchen gardens. Nor was there worry over clean water because the brick-lined wells remained without pollution. After the floods, which occurred two or three times during the rainy season, the agricultural land in and around Dibrugarh became fertile due to siltation, locally called *palash para*. After each inundation of the paddy fields the harvest in most cases was exceptionally good. Vegetables grown after the floods were found to be of good quality, specially leafy vegetables like cabbage, cauliflower and mustard, as well as carrots, potatoes and turnips. The town was full of wild vegetables such as *dhikia* (a kind of fern), *khutara* (a leafy vegetable), *matikadene* (medicinal), *manimuni*, *videli lata*, etc. Besides these were medicinal herbs which were traditionally used as antiseptics and pain-killers, remedies for coughs and colds, stomach diseases and so on.

This was the ideal ecological situation in and around the Brahmaputra river in upper Assam prior to the great earthquake. There was a natural balance between man and the river and at no time did people hate the river for its fury. The Brahmaputra was considered sacred and secular at the same time. During Magha Sankranti people preferred to go for a holy dip in the Brahmaputra rather than in the Ganga.

Due to the earthquake, there was topographical disturbance in the river bed with deposition of soil, gravel, tree trunks and branches coming from the badly damaged mountain. Because of the disturbance in the soil a strong undercurrent started cutting the soft soil of the bank on the Dibrugarh side. It was a sight to see how houses and trees collapsed and disappeared in the turbulent river. Engineering measures were taken to stop the soil erosion. Several dykes of boulders were built across the river to divert the dangerous undercurrent along the river bank covering the entire eroded zone. This measure saved the town but created problem for the areas outside the protective cover of the dykes.

Because of the flood control and soil erosion measures there was a gradual change in the river ecology in and around Dibrugarh town. Its impact on day-to-day life was evident at a later stage. Some of the significant points are recounted below.

1. Dykes built with boulders to divert the undercurrent of the river along the bank protected the township yet created problem for the areas outside the protective cover. Fishing, which was a regular feature near the river bank, became impossible. A whole village of fisherfolk living on the bank were displaced and had to change their life-style.

2. As has already been indicated, with the engineering success in controlling the erosion attention was given to flood control. The dam which was constructed along

the river bank covering the entire the length of the town, although it stopped flood water entering the town, in a few years' time the results of the flood control measures were reflected in the changing river ecology and the corresponding impact on the life-style of the people. The river's fury became a nightmare because of breaches during peak flood times and the possibility of flash floods.

3. Since Dibrugarh town lies in a heavy rainfall zone, during the rainy season water started accumulating inside the town and the low-lying areas. This became the source for health hazards. The north-western part of the town faced this problem constantly, which was a cause of worry for the Public Works Department. To solve this new problem a drain was dug through the length and breadth of the town for stagnant water mainly in the rainy season. The canal served its purpose for some time but became a source for change in ecology and the environment with gradual water pollution due to deposition of debris and blockage at places.

We have seen two contrasting realities when we take into account the pre-earthquake ecology and the post-earthquake ecology in Dibrugarh. In the pre-earthquake period there was complete harmony between the people and the river ecology. Floods were tackled in an indigenous way and were hardly considered a menace. The recurring floods were responsible for the fertility of the soil and for cleaning the stagnant water of the town. They were also responsible for a source of protein because of the large quantity of fish caught.

In the post-earthquake period, because of engineering measures, there was a gradual change in the river ecology in and around Dibrugarh town which resulted in socio-economic problems. Some of them are described below.

1. The dam which was erected to protect the town from floods has became a source of fear for the people in the recent past. It has created a constant threat of flash floods in heavy rain due to a possible breach in the dam. People of the town living adjacent to the river have had to be shifted to multi-storied buildings or to high places a couple of times in the past. Arrangements for a public address system had to made to inform people about the flood situation and prevent panic.

2. Another factor reflected in the agricultural sector was due to the stoppage of annual silting. The people of the area after the earthquake faced the problem of normal growth and production of quality crops and vegetables. This resulted in the use of chemical fertiliser and resultant deterioration in kitchen garden produce.

3. Fish became more expensive — because of the dyke and the natural drying of the ponds.

4. The drain around the town has become a health hazard. This drain is now a constant source of water pollution.

5. In pre-earthquake times Dibrugarh was a green town. Due to the change in the river ecology there are now fewer trees, herbs and shrubs, specially medicinal herbs.

There are many other observations relating to the changing river ecology in and around Dibrugarh. The primary idea here is to show that there is a need for understanding the traditional wisdom of the people living in a particular ecology and infusing their traditional knowledge into ecological and natural crisis management. The river ecology in Dibrugarh, which was once attuned to the life-style of the people, has been alienated by engineering measures and other development work without considering need-based long-term planning.

This is one of the examples of modern ecological management in which the significance of the cultural dimension has been totally neglected while tackling changing river ecology. In modern scientific parameters, the importance of the interdependence of the cultural component is not central but peripheral to the planning process. That is why disastrous after-affects are often noticed. As a matter of fact, in ecological crisis management by scientific means, the short-term results overshadow long-term holistic requirements. This is quite apparent in the present study of changing river ecology in Dibrugarh region.

Keeping in view the traditional knowledge and experience of the people who have lived their lives in river ecology, the following long-term planning and ecological management would have been the right prescription for this particular region:

1. Soil erosion by the Brahmaputra is a natural process. This has happened in the past as and when there were disturbances in the river bed. It is continuing over the years in different dimensions.

2. Erosion should have been allowed to continue naturally till it reached its stage of saturation. This would have allowed the normal flow of the river and gradual cleaning of debris from the river bed in course of time.

3. Instead of constructing an artificial dam to prevent river water overflowing the bank and low-lying areas, the natural process of flooding should have been allowed to continue. With the gradual removal of debris either naturally or by mechanical means, the fury of the floods would have eased in course of time.

4. The traditional ecological crisis management system should have been studied by planners to make it more effective in dealing with the recurring floods and soil erosion.

10

The Warlis and the Dhangars
The Context of the Commons

Ajay Dandekar

In this paper we shall discuss the specific problems faced by communities occupying different econiches and different geographical and environmental zones, the Warlis and the Dhangars, hunter-gatherers and cultivators and pastoralists of Konkan and western Maharashtra. Occupying opposite ends of the continuum, with one being sedentary and the other semi-nomadic, they are confronted with a problem similar to the tragedy of the commons, due to reasons, it will be argued here, which are external to them yet have affected them severely. In the first part of this paper we shall briefly discuss the context within which the problem of land use is faced by the Warlis and the Dhangars. The subsequent sections discuss traditional knowledge systems and resource use against this background.

Bio-diversity: plants

The following are the chief trees found in the Thane forests: *ain*, *Terminalia tomentosa*, is tall and very useful. Its wood is durable and hard and is used both for building and as fuel. The bark is much valued in tanning, and its sap yields a gum which is largely eaten. *Alu*, *Vanguieria spinosa*, has worthless wood, but its leaves are useful as fodder. *Amba*, *Mangifera indica*, the mango, is valuable both for its timber and its fruit. There are three well-known varieties, *aphus* (alphonso), the best; *pairi*, also excellent; and *raival*, the common sort. The first two are believed to have been brought from Goa by the Portuguese. *Ambara*, *Spondias mangifera*, is a large tree with soft coarse-grained useless wood. The fruit has an astringent bitter taste. *Apta*, *Bauhinia racemosa*, a small fibrous tree, has leaves used for making bidis. *Asana*, *Briedalia retusa*, a good timber tree, whose wood can last under water, is much used for well kerbs. Its fruit is one of the wild pigeon's favourite articles of food. *Ashi. Morinda citrifolia*, has very poor wood, but its roots yield a scarlet dye. *Avla, Phyllanthus emblica*, yields the emblic myrobalan, which is very bitter but much used in pickles and preserves. Its wood is strong and durable in water, and its leaves contain 14 per cent of tannin. *Babhul, Acacia arabica*, though too small to be of much value as a timber tree, makes excellent firewood and yields pods of which cattle and sheep are very fond. *Bakul, Mimusops elengi*, is a large and handsome tree well-known for its fragrant flowers which are strung into garlands and worn by women. *Beheda, Terminalia bellerica*, and *hirda, Terminalia chebula*, though their wood is poor, are both well-known for their myrobalans. The *beheda* can be told from the *hirda* by its much greater size and its bad-smelling flowers. *Bhava, Cassia fistula*, is a beautiful tree, especially towards the close of the cold weather when it is hung with long clusters of pale yellow flowers; its wood is valuable and its pods are much used in medicine. *Bhendi, Thespesia populnea*, though rarely found in sound condition, has good wood which is used for making the spokes of wheels and cart poles; its flowers are a cure for itching. *Bhokar, Cordia myxa*, is a fibrous tree whose leaves are a useful fodder and whose fruit is much eaten; it yields a viscous gum. *Bibla, Pterocarpus marsupium*, a large tree, yields a useful gum; its wood, though of fair quality, does not last long. *Bibva, Semecarpus anacardium*, the common marking-nut tree, is very little known but for its nuts; the wood is in no way useful.

Bondara, Lagerstroemia flos-reginae, is a very beautiful flowering tree with red, strong wood. *Bur, Zizyphus jujuba*, is a common tree bearing small fruit which is much eaten by men, beasts and birds. *Burkas, Elaeodendron roxburghii*, is an ordinary tree whose wood makes good fuel. The tree is named *tamruj* in Bombay and its wood, whitish or light reddish brown, is even, compact and durable. It works easily and takes a fine polish. *Chamal, Bauhinia speciosa*, a tall handsome tree, has very soft and close-grained wood. *Chapha, Michelia champaca*, the well-known flowering tree, has close-grained wood when fully grown. *Chamari, Premna integrifolia*, a large shrub or middle-sized tree, has a white, moderately close-grained wood used for rafters. *Chithari, Caesalpinia sepiaria*, is a splendid hedge plant, and its bark is of much service in tanning. The Tamarind, *chinch, Tamarindus indica*, a large and handsome tree, has hard wood which is used in a variety of ways. *Ohira, Erinocarpus nimonii*, is a common tree which grows rapidly and forms good coppices. Its high stems, though not very durable, are much used for rafters. *Dundoshi, Dalbergia lanccolaria*, is a small tree whose wood is used for making field tools. *Dhaman, Grewia tiliaefolin*, is a small tree yielding small edible fruit, tough wood and bark that provides a strong fibre. If rubbed over the affected part, the bark allays the irritation caused by cow-itch. *Dhavda, Anogeiessus iatifolia*, a very valuable fibrewood tree, produces a gum which is eaten by the people. Besides as fuel, its tough wood is much used for axles and poles and also in cloth printing. The leaves yield a black dye and are very useful in tanning. *Dhayti, Woodfordia floribunda*, a small shrub tomentosa, is a middle-sized tree with smooth grey bark which gives out a thick milky juice. *Gehela, Randia*, is very little known but for its fruit, which is used to poison fish and for its medicinal properties. *Gharbi, Entada scandens*, is a very large creeper bearing pods about four feet long. The seeds are turned to use in several ways, small snuff-boxes and other articles being made of them.

Ghot, Zizyphus xylopyra, supplies fodder for cattle and yields nuts whose charcoal is used as blacking. *Gorakhchinch, Adansonia digitata*, said to have been brought by the Arabs from Africa, grows to an immense size. Its wood is believed to possess antiseptic properties, and its bark to be capable of being made into paper. The pods are used by fishermen as buoys for nets and the seeds as febrifuge. *Iled, Adina* or *Nauclea cordifolia*, is a large and handsome timber tree. Logs more than thirty-five feet long are sometimes cut from one. For their durability in water and their length the logs are much prized for fish stakes. *Humb, Saccopetalum tomentosum*, is a fine and tall tree bearing edible fruit. The wood, though suited for house building, is little used. *Jambul, Eugenia jambolana*, is a useful tree whose wood is very durable under water, and, when of large size, makes good planks. Its fruit is eaten and its bark is much used in tanning. *Kakad, Garuga pinnata*, is a common tree making fair fuel and supplying wood used for the beams and posts of huts and sheds. Its bark is soft and elastic and is much used for flooring cattle sheds. Its fruit is not unlike the *avla* in appearance. *Kalak* or *padai, Bambusa arundinacea*, is the well-known and very useful giant-armed bamboo. *Kalamb, Stephegyne* or *Nauclea parvifolia*, is a large timber tree used like *hed* for making fish stakes. *Kanchan, Bauhinia variegata*, is a tree of little consequence, supplying but very poor wood. *Kandol, Sterculia urens*, is an ordinary tree bearing edible fruit. Though its wood is useless, its bark is fibrous and its leaves are often used in native medicines; its sap yields a poor gum. *Karambel, Dillenia pentagyna*, bears fruit on which deer feed; its wood is worthless. *Karnad, Carissa carandas*, is a small but well-known tree bearing edible berries. *Karanj, Pongamia glabra*, is a handsome shade tree; the leaves are used as manure, and from the seeds an oil is extracted and used as a cure for itch. *Karvati, Streblus asper*, is a small tree, the dry leaves of which are used like sandpaper to rub and clean woodwork. *Karvi, Strobilanthus grahamianus*, which reaches its full growth in eight years, bears a cone-shaped mass of calices from which appear beautiful blue flowers. After the flowers fall the cones become covered with a sticky exudate called *mel*. The seeds remain in the cones till they dry and fall out. The stems are largely used as wattle for huts and cottages. *Kavath, Feronia elephantum*, is a strong tree yielding fruit much used in cooking. It produces valuable gum. The oil made from its fruit is supposed to be good for leprosy. *Khair, Acacia catechu*, is a very valuable tree both for timber and for fuel; from its juice the substance known as ҫatechu is made. *Khirni*,

Mimusops hexandra, famous as a shade and fruit tree in north Gujarat, does not flourish in Thane. *Khivan, Helicteris isora*, is a small fibre tree whose seeds are supposed to be a cure for snakebite.

Kinhai, Albizzia procera, is a large and graceful tree of very rapid growth; its heartwood, which is dark in colour, is very durable and strong, and is much used for making rice-mortars, *ukhli*. Its bark, pounded and thrown into ponds and pools, stupefies fish. *Kokamb, Garcinia purpurea*, a common tree, yields a very pleasant fruit. By boiling the seeds, an oil is obtained which is much mixed with clarified butter and is often used as an ointment for sunburn. *Koketi, Sterculia guttata*, yields fibre and an edible fruit. The wood is very poor and is rarely used. *Koshimb, Schleichera trijunga*, is a useful tree growing best in ravines. Its very heavy and dark red heartwood is mostly used in making oil and sugar mills. Its leaves, especially the young leaves, are elegantly cut into six leaflets, three on each side, and have very beautiful red and yellow tints. *Kuba, Careya arborea*, is a fibrous barked tree furnishing a fairly good wood used for field tools. The bark is commonly used in dyeing. *Kuda, Wrightia tinctoria*, is said to have medicinal properties. When of large size the wood is good. *Kura, Ixora parviflora*, is a small tree used for torches. *Mershingi, Spathodea falcata*, is a rare tree whose wood, though of a fair quality, is not much used. *Moha, Bassia latifolia*, is a well-known tree whose flowers yield liquor and whose fruit yields oil. Its wood, though of a good quality, is seldom used. *Mokha, Schbrebera swietenioides*, a middle-sized tree, yields fair firewood. The wood is close-grained, hard and durable, and has some of the qualities of boxwood. *Nana, Lagerstroemia lanceolata*, is generally used as firewood and sometimes for fish stakes, and is also fit for house building.

Nandruk, Ficus retusa, is one of the best roadside trees. *Nimb, Melia indica*, well-known throughout the district, is much esteemed for its medicinal properties. *Nivar, Barringtonia racemosa*, bearing spikes of beautiful pink flowers, is common in hedgerows on the coast. A tree of the same name, *Barringtonia acutangula*, grows near salt water beyond the tidal range. The wood is tough and heavy, and among other purposes is much used for making well kerbs and boat knees. The tree bears an edible fruit, and its bark is a fish poison. *Padvai* or *Pejvi, Melia azedarach*, is a large and handsome tree of the *nimb* kind. Its hard berries are strung together and worn as necklaces. *Palas, Butea frondosa*, is common. Its wood, though of fair quality, is not much used for building or other purposes. Its flowers yield a dye and the roots a fibre. A watery fluid gathered from its roots is considered a cure for fever. *Pangara, Erythrina indica*, is a middle-sized quick-growing tree. Its wood, known as *moshi* wood in Madras, is used for making rafts, and when hollowed, it makes good cattle wood. *Panjambul*, or water *jambul, Eugenia salicifolia*, grows generally on river banks. Its wood is used for making rafters. *Payar, Ficus cordifolia*, is a large shade tree, but from its awkward shape is less suited than either the *ved* or the *nandruk* to roadside planting. *Petari, Trewia nudiflora*, a small bush-like tree, has a soft wood which is used for several purposes. *Phanas, Artocarpus integrifolia*, the well-known jack tree, bears a large fruit which is much prized by all classes. *Phalari, Albizzia stipulata*, is a large tree at Vadavli, 20 miles north of Bhiwandi, with a girth of 46 feet 9 inches.

Pun, Sterculia foetida, resembles *koketi* in almost all points. *Ranundi* or forest *undi, Ochrocarpus longifolius*, yields fair wood and a favourite fruit. *Ritha, Sapindes emarginatus*, the common soapnut tree, is grown in many parts of the district. Teak *sag, Tectona grandis*, though never found large except in some remote places, grows throughout the district in great abundance. An oil employed as a remedy in certain cattle diseases is extracted from its wood. *Savar, Bombax malabaricum*, the well-known silk cotton tree, has very light wood which is hollowed for canoes and water troughs. It grows to a large size. Its cotton is used as tinder. *Shembat, Odina wodier*, yields fair firewood. The wood is also used in building huts. *Shiris, Albizzia odoratissima*, is a large tree whose leaves yield good fodder. *Shisav, Dalbergia latifolia*, is a useful timber tree, but seldom grows to any great size. *Shivan, Gmelina arborea*, is a large tree of the teak kind yielding edible fruit; its glossy wood takes a high polish and is much used in panelling. *Sura, Casuarina equisetifolia*, grows freely near the sea especially in Salsette; its wood is heavy, strong and tough and makes good fuel. *Tarbor, Flacourtia*, or *Xylosma*, a tree found generally on high hills, bears a sub acid red-coloured fruit enclosing three or four seeds in its strong and thick pulp. It is not known if its wood is in any way useful.

Tembhurni, Diospyros melanoxylon, is everywhere common. The black heartwood of old trees is used for cart wheels and for bracelets, and, instead of sandalwood, is ground into a paste and smeared over the face and body after worshipping the gods. The leaves, like those of the *apta*, are so much used in rolling cigarettes that shiploads are every year sent to Bombay. *Tetu, Calosanthes indica*, a useless tree as far as its wood goes, is said to have healing buds and leaves. *Tivar, Avicennia tomentosa*, a firewood tree, generally grows in salt marshes. *Tivas, Ougeinia dalbergioides*, a large but scarce tree, grows best in the north of the district. Its hard and heavy heartwood is used for house building and for field tools. *Tokar, Bambusa*, is of two kinds, the common unarmed bamboo, vulgaris, and the male armed known by the name of *bhariv tokar. Toran, Zizyphus rugosa*, is a creeping shrub, which, when cut young, sends out a watery fluid. Its tough and strong wood is much used for making field tools. *Umbar, Ficus glomerata*, is the wild fig tree. *Undi, Calophyllum inophyllum*, is a very handsome tree growing near the coast. The wood is very useful, and from its nuts a thick oil is extracted. *Vad, Ficus indica*, is a well-known shade tree. *Varas, Spathodea quandrilocularis*, has soft, easily worked wood and leaves much eaten by cattle.

Vavli, Ulmus integrifolia, is a large and common firewood tree whose leaves are given to cattle as fodder.

The Warlis, according to the gazettes (DG Thane District 1984:182) are mainly located in the Dahanu Taluka of the Thane District. They are also to be found in the adjoining areas of Murbad, Talasari, and other areas of the Thane District. Some of the Warlis are also located in the adjoining district of Nasik. It is generally believed that the Warlis once inhabited the region near Dharampur. Megasthenes describes this region as the Varalata, and thus, perhaps, the Warlis acquired the name that they are known by today (*Sanskriti Kosa*, 19, 608).

An interesting legend is a fair indication of the position and the prestige that the Warlis once enjoyed in the region that they occupied and the reasons why they lost these. 'The Koli Raja, Popera, invaded the Warli kingdom of Jawhara. Popera demanded only that much of land that could be covered by cattle hide. The Warli King agreed to this demand, since he felt that it was a reasonable demand to make. Popera then covered the entire kingdom of Jawhara with the cattle hide and thus the Warlis lost their kingdom'. The Warlis even today remember this legend fondly and the folk memory thus preserves whatever remains of the past in their mind-set.

The Warlis completely identify themselves with nature and their identification with the forest is legendary. It is this identification with the forest that has now become a problem, especially since colonial forestry and the draconian laws of the Raj. The forest plays a pivotal role in shaping the Warli mind-set. The field-work carried out in the Ashagadh and Dahanu regions reveals not only complete identification with the forest but also seasonality, which is in fact central to the Warlis. In order to understand the problems of resource management, which incidentally are external to the Warlis, a brief account of the 'fight for the forest' (Gadgil and Guha 1992:146) is required.

The forest communities, especially the hunter-gatherers and the pastoralists, have always been subjected to pressure by the agrarian communities. At times such pressures have been successfully resisted;but the colonial forest laws proved to be a watershed in this fight for the forest. The emergence of forests as a commercial entities altered the situation and the colonial state asserted its control over them, which in turn meant an active intervention in the day-to-day lives of the communities who depended on the forests for their survival. The colonial state not only took effective control over the forest, it also changed property rights, rights of use, traditional rights and obligations. This was in sharp contrast to the earlier system of local use, based on traditional rights and obligations to the use of the forests. The colonial state also promoted species which were of little use to the local population, namely teak, pine and deodar, in different ecozones, while it sought to replace oak, for instance, which again went against the interests of the local communities (Gadgil and Guha 1992:147).

The forest laws of the colonial state affected the communities occupying the different echo-niches in different ways. The Chenchus were, for instance, denied their traditional right of hunting and were forced into a subordinate relationship with the powerful cultivators of the region. This in turn resulted in their being driven into banditry (Furer-Haimendorf 1943). We can in fact map out the cumulative effect of the forest laws on the hunter-gatherers in more than one way. As Elwin noted, the Baigas of the Central Indian Plateau lost much of the hunting skill gathered over a long period of time, though they live for the hunt and the meat existed (Elwin, 1939). A number of such instances could be cited where communities have suffered due to forest laws.

The Warlis too were severely affected by the laws and the cascading effect that they had on their ecosystem. The Warlis were pushed into rice cultivation and the original affluent society (Sahlins 1971) was reduced to struggle to make its living. Today the Warlis find themselves in a state of transition. This transition is vividly reflected in the seasonal cycle and in the life-style that the Warlis have been forced to adopt.

Customs of Marriage and Festivals of Death

Marriage is the most important ceremony in the community. The Warli marriage lasts for four or five days and many minor rites are scrupulously performed. Marriage is not so much a sacrament with the Warlis: it is a contract in as much as there is an agreement in the form of betrothal and a consideration in the form of a bride-price.

Girls are usually married at the age of seven or eight years and boys at twelve. Marriage within the clan is prohibited. Parallel cousin marriages on both paternal and maternal sides are prohibited.

Polygamy is allowed but has been stopped due to local influence. The system of *gharor* exists, in which a man is permitted to marry a girl by offering his services to her father. A man and woman are also allowed to lead a marital life without undergoing a regular marriage ceremony. The regular marriage may be performed at their convenience later, even after children have been born to the couple.

Divorce is granted by an assembly of a few influential men. Divorce is granted on account of adulterous connections on the part of the wife and criminality. At the time of granting divorce the old and new husbands take cups of *palas* (leaves) filled with tea into their hands.

A stick is kept on their cups which is later on broken in the middle by the chief of the Panchas.

If a man dies his widow, with her consent, is allowed to marry her late husband's brother even if he has a wife. Remarriages are allowed. A man whose wife is dead can marry again by *pat* marriage. Widows and divorced women can also remarry by *pat*.

A birth in a family is an occasion for joy and various ceremonies are performed. The children live with the father and go with their mother in case of divorce.

Ideas about chastity and morality are not very rigorous. Pre-marital sex relations are not considered serious. At the most the young man and woman are asked to get married. If the girl develops pregnancy as a result of such relations, the seducer is forced to marry her under threat of a heavy fine. In case a women if found in illegal connection with a person of a lower tribe she is outcast. There is no problem of illegitimate children among the Warlis.

The institution of adoption is widely prevalent among the Warlis. It is very rare that a man has no issue. If one wife is barren, he can marry another. If he has only daughters, he may choose such bridegrooms as may be willing to stay with his own family. It is only when a man has no child and is rich enough to possess a well-built hut, cattle and corn, that he adopts a son. The man usually selects a boy from his clan, with the consent of the boy's father or guardian. No ceremonies or rites are performed. A few relatives and influential men from the village are invited and served with toddy in order to make it known to the public that the boy has been given in adoption. The natural father has no claim over his son after the adoption is publicly declared.

An adopted son takes the name of his adoptive father and his family. He is however prohibited from marrying a girl from his natural father's clan or from his new one.

Grown-up boys erect their own huts and live with their wives separately from their parents. So the question of inheritance of household property never arises.

A very few Warlis have land of their own. A majority of them are tenants of landlords and *sawkars*. The property owned by a Warli is inherited by his sons. Similarly, a *charor* inherits the property of the father-in-law if the latter has no sons, and stands on an equal footing with his sons.

The death anniversary ceremony is called 'kaj' by Warlis. The anniversary is observed for the first time preferably in the month of Margshirsha (December) or on any convenient day. The anniversary is not necessarily observed on the completion of a year and is not repeated. The ceremonies relating to the anniversary begin in the evening and last for the whole of the night and the day after. The male and female relations and inhabitants of the hamlet are invited and served with food and drink. For this purpose a small booth with six bamboos is erected outside the hut in the yard. The roof of the booth is thatched with thorny bamboos and grass. The ground in the booth is cleaned with cowdung and flowers and red lead are sprinkled on it. A winnowing fan with a little rice and a coconut in it is kept on the roof of the booth. Two lines of rice are drawn in this *mandap*. Between these of two lines a human figure is drawn by means of red lead as an image of the dead. A nickel coin is placed on the figure and some coins on the rice lines. The figure is then covered with cloth.

Two more lines are drawn with grain husk outside the *mandap*. A heap of grain husk is placed between them. An earthen pot filled with fresh water is placed on this heap. One more heap of husk is made at a little distance, on which is placed another earthen pot of the same size. Red lead masks are applied to both pots. A coconut is placed on the second pot. A string is tied from the roof of the booth to the mouth of the second pot. To this string twelve betel leaves are tied.

Small rice cakes, cooked beans and vegetables are brought in a little basket as an offering to the *pitar*. A portion of this offering is placed in a *dron* (a cup made of leaves) and fixed in the mouth of the first earthen pot to which no string is tied. Another *dron* is similarly filled and taken up to the top of the *mandap* and brought down to the ground five times by the chief mourner and placed in the winnowing fan on the roof of the booth. These offerings are made at midnight. If the deceased is a woman, whether she died as a *suvasini* or a *widow*, a glass bangle and *kumkum* are offered, among other things.

The conductor of this ceremony is the Kamadi. He sings death songs throughout the night to the accompaniment of musical instruments. The Kamadi himself beats a handy drum. His assistants play on cymbals. At the end of each song the singer shouts the name of deceased, which serves as a signal for the women to begin crying loudly. This general weeping lasts for three to four minutes and is almost mechanical. The singers are served with drink at intervals.

In the morning a lamp is lit and all the relations of the dead are called forth to touch the string hanging from the roof of the booth. The chief mourner touches the string first and all others stand behind him in line touching the person in front. The chief mourner then waves a lamp to the booth. This is *divalya*, waving of lamp.

The Kamadi resumes singing. A medium sits in the booth opposite the singers with earthen pots in front of him and tries to get the spirit of the dead into him. He violently shakes his body and songsters sing loudly. All the persons eagerly watch the coming of the *pitar*. He goes during afflatus to a place formerly visited or inhabited by the dead. He finds something which was presumed to be placed by the dead. By this act, the people believe that the spirit has already entered his body. He also acquaints the people with incidents which occurred in the lifetime of the dead. Some of the secrets of the dead are also revealed by him. He catches some of the relatives of the deceased and takes them to places familiar to the dead. This goes on for a short time and the medium again sits in the booth. The relations of the dead embrace and hug him one by one, weeping bitterly all the while and sincerely believing that they are meeting the deceased, only in different form. This quietens down after a time.

In some places the medium invokes the spirit of the dead during afflatus, makes a small hole in the hind portion of his head above the neck with a sword or a knife, and drops a little blood in the earthen pot. This process, which is called *doki kapne* (head cutting), is entrusted to a member of a particular clan in the locality. The idea of the offering is that no offering is perfect unless it culminates in the giving of human blood.

In respect of the anniversary ceremony of a dead person who was only buried and not burnt, a figure is made of rice flour at the end of ceremony and burnt near a pool or stream where a final purificatory bath is taken.

In the afternoon the pots are taken to a stream or pool and broken there. All take a final purificatory bath. This terminates the anniversary ceremony, which is never repeated.

A single ceremony can be performed for more than one person during the year. In this event the expenses are shared by all concerned. But a large portion has to be borne by the one at whose place the ceremony takes place, and the *pitar* he worships is regarded as principal. A poor man who finds it monetarily difficult to perform the ceremony avails himself of the opportunity of sharing expenses with somebody else in the village. Without such a performance, it is believed that the spirit of the deceased does not become free from bondage and the family may incur its wrath in the form of disease or other calamities. These ceremonies are performed within a year of death and on may on no account be postponed. A member of the family in which a death has taken place cannot marry unless these death rites are performed.

Seasonality

Warli life revolves around the cycle of seasonality, which for them begins with the advent of the monsoon. The Warlis have developed an amazing variety of eco-indicators with the help of which they can predict the onset of the monsoon. Minute change in the time of sunset and the cry of the *pavasya* (bird), are two of them. They also identify change in the *ayan sthan* of the sun to predict the onset of the monsoon. The arrival of the monsoon heralds the season of plenty for the Warlis, as the first crop of paddy becomes a virtual certainty for them.

Warlis avoid eating certain things from the first showers of rain to the time of threshing new corn: coconut, plantain, betel leaf, betel nut, turmeric, sugarcane, beans, cucumber. etc., are taboo to them. These are avoided because they must not be partaken of unless offered to God and the deity of corn. The head of the family has to observe this taboo. Young men who are being trained under a Bhagat, the Bhagats themselves, snake charmers and medicinemen do not eat fish or flesh either.

The successful completion of sowing operations is celebrated by the festival of Koli-bhaji. The entire family gathers around the *deva medhi* (principal pillar that supports the structure of the house) and prays for the *pavasya deva*, the rain god. Cereals and rice are offered to the rain god and to the forest and to all the living beings of the forests. Offerings are also made to ancestors, and the family then prays for the well-being of all. The newly arrived crop is celebrated by the festival of Navabhat, literally the new rice. The rice is offered to ancestors and to the forest. The rain god is offered the new rice and the Warlis dance to the *tarpa*, a musical instrument.

The next important festival is after the paddy is harvested. The Warlis then are in the season of plenty. Marriage ceremonies take place, and important functions which might have been held up due to a variety of reasons are performed now.

This season of plenty comes to an end in March, and the wait for the rains begins in right earnest. The Warlis report that the situation was not so bad when the forest was thick, as they had access to it and the game it provided. Because of the forest laws of the colonial state, continued after Independence, the Warlis have been denied their traditional access to the forest and have perforce had to transform themselves into cultivators.

This cycle of seasonality occupies an important niche in the world-view of the community. Its importance is also reflected in the way the Bhagat transmits knowledge to the next generation. Usually the fifth day in the month of Shravan is earmarked for the initiation of the younger generation into the traditional knowledge system. The teacher takes his students to the forest and introduces them to the medicinal uses of various plants and teaches them the methods of preservation of the varieties of paddy. The Bhagat also tells the young to respect the living beings in the forest and in the settlements. This respect is so complete that the Warlis never go for a hunt unless there is absolute necessity, and they ask the pardon of the guardian deities of the forest before they commence hunting.

The Warlis are now coming under a stress due to factors such as the denial of access to the forest and forest products. This has resulted in the tragedy of the commons, as some have argued, but in an entirely different context than visualized by Hardin (1968). The tragedy of the commons as propounded by him is a powerful and controversial theory. It poses irreconcilable contradictions between individual and system interests. It locates the source of the problem in common property, broadly understood to mean free and unregulated access to scarce resources (Macay and Acheson 1990:1). We shall discuss the tragedy of the commons in the context of the pastoralists also, as it has been attributed to them as well by sedentary society. It will, though, be our endeavour to argue that the tragedy, though it has occurred, has been hastily applied to pastoralists and hunter-gatherers, in this case the sheep-keeping Dhangars and the Warlis of Western Maharashtra. It is therefore important to understand Hardin's proposition and how it may work at different levels due to communities utilising a variety of methods to combat scarcity and make a living which is ecofriendly. Hardin argues that all the resources owned in common — air, oceans, grasslands, forests, space and so on — will be over-exploited.

The Dhangars

Now when we start from the *wada* at Jawli, our first halt is at Naikoba Wadi. Next day we start from this *wadi* and, using the water in the nearby ponds and the grass, we start going towards the west coast. At times we find that pasture is not enough to sustain us, yet we have no alternative but to go on. From Phaltan we go towards the coast and reach Kajal and then on to Lonand. From there we reach Bhajor, where we do all our shopping. Next we descend the *ghat* and offer a sheep as sacrifice to the goddess. After that each of the flocks splits and I reach my village near Mahad. The farmers are usually waiting there for me because the sheep have to be penned in the field. We decide on the field and pen the sheep. Each farmer gets his turn and they get enough manure for their crop.

We have been going to these villages traditionally and there is an understanding that one family will not encroach on another's territory. In my memory such cases have been rare, but whenever they have happened the community has taken severe action against the erring family.

This description is from a Dhangarwada of Sakharam Lakde and his yearly transhumance to the west coast. This practice has been a hallmark of sheep pastoralists of the semi-arid plateau, and it involves the communally owned and operated pasture lands. The method of dispersal and the even distribution of the pastures has taken care of the sustainability of the pasture land.

Enthoven in his observations has listed 22 endogamous and 108 exogamous groups of Dhangars (Enthoven 1920:311). Enthoven, precise in his calculations, noted that there were 467,622 Dhangars in all and that they were found 'all over Deccan, Konkan and the Southern Maratha country' (*ibid.*). Six decades later, Irawati Karve in her observations recorded that the Dhangars were found in what is today known as 'Madhya Maharashtra' (Karve 1968:20). Kailash Malhotra in his most recent findings notes that the estimated population of Dhangars is nearly three million, and these people are spread over all the twenty-six districts of Maharashtra (Malhotra 1984:298). He further notes the major occupation of the Dhangar caste cluster. According to his figures, sheep-rearing Hatkars. Ahirs, Thellari, sheep-rearing and wool and blanket weaving Khutekasrs and Kannade. blanket weaving Sangars, buffalo-rearing Dange, and the meat-selling Khatiks occupy a predominant position over other castes. Compared with these communities the Nikhar, Ladshe, Hande, Kurmar, Kannade, Telangi and others number only a few thousand, and obviously are a minor component of the Dhangar spectrum (for details see Malhotra 1978,1979,1979b,1980; Malhotra and Gadgil 1981). These figures also include cattle-keepers, and hence we may not get a clear picture of the sheep-keeping population of the area. But if we look at the Bombay Presidency gazetteers and compare the total with the post-Independence demographic chart, a significant correlation is established. The Hatkar Dhangars, according to the latter figures, are 573,000 in number and are found in the districts of Ahmednagar, Akola, Amravati, Aurangabad, Bhir, Buldhana, Dhulia, Jalgaon, Kolhapur, Nanded, Nasik, Osmanabad, Parbhani, Pune, Sangli, Satara, Sholapur, Wardha and Yeotmal. The estimate arrived at by Enthoven does not appear to be far-fetched.

Significantly, Malhotra also notes that 'their main concentration, however, is in the semi-arid tract of central Maharashtra, which has a rainfall of 800 mm or less per year' (Malhotra 1984:450-1). The district gazetteers come remarkably close to the figures mentioned above. Sontheimer's observations, based on his field data, correspond with other observations. We can thus safely conclude that the sheep-keepers today, and since the time from which demographic data are available, are a major factor in the semi-arid zone.

There are certain other indicators in the data that suggest that the Hatkar Dhangars were not originally sheep-keepers and in fact are late entrants into the field. The Khillari Hatkars have been described as 'land-holders, potters, messengers, house keepers, shepherds and money changers' (DG Sholapur 1884:87). Captain Fitzgerald, as quoted by Syed Hussain, observes, 'the general idea is that originally there were twelve tribes of Bargi-Dhangars who came from Hindustan, and the country around Hingoli was called Barahatti' (cited by Sontheimer 1989:126; for original quote see Hussain 1920:248).

Lastly, it should be recorded that the list of the 22 endogamous and 108 exogamous groups of Dhangars, as provided by Enthoven, is not exhaustive. For instance, the Bargi Dhangars do not figure in the list because, according to Enthoven, they 'claim to be Marathas and were perhaps Bargirs or the mounted troopers during the times of the Marathas' (Enthoven, *op cit.* 311). But as Sontheimer has recorded, the Bargis could well have been the twelve tribes from the Bara-Hatti.

Thus today a significant proportion of the Dhangar population which is still engaged in pastoral practices consists of sheep-keepers of Madhya Pradesh.

The Gavlis and buffalo and cattle-keepers, who are also called Gavli-Dhangars, are located between 19^0 N to 13^0 N latitude, over 11 districts and 47 tehsils of the three states of Maharashtra, Goa and Karnataka (Malhotra 1984:450-1). In one significant observation, scholars have noticed that Gavlis lack any known genetic defence against malaria (Undevia *et al.* 1973) and thus seem to consciously avoid malarial tracts of the region mentioned above (Gadgil and Malhotra 1982).

The high-rainfall tract occupied by the Gavlis lies beyond the 'intersect' and the Maval and to the west of the semi-arid zone. The environmental conditions of the Western Ghats are conducive to buffalo herding. Over this Western Ghat range the Gavlis are variously known as Gavli-Dhangars, Mhaske-Dhangars, Dange-Dhangars and Gollas. But since they are a single homogeneous group they will be designated as Gavlis throughout this work.

Apart from these two major pastoral groups that occupy the semi-arid zone and the Western Ghats today, there are a few other groups that exist outside this area. We get references to minor pastoralists from Chandrapur, Wardha, Amravati and Nagpur districts, areas of relatively stable rainfall. This area does not form the central focus of this study, nevertheless a brief discussion is necessary before we move on to the other aspects of the pastoral landscape of the Western Ghats and the semi-arid zone.

The Gopals have been equated with the Gollas (Gavlis) by Enthoven. They are a 'wandering tribe of cattle owners and beggars' who appear to have originated from a group of children offered to the gods by several other tribes. The Gopals apparently are derived from Marathas, Kunbis, Dhangars, Kasars, Sonaris, Salids, Vanjaras and Mahars. They divide themselves into five subdivisions. These are: Maratha Gopal, Vir Gopal, Pangul Gopal, Pahalvan Gopal and Gurathi Gopal. These people subsist primarily on milk and milk products and are located in the north-eastern corner of the state of Maharashtra.

The Govaris are the cattle-herders of Vidarbha and the adjoining areas. They are largely distributed in the Bhandara, Amravati and Gadchiroli districts. Their population in this region has roughly been calculated at one hundred thousand. Though they are traditionally cattle-herders, they have diversified into agriculture and many are also wage labourers, (Census 1931:88-9; 286-91; 332-88).

The Nandiwalas are a non-pastoral nomadic community located in the Ahmednagar. Aurangabad, Nasik and Pune districts of Maharashtra. Their largest concentration is to be found in the district of Ahmednagar. Their traditional occupation is the display of Nandi (the bull) in villages, though this does not rule out a plausible link between them and the pastoralists in the recent or distant past.

The Nandiwalas divide themselves into three groups: Tirmal Nandiwalas, Fulmani Nandiwalas and Devwallas. An ethnographic survey (1982) carried out amongst them indicates that the migration of Tirmal Nandiwalas took place some 800 years ago from the present state of Andhra Pradesh. The Fulmani Nandiwalas migrated a couple of centuries ago. The Nandiwalas are also engaged in the buffalo trade, and this becomes interesting in the light of the entire spectrum of trade and nomads in the past.

The Golkars and Yadav Gaulis are two other groups found in the Gadchiroli district and the Achalour taluka of Amravati district. They are traditional breeders and herders of cattle.

Though the groups mentioned above are roughly scattered over a stable rainfall zone and are marginal to this study, nevertheless they are important to understand the spatial dimension of pastoralism.

The subsistence of any pastoral group depends on the primary herd animal on which it has based its herd system. The requirements of the primary herd animal in turn determine the use of echo-niches, pattern of migration and the necessity of interaction with the other subsistence systems.

The choice of the primary herd animal is determined by environmental and biological considerations. This is not to deny the role of political, economic and cultural factors in the choice of herd composition. For instance, as Lattimore has so cogently argued, the expansion of a dominant and exploitative Chinese civilisation caused a decisive shift on the frontiers of China, where mobile herding became an act of resistance, even freedom (Lattimore 1989; Krader 1957; Sahlins 1936). Though a general applications of Lattimore's leitmotif is problematic, it still is an important argument: pastoral systems may not develop just because the echo-niche already exists, there might be other political and cultural reasons. We also have the example of the Bedouins of Arabia, who keep horses because they are prestigious, though they are quite unsuited to the environment.

But so far as primary herd animals are concerned, it appears that their choice is necessarily dependent on eco-factors. As Stauffer has argued, the number of sheep and goats maintained by the nomads may also depend upon the distance between markets and pastoral settlements (1965:292). So along with the environmental context as a major factor, a number of other variables operate in the determination of the species composition of a herd.

Sheep, goats, cattle, buffaloes and horses (as pack animals) are the primary herd animals that constitute the herd system. A brief discussion on the nature of these species is required before we turn to other aspects of pastoralism.

The domestic sheep can tolerate a complete lack of shade and scarcity of water but cannot tolerate slushy conditions. The semi-arid tracts of Maharashtra offer the optimum habitat for shepherds. Below is a table indicating the number of sheep which the entire semi-arid zone holds.

DISTRICTS	SHEEP	GOATS
Pune	320030	325467
Satara	271257	
Ahmednagar	228888	501263
Sangli	227954	
Sholapur	192139	
Nasik	132410	349490
Kolhapur	108075	
Osmanabad	76411	

The Hatkar Dhangars, with an estimated population of 573,000, are distributed in the 19 districts of Maharashtra; their major concentration is in the semi-arid tracts of central Maharashtra, which has a rainfall of not more than 750 mm.

The location of the present-day camp-sites of the Hatkar Dhangars is within an imaginary box beyond a vertical line that connects Junnar in the north to Ajra in the south. The north-eastern boundary is delimited by the Ahmednagar plateau and is sharply demarcated in the south by the Mahadeo range and the Khanapur-Jath plateau. The eastern boundary of this box can be stretched to Osmanabad, where the semi-arid tract rainfall gives way to more stable rainfall. In the area defined above, we basically come across two types of Hatkar Dhangar settlements:

(a) The majority are now are located at the edges of villages. Here we find that most of the Dhangars have taken to agriculture and animal husbandry and have more or less given up pastoral nomadism (by pastoral nomadism we mean a distinct economic activity where the majority of the population is engaged in herding. See Khazanov 1984).

(b) Some settlements are away from villages. Fully nomadic Hatkar Dhangars inhabit these settlements and wear a red turban to distinguish themselves from their sedentary neighbours.

Ethnographic enquiries have revealed that the optimum size of a band of mono-clan Hatkar Dhangars consists of about 20 household units, and each household is composed of 5 or 6 persons (Malhotra 1984:452; Sontheimer 1975:139 ff.). The shepherds reports that they require a minimum of 100 sheep to maintain a family of 5 or 6 persons. This figure is interesting and may help us in throwing light on the biomass of the flock *vis-a-vis* the area.

The most important seasonal movement of the Hatkar Dhangar clans takes places at the end of the monsoon season. The sheep-keepers are forced to vacate their seasonal monsoonal settlements in the semi-arid zone by October-November (Ashvin-Karttik) and have to migrate to Konkan. They return by June-July, the entire cycle of migration being shaped by the onset and the withdrawal of the monsoon.

The migration route will be analysed in a different context in the next sub-section. Here we will discuss the actual route and the distances covered. The discussion is primarily based on observations made by people in the field over a couple of decades. All the routes discussed below are subject to change. Primarily Dhangars take the following routes to the Konkan:

1. Settlements in the vicinity of the area from Jejuri to Phaltan in the Upper Karha Valley start from beyond Jejuri and follow the route linking Jejuri-Saswad-Hadapsar-Chinchwad-Dehuraod-Talegaon-Khumset-Lonavala (Bhor-ghat)-Khopali to Roha Taluka of Kulaba District.

2. Another route frequented by the Dhangars links Phaltan with Mahad through Vadale-Phaltan-Kalaj-Lonand-Bhade-Sirkhimvadi-Rajwadi-Bhor-Manjari (Varandha pass).

3. Settlements near Gulunce and Baramati take the Bhade-Jejuri-Hadapsar-Kothrud route to Pauna valley and stop and spread out near Paud.

4. Settlements forming an arc from Dahiwadi-Mhasawad-Pandharpur follow the Diwad-Khatav-Khamgaon-Kuroli route to Satara and then through the Bamnoli pass to the west coast.

5. Settlements hugging the edge of Maval in the south near Pattankodoli in Kolhapur district go towards Arewadi in Osmanabad district.

The settlements that do not cross into Konkan stop at the Junnar-Pune-Satara-Karhad-Kolhapur axis, the heartland of Maval. As noted elsewhere, all the Dhangar groups do not cross Maval. One of the main reasons for this seems to be opposition from the sedentary population. Recently one group from Phaltan has started going towards Marathwada for the same reason (personal communication). This partly explains the existence of a Dhangar worship centre at Bahadurwadi, to the west of Kolhapur in Maval.

The migration route generally follows an east-west direction from the semi-arid zone. The migrations are uninterrupted and last for 15-20 days. There is no interaction between the villagers and the nomads during the actual period of migration.

Migration Route: Crop Zones

The Dhangars' seasonal camp-sites are located in an area that is characterised by dry mixed deciduous and thorny forests. Scanty, precarious and often unreliable rainfall supports vegetation of thorn forest, dominated by *Acacia catechu* and *Acacia tundra*. The migration route takes the Dhangars to the semi-evergreen and monsoonal evergreen forest formations of the Western Ghats.

Bajra (*Holsus spicatus*) is the leading crop of the scarcity zone. The reasons for this are not far to seek. This crop can be grown on inferior soils and does not require much watering. It is sown by the end of June and is harvested by October. This entire area is the slowly undulating wild plateau tract supporting a thin millet cultivation here and there. I would, with many others (Sontheimer 1975), like to imagine that the Sangam poets could have found another 'Mullai' in the Deccan, but without jasmine creepers, though! (*Mullai* is the pasture land among the five landscapes (see Zvelebil 1975:1982)).

The migration route crosses the 74^{0} longitudinal line into Maval proper, which also marks the crop transition from *rabi* to *kharif*. *Jowar*-paddy-maize-*bajra* are the leading crops of Maval. *Kharif jowar* and paddy are sown in June-July and ready for harvesting by November. Today the extension of irrigation has facilitated a second *rabi* crop.

The migration route terminates in Konkan, an area predominantly under paddy cultivation. Paddy here is complemented by a coconut-mango-*nachani* combination.

Stay in Konkan

The Dhangars on an average spend 7 to 8 months in the Maval and Konkan. In Konkan the settlement splits into its nuclear components after the summer pastures are reached. The fields in Konkan are smaller than their counterparts on the plateau, and thus 80-100 sheep are adequate for penning in one field. In exchange for sheep manure the Dhangars receive rice, which is transported back to the plateau. The Dhangars primarily subsist on *ragi*

(*Elusine corocana*) while they are in Konkan.

The families of agriculturalists and the fields where the sheep are penned have ties. One informant divulged that these ties go back at least four generations, and this was confirmed by the agriculturalists from the plateau.

The sheep are moved to various villages in what can be termed a local migration. The requirement of manure is usually felt after the harvesting of *kharif* paddy, not before March. in Konkan, when the operations for the *kharif* crop begin.

The Return

The Dhangars vacate Konkan with unusual alacrity at the onset of the monsoon. The sheep cannot tolerate slushy conditions, and they therefore have to keep ahead of the ferocious downpour in Konkan and on the ghats. But the Dhangars tend to spend some more time in Maval, where sometimes the resources of 3-4 settlements are mobilised to provide manure for the larger fields. At times 2,000 to 3,000 sheep are penned in the fields. The return to the seasonal monsoon camp is conditioned as much by the monsoon as by the requirement of the agricultural system. The sheep finally return to the summer camps at the end of June or the beginning of July, i.e., Ashadh.

Symbiosis

We are attaching a chart which explains this entire migration circuit, manure requirement and the seasonality of crops.

1. The Dhangar migration circuit and the cropping cycle reveals that no manure is required by the sedentary agricultural population in October-November. No exchange between the two subsistence systems take place.
2. Not only is no manure exchanged, but the Dhangars have to avoid the fields, for the *kharif* crops are still standing and the *rabi* preparations are still at least a month away.
3. The requirement for sheep manure is intense in Konkan by March, when the usual preparation for the *kharif* crop begin. Similarly, the *rabi jowar* is harvested by March in Maval and *kharif* operation begin there by April.
4. This means that between the months of November-December and March-May there is a demand for manure by the agricultural system.
5. After May, the sheep-keepers becomes foreign elements and thus find it difficult to

manage decent pasture land for their sheep.

6. It is quite surprising to note that clarified butter, meat and blood, major items of exchange elsewhere (Barth 1962; Swift 1977) are not major items of exchange in the Dhangar scheme of things. Sheep manure, on the other hand, is extremely valuable.

The key to this seemingly symbiotic relationship lies in the exchange network based on sheep manure. This relationship, given the pulls on each side, is held together because of the mutuality involved.

The possible tension point that emerges out of this complex web of relationships is the foundation of the system itself. Given the tendency of sheep to move into standing crops or tended fields, and of nomads to encourage it on one side, and a fear on the part of agriculturalists that the nomads can and may refuse sheep manure or drive a hard bargain, a precarious balance is deliberately maintained.

This tension reflects itself in yet another significant way. Ethnographic accounts suggest that the migration to Konkan is a relatively recent phenomenon, and that the earlier circuit extended only up to Maval (Sontheimer 1975:161). This excursion into Konkan is perhaps due to the increasing pressure of the expansion of agriculture and resistance of the sedentary agriculturalists to have the nomads in their fields. Though it is clear that with the spread of irrigation the 'sedentists' will gain the upper hand in the mixed agro-pastoral economy, but earlier the situation would have been different. In a situation where agriculture itself is confined to pockets, the pastoralists would play a critical role in maintaining the system, with the supply of manure as the crucial variable in the relationship.

The symbiosis between the two subsistence systems is thus fraught with tension. We have not come across any explicit points of tension but there are indicators, like the extension of the circuit itself. This symbiosis, we suspect, is a *modus vivendi* guided not just by economic considerations but more by the correlation of forces ranged on each side. The complexity occurs also because of the various econiches that are utilised by other groups that intrude in the migration circuit.

Lastly, the circuit and the general movement from east to west and back are indicators of the movements of the pastoralists in the past, thus establishing the 'commons' in history.

The tragedy of the commons argues that the use of common property resources inevitably leads to the degradation of these resources. There have been powerful arguments in favour of the tragedy of the commons. These arguments have been used to justify the deprivation of the CPRs to the hunter-gatherers and the pastoralists, the two communities who have nursed these resources over thousands of years and continue to do so.

In this context the degradation of the CPRs cannot be attributed to their use by the Warlis (in the case of the forests) and the Dhangars (in the case of pasture lands). The degradation of the CPRs in both cases is in fact attributable to commercial interests and the greed of market forces. The answer therefore does not lie in depriving these communities of their traditional rights on the CPRs but in taking a hard look at modern development processes.

References

Barth, F., 1969, *The Basseri of South Persia*. London.

Bombay, 1884, *Gazetteer of the Bombay Presidency: Thane.*

Enthoven, R.E., 1920, *Tribes and castes of Bombay Presidency*. Bombay.

Elwin, Verrier, 1939, *The Baiga*. London.

Furer-Haimendorf, C. von, 1943, *The Chenchus: jungle folk of the Deccan*. London.

Gadgil, M. and R. Guha, 1992, *This fissured land*. New Delhi.

Hardin, G., 1968, 'The tragedy of the commons'. *Science*, 162

Joshi, M., comp., 1974, *Sanskriti Kosa*, Vol 8, Bombay.

Karve, Irawati, 1969, *Maharashtra, land and people*. Bombay.

Krader, L., n.d., 'Culture and environment in interior Asia', In *Studies in human ecology, social science monograph*. Washington.

Lattimore, Owen, 1989, *Inner Asian frontiers of China*. Oxford University Press.

Malhotra, K., 1978, 'Natural selection and colour blindness: fresh data on Indian castes', In *Genetic research*, 31.

———, 1980a, 'Inbreeding among the four Dhangar castes of Maharashtra, India'. *Collegium anthropoloquium*, 3

———, 1980b, 'Matrimonial distances among four Dhangar castes of Maharashtra', *South Asian Anthropology*, 1

———, 1984, 'Population structure among the Dhangar caste cluster of Maharashtra'. In J.R. Lukacs, (ed.), *The People of South Asia.*

Malhotra, K. and M. Gadgil, 'The ecological basis of the geographical distribution', In *People of South Asia.*

McCay, B. and J. Acheson, 1990, 'Human ecology of the commons', In B. McCay and J. Acheson, (eds.), 1990, *The Question of the Commons*. Arizona.

Sahlins, M., 1963, *Tribesmen*. Englewood Cliffs

———, 1971, *Stone age economics*. Chicago.

Sontheimer, G.D., 1975, 'The Dhangars', In L.S. Leshnik and G.D. Sontheimer, (eds.). *Nomads and pastoralists in South Asia.* Wiesbaden.

———, 1989, *The pastoral deities of western India.* New York.

Undevia, J.V. *et al.*, 1973, 'G-6 PD deficiency and abnormal haemoglobin among the Dhangars of Maharashtra'. *Proceedings of the Conference of Indian Physicians.* Udaipur. 1973. Abstract No. 41.

11

Cultural Dimension of Ecology
A Case Study of the Oraons

Virginius Xaxa

THIS paper aims at understanding the place that the natural order assumes in the life of the Oraons, one of the major tribal groups in India. This is done by examining some features of Oraon culture — culture understood in the sense of the way of life of a group. All the same, the focus in this paper is not on how nature and the environment are articulated in riddles, stories, myths, legends, etc. Though these do tell us about the ways in which nature is perceived, they may not tell us how people actually relate to nature. Accordingly, the paper deals with aspects of culture that are being lived in the day-to-day lives of the people.

The paper is divided into three parts. The first part outlines the place of nature in the life of the Oraons. The second tries to understand the nature of the interface that obtains and the values making such interaction possible. In the last part we explore the modes through which the Oraons sustain the order that exists.

I

An important aspect of Oraon culture that is intimately related to environmental features is food habits. The Oraons are primarily agriculturists. Their usual diet consists of rice, *dal* and vegetables. Fish and meat are occasionally consumed. What is striking, however, is that leaves, flowers, seeds, roots and fruits are an integral part of the Oraon diet. These are procured from the forest. Only a few are grown by the people themselves. A study has shown that there are about 21 kinds of common native plants whose leaves are eaten by the Oraons. The number of common native plants whose flowers, roots, seeds, fruits and whole plants that are eaten stand at 10, 10, 15, 25 and 6 respectively. In all, there are 87 kinds of common native plants which are related to the food of the Oraons.

The construction of houses, household items and other artifacts too show a linkage with the environment. Chotanagpur is a land of forests. Many products are obtained from the forest. Some of these are major products and others are minor ones. The Oraon house is usually made of mud walls and tile roofs. All the same, house construction requires the use of timber and bamboo.

It is for minor products that we find greater concern among the Oroans. The Oraon household includes such items as mats, cots, wooden stools, baskets, cups, plates, cushions, rope, mortar and pestle and oil presses. All of these are made from forest products. Hunting implements such as bows and arrows, slings, spears and swords are made from forest products. Similarly, fishing tools such as baskets and traps of various kinds are made of bamboo. Fishing nets are made of twine. Umbrellas are made with the handle and ribs of bamboo covered with *gungu* leaves. Even the hooded waterproof coat is made of the *gungu* leaves.

Knowledge of the treatment of diseases is another sphere where we find a close relation between the Oraon community and its environment. Treatment of diseases is invariably based on the use of medicinal herbs found in the region. There are about 34 kinds of disease which are treated with such medicines. These include pain (headache, toothache, stomachache, eye pain, ear pain, migraine), fever (high, ordinary, malaria), wounds, constipation, diarrhoea, dysentery, epilepsy, rheumatism, insomnia, tetanus, eczema, etc. These are treated with medicines based on leaves, roots, the bark of trees, and with plants which grow wild in the jungle. Some of them are grown in their fields by the people themselves.

The major customs among the Oraons, as with any other community, are connected with birth, marriage and death. The linkage of customs with the ecology is best reflected in customs connected with marriage and death. There are many customs preceding marriage with which the environment is very closely connected. There is the custom of men going to the forest to fetch firewood and women to fetch *sal* leaves for preparing cups and plates. The preparation of the marriage mat and marriage baskets of various sizes are other customs. Setting up a *marwa* is, however, the most significant. Nine *sal* saplings with leaves on top are planted in the courtyard in three rows. The middle one of the second row differs in its height. Also planted are branches of bamboo, *sidha*, *bhelwa*, mango and *mahua*. The mango suggests perpetuity of descendants, the bamboo symbolises progeny, the *sidha* fidelity of husband and wife, the *bhelwa* protection from the evil eye and the *mahua*, love between the couple. The marriage ritual would be incomplete without this invocation of trees and plants.

During funerals the Oraons practise burial and cremation. Bodies are buried when crops stand in the field. In this custom, various shapes of branches cover the bottom of the grave, lengthwise and crosswise.

Important festivals of the Oraons pertain to the forest, hunting, agriculture and cattle. Besides these, there are socio-religious gatherings known as *jatras*, which take place at the commencement of different seasons. It is not possible to discuss all their festivals. I shall confine myself to a few for the purpose of illustration.

The spring festival, known as *sarhul*, is celebrated when the *sal* tree is in full blossom. In this festival the Oraons perform the symbolic marriage of the sky with the earth. This is done to ensure the fertility of mother earth. On this day a propitiatory sacrifice is offered to the old lady (the village goddess) who is believed to abide in the sacred grove of the village. *Phaggu* is a festival which is observed towards the end of February or the beginning of March. On the evening previous to the feast, a young castor (*Palma christi*) plant and a *semar* (*Bombax malabaricum*) branch are planted in an open place. Around these some hay, firewood and dry leaves are heaped. The village priest sets fire to the hay. When fire burns at its brightest the young castor shrub is cut into pieces with an axe. Immediately the young boys of the village light torches from the bonfire and throw the burning torches at fruit trees, saying, 'Be loaded with good fruit'.

II

What these selected illustrations show is the scale of interaction that prevails between the community and its environment. Whereas the community's dependence on nature is overwhelming, it is far from being passive. The community acts on nature and transforms it into forms that are of use to it. However, the use of environmental resources is limited to the extent necessary for the community. It is this which leads to harmony between community and environment. Such harmony is, however, possible because of the overriding social values that guide Oraon society. These are the values of equality in society, collectivity in economy, accommodation in history, ethical living in philosophy, folkism in literature and group participation in art and music. On account of these, the attitude the Oraons have towards nature is one of rational adaptation and not of mastery over the world.

Crises in this harmony result from a number of sources. The opening up of the economy to the market and therefore profit is an important factor but is not the only one. Societies guided not by profit but by their assessed needs have been equally instrumental in the destruction of environmental wealth.

What seems to be at the back of disharmony is the attitude of rational mastery over the world rather than rational adaptation to it. What has led to this shift seems to be a spirit of competition and domination rather than cooperation, the hallmark of traditional societies.

III

After having tentatively explained what makes possible harmony between community and environment, we shall explore the ways in which the Oraons contribute to sustaining the existing order. We have seen how nature enters into the very fabric of Oraon society — their food, houses, domestic goods, artifacts, rites, rituals, customs, festivals, etc. This shows how the natural order enters into the social order of the Oraons. The two orders are not separate, discrete, autonomous. Rather, they are integral to each other. At the same time, the social order is also a moral order to the Oraons. Hence there are ways through which the moral order is maintained. In Oraon society, these orders are maintained either through prohibition or propitiation. Taboos surrounding the use of environmental features are varied. These are observed on different occasions and by different sets of people. Restrictions surrounding hunting or the commencement of a season or totemic institutions may be taken as illustrations. Propitiation of village deities in charge of different environmental features is another way by which the moral order is thought to be maintained in Oraon society.

12

Ecological Cultivation in the Karanpura Region
A Case Study

Sachchidananda and Rajiv Ranjan Jha

WHAT precisely is ecological farming? Is it something similar to natural farming and traditional agriculture? Is there any similarity with sustainable agriculture? How does it differ from modern and organic farming? Without entering into any exhaustive discussion on the subject, we can say that there is a convergence among all, i.e., natural, traditional, organic and ecological farming. We quote below an expert opinion on the issue recently presented by Gandhimati and Lanting (1994) (Table 1).

'Eco' is derived from the Greek *oikos*, meaning house or household. In current usage it implies the wisdom and authority to manage the interests of the household. In an ecological farming system the idea of an orderly household is expanded to include the managed environment, comprising the cultivated land and its surroundings, the plants contained or grown thereon, and all the animals associated with it.

Terry Gips (1986) stated that sustainable agriculture should be ecologically sound, economically viable, socially just, humane and adaptable. It has been explained by Coen *et al.* (1992) as follows:

Ecologically sound: The quality of natural resources is maintained and the vitality of the entire agroecosystem — from humans, crops and animals to soil organisms — is enhanced. This is best ensured when the soil is managed and the health of crops, animals and people is maintained through biological processes (self-regulation). Local resources are used in a way that minimises losses of nutrients, biomass and energy, and avoids pollution. The emphasis is on the use of renewable resources.

Economically viable: Farmers can produce enough for self-sufficiency or adequate income, and gain sufficient returns to warrant the labour and costs involved. Economic viability is measured not only in terms of functions such as conserving resources and minimising risks.

Socially just: Resources and power are distributed in such a way that the basic needs of all members of society are met and their rights to land use, adequate capital, technical assistance and market opportunity are assured. All people have the opportunity to participate in decision-making, in the field and in the society. Social unrest can threaten the entire social system, including its agriculture.

Humane: All forms of life (plants, animals, humans) are respected. The fundamental dignity of all human beings is recognised, and relationships and institutions incorporate such basic human values as trust, honesty, self-respect, cooperation and compassion. The cultural and spiritual integrity of society is preserved and nurtured.

Adaptable: Rural communities are capable of adjusting to the constantly changing conditions for farming, population growth, policies, market demand, etc. This involves not only the development of new, appropriate technologies but also innovations in social and cultural terms.

Coen *et al.* (1992) state that 'farming practices that enhance, or at least do not harm the environment and are aimed at minimising the use of chemical inputs, rather than completely avoiding them as in organic farming, is Ecological Farming'.

Fukuoka (1985) has a strong belief in natural farming and states that there is no need for ploughing and weeding and mixing fertilisers and pesticides on the land.

In the Karanpura region we found that many farmers were turning away from their traditional mode of agriculture to modern farming systems. It was a farming totally dependent on modern fertilisers and hybrid and improved seeds. As a result the soil has lost its fertility and led to massive unemployment and migration to other states.

There is a difference in opinion among scientists on Gip's definition, and its success also depends on the type of farmers, the community and the state and the government's policy. To provide sufficient food for the survival of the community from their existing natural resources, recourse has to be taken to low-cost input agriculture practices. This will help in the revival of traditional cultural heritage by which women can be strengthened socially, economically and politically.

The Need for Ecological Cultivation in Santhal Pargana

Santhal Pargana is one of the divisions of south Bihar. It comprises five districts, Godda,

Table 1

Approved	*World Vision*	*Purpose/ goal*	*Life Style*	*Mechani zation*	*Nutrient Management*	*Pest & Disease Control*	*Weed Control*
HIGH EXTERNAL INPUT AGRI-CULTURE	Free Market Forces, Profit Exploitation of Nature	Profit Motive	Consumer-ism Capital goods	Heavily Mechani-zed	Application of fertilizers on economic criteria.	Preventive spraying according to fixed sche-dule; all methods of pest & disease control are al-lowed; criterion for cho-ice is profit.	Herbic-ides & all other available methods
INTEGRATED FARMING	Free Market; but look after the weak; re-sponsibility for World + future	Profit but maintain Ecology	Consume-rism within limits prolong the benefits	Only when needed	Organic ma-nure base + corrective chemical fer-tilizers (close monitoring of the nutritional need)	Integrated pest manage-ment, Only specific not systemic, not broad spe-ctrum pesticides which are biodegradable can be used	Cultural methods + mech-anical control
LOW EXTER-NAL INPUT FOR SUSTA-INABLE AGRI-CULTURE	Equality; empowerment of farmers; st-art with reality eco should not be disturbed	Reduce depe-ndency on ex-ternal inputs by rationaliz-ing use of in-ternal resources	As good as possible wi-thout dam-age to other & environ-ment	Only when it is not dependent on outside	As much as possible orga-nic matter, fertilizer if it is not making farmers dependent	As much as possible th-rough crop husbandry, use of local biological methods; specific pestici-des (Biodegradable), Int-egrated Pest Management	Cultural methods + mech-anicals control
PERMA-CULTURE	Future Society as small auto-nomous social units; goodlife harm any with nature	Maintain all natural cycles specially the energy cycle	Simple good life, high technology	Only when it can be controlled by the social unit	Basic organic manure + corec-tive chemicals if necessary & if it is not making far-mers dependent	Same as above	Same as above

Approved	*World Vision*	*Purpose/ goal*	*Life style*	*Mechanization*	*Nutrient Management*	*Pest & Disease Control*	*Weed Control*
ORGANIC FARMING	Rejection of present society + values; use natural products healthy life	Have respect for the procss in nature	Very very simple, healthy life no luxury	Mechanization high level (1) Human Labour (2)	Manure, biomass, no fertilizers	Only Bordeaux-Mix is allowed + pest control through repellent, trap crops companion crops, artificial release of predators not allowed.	Selective weeding
NATURAL FARMING	Human as part of natural spiritual individual	No interference in nature only sowing and harvesting	Simple Natural & healthy (stoic) life	Human labour + simple tools	What is taken from soil is returned	No pest or disease control is done	No weed control
BIOLOGICAL FARMING	Rejection of present society + values; use natural product healthy life	Respect nature + food quality	Very very simple, healthy life no luxury	Human Labour + simple tools.	Manure, biomass, no fertilizers	Only Bordaux-Mix allowed + pest control through repellent, trap crops companion crops, artificial release of predators not allowed.	Selective weeding
BIO-DYNAMIC FARMING	Rejection of present society + values; use natural product healthy life	Empathy with nature farming in line with invisible forces	Very very simple, healthy life no luxury.	Human Labour + simple tools.	Organic manure + ground rocks (minerals)	No. of specific concoctions are used	Selective weeding

Dumka, Deoghar, Sahibganj and Pakur. Santhal Pargana is included in the area covered by the Jharkhand Autonomous Council.

There was a time when the Santhal Pargana division of Bihar had rich natural wealth. The region was covered with thick forest and received heavy rainfall during the monsoon. At present, barely 13 per cent of the land is covered by forest. The forest is the dry deciduous *sal*, and what we see today are naked hill slopes and barren land which has lost fertility. Five rivers, Mayurakshi, Chir, Ajay, Mor and Brahmani, flow in the area. Besides, there are hundreds of monsoon streams, drains, rivulets and several perennial streams. Because of the destruction of the forest, the water retention capacity of the soil has decreased. The level of water has gone deep down, thus affecting the ecology of this region in several ways. Many wells and streams have dried up. During the summer all sources of water dry up leading to inconvenience for human, animal and plant life. The forest, which once had timber trees and about 1,200 species of plants, has withered and biodiversity has been reduced.

The Rajmahal hills in this division were well-known for the rich deposition of fossils but are now devoid of plants and wild birds and beasts like tigers, elephants, bears, wild boar, peacocks, etc. These are hunted by the Santhals and have disappeared because of the shrinking forest cover. The region has also a rich mineral resource base comprising china clay, fire clay, gypsum, quartz, coal and road metal. For human development, several dams were constructed in this region, which led to the displacement of tribals and other inhabitants. They have been deprived of their land and belongings as many areas were submerged in deep water, thus doing heavy damage to the ecological balance of this region (Verma *et al.* 1994; Sachchidananda and Jha 1995).

Beginning of Ecological Cultivation

Early in 1982 Sri Bajrang Singh, the secretary of the Badlao Foundation (BF) and an activist in the JP movement in Bihar, came in contact with the late Mr Khudi Ram Sen Gupta, a famous Gandhian. They moved to Kewatjali near the Mihijam and began the struggle to restore the ecological balance in the region in which 39 villages were submerged by the erection of the Maithan dam. Employment generation for the landless and homeless people was first started for tribal women. The stiff fight to restore the degraded ecosystem helped people to stand on their own feet once again.

Some years later another dam was going to be constructed on the Patro at Budai, a village in Madhupur block of Deoghar district. The irrigation department had surveyed the area for the construction of a big dam by which 43 tribal villages would be submerged. The infrastructure for the dam was already created. People's experience of such dams was painful. The Maithan example was fresh in their minds. All the leading NGOs of the region came together to oppose the construction and forced the government to abandon the project. It was proved that people's unity for a just cause is a powerful force.

During the struggle against the irrigation department at Budai, Bajrang Singh had come in close contact with an ex-serviceman, Sri Binay Singh, a local villager. The latter had 14 years' experience in the conservation of forests and in wasteland development. He went for a six-week training course at Pondicherry conducted by ETC/AME, Holland, in early 1986. He initiated the idea of reviving traditional agriculture with low-input agricultural practices in and around Budai, by which the farmers would desist from the use of fertiliser and hybrid seeds. He planned to conserve the natural wealth and to develop an alternative to modern agriculture without disturbing the components of nature, water, land, forest and animals. Being a local resident, he was well acquainted with the slow penetration of fertilisers, pesticides, monoculture practices and hybrid seeds in this tribal dominated region.

The Netherlands Organisation for International Development Cooperation had initially agreed to support the project 'extension and training for ecological cultivation' in 1986. A team of four young members under the direction of the late Binay Singh started work in two extension centres at Porida and Budai. Porida was situated in a non-forested area whereas Budai was in the forest zone. Each extension centre consisted of 10 villages. By the end of 1989 the contact programme with villagers was completed. Then there was training of staff members and all relevant information related to the future strategy was collected. The agricultural practices of tribal and non-tribal farmers were analysed. The areas more ecologically viable for the next phase were identified. The factors of social justice and economic soundness were also discussed for the selection of the what was later termed ecological farming.

The next phase was started in late 1989 and continued till the beginning of 1990. In this, training and extension of ecological cultivation was spread in Jamtara and Jarmundi CD Block. The follow-up of the old project was continued in Madhupur CD Block only in the Budai area, i.e., the forest zone, but 10 new villages were added to the 10 old villages of the Porida extension centre. The farmers' selection for introduction of ecological cultivation, their training, exposure, etc., were the major components of the work. The non-formal education centres in all the villages were involved in the programme. Green manure was for the first time introduced in the region in 1989, when 40 farmers of 10 villages grew *daincha* (*Sesbania sesban*) in their paddy fields.

An extensive programme of ecological cultivation with demonstration plots was started in 1992 for the sustainable development of the area. The headman of Karanpura had donated 2 acres of community land for the establishment of a demonstration centre on the outskirts of the village. The main extension office at Madhupur, about 29 km from the operational area, was finally shifted to Karanpura in March 1995.

The project continued up to August 1995, and after that the BF decided to go in for more elaborate activities related to land and water development, animal husbandry, strengthening of women's organisations and some innovative income generation schemes for women.

Why Farmers Opted for Ecological Cultivation

A survey was made of farmers who had adopted ecological cultivation to find out which communities had opted for it, the age group to which it appealed most and whether landholding and education had anything to do with it. The survey also revealed the actual land under ecological cultivation and the farmers' reasons for going in for this kind of cultivation.

1. COMMUNITY-WISE BREAK-UP OF THE ADOPTERS

Communities	*No. of households*	%
Scheduled Castes	3	5.45%
Scheduled Tribe	24	43.63%
Backward Castes	17	30.90%
General	11	20.02%
	55	100.00

It was revealed that the bulk of the adopters were tribals. They were followed by the backward castes.

2. AGE-WISE BREAK UP OF THE ADOPTERS

Age bracket	*No. of farmers*	%
Below 20 years	1	1.81%
21 to 30 years	12	30.93%
31 to 40 years	25	45.45%
41 to 50 years	10	18.18%
Above 50 years	2	3.63%
	55	100.00

Farmers between the ages of 21 and 40 years have gone in for ecological cultivation. It is clear that it appeals to the younger farmers.

3. BREAK- UP OF FARMERS BY LANDHOLDING

Acres	*No.of farmers*	%
Less than one acre	1	1.81%
1 to 2 acres	15	27.28%
3 to 5 acres	18	32.72%
Above 5 acres	21	38.19%
	55	100.00

This table reveals that the rate of adoption goes up with landholding

4. FARMERS' BREAK-UP BY EDUCATIONAL LEVEL

Educational Level	*No.of farmers*	%
Illiterate	22	40.00
Literate	15	27.20
Upto class IX and above	18	32.72
	55	100.00

It is seen that educational level has no correlation with the adoption of ecological cultivation.

5. LAND UNDER ECOLOGICAL CULTIVATION

Land in acres	*No. of farmers*	%
Less than one acre	17	30.90
Up to 2 acres	22	40.00
Up to 5 acres	14	25.47
More than 5 acres	2	3.63
	55	100.00

It was found that the farmers going in for ecological cultivation did not practice it in all their plots.

Asked about the reasons for the adoption of ecological cultivation, the following frequencies were revealed:

1. Light ploughing	20
2. Retention of moisture	14
3. Produce tasty	25

4. Retention of soil fertility	1
5. Lower cost of cultivation	10
6. Crops become disease and insect resistant	7
7. Environment-friendly	4
8. Conducive to good health	1
9. Use of compost	9
10. Use of local seeds	8
11. Can be practised even in poor rainfall	11
12. Seeds are strong and healthy	13
13. More straw yield	9
14. Assured crop	7
15. Produce does not rot	4

The five most important reason for the adoption of ecological cultivation in order of priority are the following:

1. Tasty produce.
2. Light ploughing.
3. Soil moisture is retained.
4. Seeds are strong and healthy.
5. Production even with less rainfall.

To probe deeper into the matter and to get the feel of the farmers in respect of ecological cultivation, we made some case studies of farmers. Some of their observations have been quoted in the narrative below.

Laloo Thakur of Kulharia village has been farming from the very beginning by traditional means. He is a matriculate and is not able to analyse the benefits of ecological farming, but from his personal experience he can say that after doing farming by traditional means, his land has regained strength, his health has improved and economically he has profited. 'At first I cultivated paddy by applying compost and green manure. Besides paddy for the past five years, I am also cultivating potato, bitter gourd and other vegetables'.

Behrabank village of 55 households is mainly inhabited by small farmers. For increasing the yield of their crops the farmers adopted modern methods of agriculture about a decade back, but they have now returned to natural farming. For the past four years they are practising ecological cultivation of maize, paddy, potato, pulses, etc.

Gradually the villagers came to abstain from the use of chemical fertilisers. Thirty-year-old Mahesh Prasad Singh has been acquainted with Badlao for the past five years and saw farmers doing natural farming, but he was convinced only last year and now is doing this kind of cultivation on 1.6 acres of land. He observed, 'Today we make compost and spread it in our fields. Earlier we used to throw it away. Through the use of compost we have been able to save money spent on urea. My land had become tough and infertile, but this year it has improved to a certain extent. By the use of traditional seeds, even if there is less rainfall, there is a chance of the survival of crops'.

The change brought in cultivation has affected not only men but even women. They have also motivated other women to follow this mode of farming.

In Lamba village, Kanti Debiya is a widow, the first non-tribal woman who felt that the presence of the forest is necessary. She tried to induce women to protect the forest. In her words, 'to protect and revive our tradition is the first step in the field of ecological farming'. Today she is doing ecological cultivation on 4 acres of land. She also imparts training in ecological farming to children at NFE centres. Kanti Debiya expresses her views on ecological farming. 'Now all the ingredients of modern farming like seeds, manure, pesticides and implements are too costly and not within the people's reach. I am a poor woman and I have seen with my eyes the land of big farmers destroyed by the use of fertilisers. They have the means to change the soil when it becomes infertile, but it is a costly affair and not possible for poor people. I use traditional seeds, compost, and also irrigate my field in the traditional manner. The yield is not less compared with hybrid seeds, and it is a matter of delight for us that it is very tasty. Even the rice gruel is sweet.'

Was Kanti Debiya really successful in her effort? After seeing Halodi Soren of Nawada village and Sunita Devi and Tagi Devi of Dakodih, who practise ecological cultivation on their fields, we find that residents of this region have given importance to the traditional mode of agriculture, which is sustainable. Jama Devi of Kakali village and Jaso Devi of Bikhandih are also following these steps. All these women are active members of the Mahila Sabha. They participate in the monthly meetings and discuss matters such as how profitable is ecological cultivation, and learn from the exchange of experiences.

Both Jama Devi and Jaso Devi are secretaries of the Mahila Sabha in their village. This has certainly led to greater self-confidence in them. Jaso Devi's husband is in government service. Therefore her economic condition is good and she can afford to cultivate by modern methods, but she has deep faith in ecological cultivation.

They planted plants on the bund, dug pits for making compost and motivated their husbands, daughters and other members of their families to adopt ecological farming. From Baratar village men migrate to other places for wage labour. Their fields remain fallow. The forest has been destroyed. For irrigation they depend on rain alone. The cost of cultivation by modern means is high. Therefore, slowly they turned from cultivation to wage labour.

Through the efforts of the Mahila Sabha the villagers went in for dry land farming by the natural method. People realised that they can carry on cultivation even with poor rainfall if they use traditional seeds for various crops. The farmers started sowing these varieties of seed on barren cultivable upland. The main reasons for turning to ecological farming are low capital input, less labour, assured crop, little harm from pests and insects, high yield and health-giving farm produce. The life of the soil is retained if essential nutrients are supplied.

The villagers are happy and came forward to sustain this mode of farming. They understand that they can no longer destroy their natural environment. They have realised that it is good to plant trees. The soil has once again become fertile and soft. They can see frogs, fish, earthworms, algae, etc., in the paddy fields during the rainy season.

All this provides the base of their faith. This has given strength to Jama Devi, whose husband is handicapped. She has faith in ecological farming. She cultivates vegetables by this method and takes pride in selling them in the local market.

The tribals are very eager to preserve their traditions. They have kept alive their traditional method of cultivation and their mode of cultivation is in tune with ecological cultivation.

Reasons for Non-Adoption of Ecological Cultivation and its Poor Spread

A quick survey of farmers not adopting ecological cultivation was conducted in the same area.

1. COMMUNITY-WISE BREAK-UP OF NON-ADOPTERS

	No. of Households	%
Community	10	20.00
Scheduled castes	05	10.00
Scheduled tribes	15	30.00
Backward castes	20	40.00
	50	100.00

It is seen that there are very few tribal non-adopters. The bulk of them come from the backward castes and the general population.

2. AGE-WISE DISTRIBUTION OF NON-ADOPTERS

Age of non-adopters	*No. of households*	%
Below 20 years	Nil	00.00
21-30 years	12	24.00
31-40 years	20	40.00
41-60 years	10	20.00
Above 50 years	08	16.00
	50	100.00

Age does not seem to have any correlation with non-adoption.

3. DISTRIBUTION OF NON ADOPTERS BY LANDHOLDING

Landholding	*No. of farmers*	%
Less than 1 acre	Nil	00.00
1 to 2 acres	12	24.00
3 to 5 acres	10	20.00
Above 5 acres	28	56.00

The bulk of the non adopters are in the higher landholding group.

4. EDUCATIONAL LEVEL OF NON-ADOPTERS

Educational level	*No. of farmers*	%
Illiterate	18	36.00
Literate	20	40.00
Up to class 9 or above	12	24.00
	50	100.00

The bulk of the non-adopters are illiterate or literate without any particular formal education.

5. REASONS FOR NON-ADOPTION

1. Bumper crop by modern methods	20
2. Imitating other farmers	25
3. More profitable	15
4. Assistance from the CD Block	18

5. Absence of any alternative to upland cultivation	20
6. Less availability of compost	22
7. Increase in soil status	8

The five main reasons for non-adoption are given below in order of priority:

1. Imitating other farmers
2. No alternative to upland cultivation
3. Bumper crop
4. Less availability of compost
5. Assistance from the CD Block

During the 1980s publicity for high-yielding seeds and fertilisers was started by government agencies. Almost in every village, under the cooperative loan scheme 8 sacks of urea were distributed to each villager. Groundnut seeds, wheat, paddy and oilseeds were given free of cost to small and marginal farmers so that they could get at least one square meal a day. These steps were to increase the productivity of their infertile land.

Kakali is a small village of 18 households. In 1985 it had only 8 households. Recalling past days, its people look at their barren land and in a sad voice regret that they fell prey to the bait of the government. Earlier they used to get at least some produce from their land, but after the use of fertilisers the cultivable land has been totally destroyed. The rice is not tasty and so is the case with potato and maize. Even the straw is useless. Above all, year by year the price of hybrid seeds and fertilisers is increasing. Thus they are caught in a trap. They can neither return to ecological cultivation because people will make fun of them, nor can they abstain from the use of fertilisers because it is matter of sustenance for their families.

After reaching this pathetic state, almost all the farmers of the village should have returned to ecological cultivation. But it was found that only small and marginal farmers adopted this method of cultivation. Under this category were mostly the Santhals. Their faith in their traditional method further inspired them to go in for ecological cultivation. They rear pigs, goats, hens and pigeons, etc. Their waste is used to make compost. The non-tribals mainly migrate to Punjab and neighbouring states to work as labourers. They are affected by the agricultural revolution in these states. They come and discuss these matters in their villages and establish direct links with the Block Development Officer and the Agriculture Extension Officer. They feel that with the use of urea and DAP, crops can be cultivated on barren land also.

There are about 100 acres of upland in and around Karanpura. Mohan Das has 1.2 acres of upland and for the past two years he has been cultivating Gora paddy introduced by the Block. This year the farmers put compost in maize but urea in paddy fields. They have been impressed by ecological cultivation. Their land was infertile from the beginning. There was also a scarcity of water. But now the situation has worsened. The land is becoming harder and for short-term gain they are destroying the productivity of the soil. This has been accepted by the farmers who have less than 5 acres of land. They use compost and green manure for paddy. For millets they use the waste of pigs but in wheat, maize and potato they put urea and DAP; otherwise production is affected. One tribal farmer, Lothra Soren, said that maize can be cultivated without the use of urea because the seed is of the local variety and he also experimented with it on 1 *bigha* of land, but nobody believes him.

Din Dayal Mishra of Behrabank says that he has 10 acres of land but he can make only 10 bullock carts of compost. 'I have to increase the yield from the land for the better future of my children. Hence it is necessary to put urea and pesticides in the fields. We require 120 kg paddy seed to sow in 1 *bigha* of land of the local variety whereas only 40 kg of hybrid seed is required for 1 *bigha* land. The yield is also doubles if hybrid seed is sown'. This was the view expressed by many farmers of Balampur, Behrabank, Nawada, Kakli, Lamba and Jorasimar villages.

This year this block is famine struck. Those who can afford pump sets have sown paddy but others could not do so. This was the helplessness expressed by the farmers who had faith in modern agricultural equipment.

But on one point all of them readily agreed. This was that the forest has been destroyed and animal wealth has decreased. There was a scarcity of raw materials to make compost. So they started using alternatives such as urea and DAP. The farmers do not make a cost-benefit analysis. They only look at the production but do not calculate the cost incurred on hybrid seeds, fertilisers and pesticides. One farmer, Kartik Roy of Kakli, was bold enough to say that a time will come when they will once again return to ecological farming. 'Last year the farmers sowed paddy seeds from the Block and the yield was good. I sold rice worth Rs. 5,000 but our animals refused to eat its straw. Even the traders were not willing to buy it. Today also I see the heap of paddy straw in my portico and feel that every year I used to sell paddy straw for Rs.500 and this year I bought it for Rs.300'.

But the use of chemical fertiliser is spreading day by day. Out of shame, the farmers of Nawada village deny that they have seen fertiliser but they accept that they use urea for the cultivation of maize. It sounds rather strange to hear that application of lime to the land was meant to reduce its acidity. It had an adverse effect. The field workers failed to spread this message in the right way. So in 1992 the farmers put lime in their fields but no compost. As a result production decreased. Now they have no faith in this method. They have seen the cultivation of cereals, oilseeds, vegetables and the plantation of fruit trees at the demonstration centre with the use of compost. But they express their apprehension and say. 'it might be that they are putting something else into it'.

In Santhal villages like Hiratand, Karanpura, Nawada, Tumbo, etc., they have now revived and kept alive their traditional art of *tasar* cultivation. They bring cocoons from the forest and wait till the larvae come out and then tie them on *asan*, *arjun* or *sal* trees. But in these villages also urea and hybrid seeds of vegetables have been introduced. The farmers are now trying to use both modern and ecological cultivation. They now understand to which crop they have to apply urea and to which, compost.

Publicity material distributed among the farmers by the Agriculture Department and commercial firms manufacturing fertilisers, insecticides, etc., stress that hunger can be obliterated only by the use of such products. For the cultivation of barren land and upland even small and marginal farmers have started using fertilisers and hybrid seeds, in the hope that they can increase their production.

Steps Taken by the Badlao Foundation to Spread the Idea and Coverage under Ecological Cultivation

Till the 1980s traditional agriculture was practised by the inhabitants of 20 villages of the Karanpura extension centre. Before exposure to the outside world and the propaganda for modern agriculture, they only sowed local traditional varieties of seeds which were resistant to drought and various pests. They grew abundant plants in rotation which provided shade, stopped weed growth and conserved moisture. They were also intercropping and putting animal waste and plant residues in their fields. In place of insecticide and pesticide, *neem* juice (*Azaderacta indica*), *sinduwar* (*Vitex negundo*), etc., were used. Cowdung was also spread on plots for pest control.

Farmers were illiterate but they knew about the green leaf covering (*Azolla*) in paddy fields. Today research has proved that *Azolla* fixes atmospheric nitrogen. There is an interaction between plants and animals. Through this mode of cultivation not only were food and fodder obtained but various valuable medicinal plants which cured both human and animal ailments.

Gips (1986) states: 'The brilliant biological structuring of such traditional agroecosystems is rapidly replaced by green revolution practices'. We found that farmers were forced to sow higher yielding hybrid seeds by which at least three dozen local varieties of seeds of rice, maize, millets, pulses, oilseeds and vegetables have disappeared. The expensive package of chemical inputs which was introduced in this region is unsuitable in the agro-biotic conditions such as the going down of the groundwater level due to massive deforestation. The ultimate result is drought and rotting of soil.

A survey was made in 1987-89 in 20 villages of Karanpura. These were divided into two equal groups, one in the forest area and the other outside it. The first step was to make contact with farmers, to study the existing traditional system and listing the activities to be undertaken in the next phase as required by the villagers.

BF first started its work in 1986 by generating awareness on the environmental situation. From this campaign the issue of ecological cultivation in Madhupur block emerged. Thus such farming practices that enhance or at least do not harm the environment were identified. It was highlighted how chemical fertilisers damage the soil. The benefits of using natural manure in the long-term perspective were emphasised. Songs, plays, posters, newsletters and video films were used to spread the message of ecological farming. A cultural team was formed to train local singers and went around many villages. The training of staff was organised, and they in turn conducted training programmes for selected small and marginal farmers, landless labourers and women. The emphasis was on soil erosion, its protection, salinisation, decreased productivity, increasing pest resistance, water contamination and the use of pesticides and fertilisers, afforestation, gender aspects, etc. The true situation in regard to fertilisers was explained to the farmers. Though these were offered to at low rates, they would not afford to purchase them when the subsidy was withdrawn. This happened after 1994 due to a hike in the price of DAP. Poor farmers could not grow potatoes and maize that year.

Awareness generation was continued in the set of 20 villages in Karanpura and later spread to 60 more villages of Godda, Dumka and Deoghar districts. From time to time new activities were incorporated. To make the new generation aware of ecological cultivation, recourse was taken to non-formal education. In 1988 ten NFE centres were started with teachers educated to at least class VI. By 1993, 35 more NFE centres were opened in three more extension centres.

The NFE centres proved a boon for this programme. The visits of children to the forest and the demonstration centre, when it was established, provided them opportunities for broadening their knowledge of ecological cultivation and environmental conservation.

All of a sudden it became difficult to convince and motivate farmers to give up the use of chemical fertiliser. So they were asked to use green manure on a piece of their land and to observe the difference over the years. This was agreed to by some farmers. The villagers realised that the use of chemical fertilisers leads to various health disorders in animals as well as human beings. From their first-hand experience they observed that yields started decreasing after reaching a peak. Steady increase of financial and material inputs was required if yield was to be maintained. The soil deteriorated and lost its fertility. It required even more water and chemical fertilisers.

At this point five farmers came forward to take the initiative. They agreed to accept scientific support for traditional agricultural practices in part of their fields. These farmers had on an average 3 acres of agriculture land and cultivated paddy, maize, potato, onion and vegetables.

These farmers were taken for a short excursion tour in 1991 to different places in the state where work related to traditional farming was being conducted by NGOs.

The BF concentrated on the revival of traditional practices for paddy because it was the major cereal. After the second year a change in soil texture and micro-organisms was observed. Farmers realised that the water retention capacity of the land had increased. Twelve local varieties of rice were cultivated with compost and green manuring. The more popular varieties were Gopiasar, Kapursar and Mainasar. Farmers mixed green manure, farmyard manure and, when necessary, *neem* leaf extract as insecticide and pesticide. The yield increased to 4 maunds, i.e., 160 kg per *bigha*. The experience of the five successful farmers changed the thinking of others. It convinced them that their traditional system was less costly and gave good results without much effort. The fields of the five farmers acted as demonstration plots which other farmers from the village and from outside could visit. Farmers who were enthusiastic about ecological cultivation formed Gram Vikas Samitis in 20 villages.

The BF provided information, seeds of green manure, cereals and vegetables collected from various parts of Bihar. Subsequently, for the empowerment of women separate Mahila Sabhas were formed in 1993. Till 1995, such organisations in 20 villages were constituted. Compost pits were dug and differences between aerobic and anaerobic decomposition by bacteria were demonstrated. Farmers were not interested in the difference between these two. They were convinced only when the compost produced by the two methods was shown to them.

The demand for *daincha* till 1989 was limited to 40 farmers. This increased subsequently. Initially seeds were brought from Calcutta. By 1994 each farmers had produced seeds of green manure in his fields and the distribution of *daincha* seeds was stopped. At the end of 1991 about 165 farmers used *daincha* seeds given to them, whereas by the end of 1995 about 385 farmers were putting *daincha* in paddy fields and also producing surplus seeds for sale.

By trial an error farmers discovered that the leaves of *palas* (*Butea monosperma*) could be used as fodder for buffaloes and as green manure for paddy crop. Intercropping of *sanai* and *kudurum* was restarted for fibre, and the residue was used for green manuring. The flower of the *kindrum* was also sold in the local market.

Farmers introduced vegetables in their *baril* land (upland) in the *kharif* season. They fenced the land with locally available plants such as *sinduwar* (*Vitex negundo*), *siju* (*Euphorbia nerifolia*), *Opuntia spp.*, *behaya* (*Ipomea cornea*), *ber* (*Zizyphus jujuba*), *babul* (*Acacia arabica*) and also constructed mud walls to stop open grazing. They also came to learn that the locally available fodder leaves from forest trees such as *piyasal* (*Ptericospermum mursumpium*), *murga* (*Adina cordifolia*), *amaltas* (*Cassia fistula*), *kachnar* (*Bauhinia purpurea*) were valuable. Even the leaves of *ber* and *babul* were collected for goats and sheep.

Gora, a dryland rich variety, was introduced in 1993 in 2 acres of land of two farmers. The seeds were initially brought from Ranchi and later the farmers procured them by themselves. In 1965, 40 acres of dryland was under gora paddy cultivation. Farmers used compost with DAP. Small farmers have now been sowing local varieties of paddy, maize and vegetables and using compost. Non-tribals used only cowdung while tribals used pig refuse and agricultural waste.

Soil pH varies from 4 to 4.5. Farmers earlier mixed ash, as it was thought to be rich in potash, to reduce acidity. After proper soil analysis dolomite (lime) was mixed, but the BF could help only 40 farmers because of its limited resources.

For fodder as well as green manuring and to enrich soil with nitrates, locally available nitrogen fixing plants such as *sisam* (*Dalbergia sisco*), *karan* (*Pongamia pinnata*), *babul*, *palas*, and others brought from outside, such as *subabul* and gerardia, were grown by farmers on the bunds of fields.

Farmers have developed small kitchen orchards to grow at least jackfruit, papaya, custard apple, mango, wood apple, *ber*, guava, drumstick, *mahua* and *sal* trees. The traditional mode of irrigation, *dhekul* has also been revived.

Documentation of more than 100 folk songs related to agriculture, forests, hills, trees and birds, in addition to songs of marriage, religious ritual, etc., was completed. From time to time booklets, newsletters and books related to them were published.

Ecological Cultivation and Integrated Development

Ecological cultivation has led to the integrated development of the people of Madhupur Block. In order to bring home the idea of ecological cultivation, Gram Vikas Samitis were formed, comprising both men an women. People were motivated to attend GVS meetings. where issues were raised, discussed and solved. Training was provided to the members of the GVS on the process of ecological cultivation.

Women were offered large participation in social life. They worked both inside and outside the house but had no say in decision-making. They are not allowed to sit with men. But now things have changed. Women of 20 villages are free from shackles. They can take their own decisions on important matters. This has led to their social and moral uplift.

Some women stated that they bring articles of daily use from the forest like fuel, fodder, broom grass, natural toothbrushes, *sakhua* leaves, etc. They do not allow others to cut trees or destroy the forest. They make brooms, leaf plates, etc., and take them to the market. This is an additional source of income for them. Some women have shown exemplary courage in the face of all odds and have surpassed men by their extraordinary work. Forest cover in and around Lamba, Hiratar, Behrabank, Nawada, Kakli and Karanpura villages has been protected by them even though it is owned by the government. They also receive the cooperation of the forest department. Only after getting permission from it can women collect dry leaves, fuel and fruits from the forest. Earlier, they used to cover long distances to collect fuel and fodder, but after the beginning of ecological cultivation and conservation of the environment they find these articles close by, thus reducing their work load.

After the formation of Mahila Sabhas many women opted for cultivation independently. Jama Devi of Kakali herself decides how and what vegetables she has to cultivate and where to sell them. Kanti Debya is adamant on the point that she can cultivate potato and maize without the use of chemical fertiliser. Men honour and abide by the decision of women for planting on community land. The women put pressure on their men to stop the use of hybrid seeds and fertilisers because it is harmful for posterity.

Women raise their voice against any feud in family or society, demonstrate against the corruption of the police and demand the proper management and functioning of government schools and hospitals. During the last two years, 20 such complaints have been resolved. They are eager to acquire their rights in Panchayati Raj. In the coming election, they are ready to contest. They have opened accounts in the Mahila Samriddhi Yojana, a government scheme, and they also visit banks and post offices. This is a manifestation of their empowerment. They have attained equality of status with men and have gained decision-making power.

After the formation of MS and GVS, anti-social elements in the villages have been eliminated. People of about a dozen villages gheraoed the house of a timber smuggler to teach him a lesson. Such an action could not have been imagined five years back.

Ecological farming can succeed only if the people and organisations feel responsible for it. In the beginning of 1992 it was decided that an irrigation well would be dug with people's participation. But the organisation did not start its work until every member of the Mahila Sabha and the Gram Vikas Samiti was convinced. They maintained details of soil excavated, articles bought, masonry charges, diesel pump, blasting material, etc. The well was completed in barely Rs.22,000 when the ordinary cost of digging such a well is about Rs.50,000.

Children attending NFE centres were also given education in cultivation. Small tips are given to them regarding the benefits of ecological farming. As a result it is seen that children make extensive plantations by the roadside, near the temple and on community land. They have planted fuel, fodder and fruit trees. Children in Behrabank alone planted 500 saplings in 1995. Women feel pride and satisfaction in feeding their children with edibles prepared with grain and vegetables grown through ecological cultivation. They taste better than food prepared from other agricultural produce.

After seeing the yield of crops and vegetable raised at the demonstration centre the villagers have gained confidence and are inspired to follow and practise such cultivation.

The tribals of this region are very poor. They cannot afford to practise modern agriculture with hybrid seeds, chemical fertilisers, pesticides and modern agricultural implements. Even it they somehow manage, while they may get larger yields, the cost would be very high. So for them ecological cultivation is cost effective. They don't have adequate funds to invest in land. It is therefore good for them to go in for ecological cultivation and make modest gains.

The Impact of Ecological Cultivation

The main objective of the BF is to ensure immediate and long-term supply of food, basic health and self-respect for the people in its operational area. All its programmes, from ecological cultivation and income generation to organisation of people's groups, are attempts to achieve this objective. Ecological cultivation has succeeded in achieving some level of stability and security. The traditional culture of the villagers ensures that its diverse resources such as land, vegetation, water, animals and forest are treated as part of the ecosystem. The people did not understand the scientific logistics of the integrated ecosystem. In recent decades, this traditional knowledge declined due to several processes, new technology, new values and environmental degradation. In the struggle for survival the villagers fail to realise that the greatest benefits from these resources can ensue only from their integrated and sustainable use, maintaining their original linkages. Soil can use waste coming from vegetation, animals and human beings, atmospheric gases and moisture and turn them into rich nutrients, thus enhancing its own productivity and moisture retention capacity and in turn producing food and nutrition for humans and animals. Any break in this chain disturbs the entire cyclical process and the food security chain is destroyed. The end result is poverty, malnutrition and ill health, which in turn enhance insecurity, apathy and helplessness.

The BF understands some aspects of this degenerative process but its programmes do not address the problems in a holistic way. Ecological cultivation seems to be limited to the application of green manure and cowdung with some stress on bunding. Its awareness building campaign against the indiscriminate use of chemical fertilisers and pesticides has definitely made an impact. But people have now fully understood the different aspects of ecological farming. Many of the farmers appear to be convinced about its efficacy but are apprehensive about adopting it completely.

There is some evidence that empowerment of the people is taking place both at the economic and psycho-social levels. Some people have benefitted substantially from agricultural development. The utilisation of local knowledge and skills has introduced viable alternatives. Ecological cultivation has much potential. The idea of a revolving fund, from which farmers could withdraw cash for seeds and return it at the time of the harvest, reduces indebtedness and ensures a reliable source for the supply of seeds. People's contribution in the form of labour for the construction of a well and the building of a schoolroom are examples that show how they have come to 'own' the development programmes introduce by the BF. At the psycho-social level decision-making by men and women through Gram Vikas Samitis and Mahila Sabhas has not only made them self-reliant but has raised their confidence and improved their self-image and self-respect.

The bottom-up approach in the BF information flow has been impressive. People have realised the need for a change in perspective. The general openness of the process involved in ecological cultivation and the keeping of accounts is a useful strategy for improving participation and removing any apprehensions.

The production from land at present sustains the people for only six months. Thus both in terms of food security and utilisation of agricultural skills the existing potential is not fully used. Ecological cultivation must focus on increasing productivity so as to sustain the growing population. Its essence is the integration of all the resources within a village in a regenerative and mutually reinforcing process.

References

Bhattacharya, K.K. and P. Bhatt, 1995, 'A NOVIB report on Badlao Foundation' (unpublished).

Food and Agriculture Organisation, 1960, *Fertilisers and their uses.*

Fukuoka, M., 1985, *The natural way of farming.* Tokyo: Japan Publications.

Gandhimati and Lanting, 1994, 'Some approaches to agriculture'. The conceptual workshop on sustainable agriculture, Bangalore (unpublished).

Gips, Terry, 1986, 'Breaking the pesticide habit'. In *Alternatives to 12 hazardous pesticides.* International Alliance for Sustainable Agriculture, pub. no.1987-1.

———, 1994, 'Matching poverty alleviation with sustainable land use'. ICCO-NGO workshop at Anantpur' (unpublished).

Pal, M. and G. Memmon, 1994, 'A NOVIB report on Badlao Foundation' (unpublished).

Sachchidananda and R.R. Jha, 1995, 'Ecology: the wisdom tradition.' Unesco workshop, Indira Gandhi National Centre for the Arts.

Sachchidananda and Anirudh Prasad, 1994, *Tribal development and voluntary action: a case study of the Badlao Foundation.* New Delhi: Inter-India Publications.

Verma, S.K. *et al.*, 1994, 'The Impact of mining on living and fossil flora of Rajmahal hills'. Department of Environment, Bhagalpur University (unpublished).

Coen, Reijntjes *et al.*, 1992, *Farming for the future.* London and Basingstoke: Macmillan.

Acnowledgement

We are thankful to NOVIB, Netherlands, for continuous financial and technical assistance, to Mr Bajrang Singh, the secretary of the Badlao Foundation, for providing facilities and co-ordinating the work, to Ms Rashmi Varma for her sincere compilation of field data, and to Mr Rana Pratap Singh for his assistance in typing documents.

The farmers of the Karanpura region are specially to be commended for their support, cooperation and patience in conducting the ecological project in their respective plots.

Finally, our thanks go to the field staff of the Karanpura Project, without whom the work could not be documented.

13

Ecology, Culture, History and World-view
The Andaman and Nicobar Islanders

T.N. Pandit

THE Andaman and Nicobar islands (also known as the Bay islands), a chain of 300-odd islands in the Bay of Bengal, are geographically one of the most scenic and beautiful and historically and sociologically one of the most interesting areas of the Indian Republic. They are situated between 6^0 and 14^0 North latitude and 92^0 and 94^0 East longitude. The evergreen tropical islands are washed by two heavy monsoons a year and the equatorial sun keeps them hot and dry from January to early May. Their total area is 8293 sq km and their total population according to the 1981 census was about 189,000. Of these 84 per cent live in the Andaman islands and the other 16 per cent in the Nicobar islands. The total population has since risen to about 2,81,000 (1991 census) — an increase of about 92,000 in a ten-year period — mostly through immigration from the mainland. Only 34 islands are inhabited, the rest lacking any permanent human habitation. As per official records, 87 per cent of the land area is still under forest cover. The island's forests are rich in tropical fauna and flora but the only mammals are wild boar, civet cat and spotted deer (introduced by the British administration in the nineteenth century). The dark blue waters of the sea abound in marine life. Very few islands have perennial streams, as most of the rainwater washes down to the sea.

The entire Andaman and Nicobar islands provide a broadly similar natural setting and environmental conditions, though micro-level variation exist, with the islands being spread over 600 nautical miles of sea. But as has been very well established by a wealth of data provided by anthropologists and human geographers, very different cultures can flourish in terms of their adaptation to similar ecologies. That is inevitable because each human group, in its collective wisdom and inclinations, makes its set of choices from among the numerous possibilities that exist, to evolve and develop cultural traditions to adapt their life-styles to the conditions in which they live.

This point is very well illustrated by studying the cultural and economic categories that exist in the Bay islands.

Hunter-gatherers

There are five small traditional hunting-gathering tribes, the Great Andamanese, the Onge, the Jarawa and the Sentinelese on the Andaman islands and the Shompen on the Nicobar islands.

Herders and horticulturists

The Nicobarese of the Nicobar islands are spread across twelve islands of the archipelago.

Agriculturists

By far the predominant population of the islands consists of migrants from the mainland who have settled here from 1858 onwards. The vast majority live in the Andamans and only a few thousand are in the Nicobars. The rural population is attached to land, practising agriculture and animal husbandry.

Subsumed under this category are also people living in urban and semi-urban areas working as unskilled, semi-skilled and skilled workers and in white-collar jobs. But we shall mostly leave this sub-category out of our main discussion.

The hunter-gatherers are today very small tribes in terms of their populations, which range from 28 to 200 or so. The four tribes who occupy a few pockets of land or forest area in the Andaman islands are of negrito stock, while the Shompen, living in the forests of Great Nicobar, are of Mongoloid stock (like the other Nicobarese). In popular parlance and even in official correspondence they are referred to as 'primitive tribes'. Along with the Nicobarese they are listed as scheduled tribes by the Andaman and Nicobar administration.

The Nicobarese live in large, well-organised permanent coastal villages. Their relatively large population of 21,172 (1981 census) is spread out in twelve Nicobar islands, and a small number have in recent years settled in the Little Andaman island. The Nicobarese are herders of pigs and horticulturists, with plantations of coconut, areca nut, yams, bananas, pandanus, etc. A majority of them are converts to Christianity, major conversions having taken place from 1945 onwards. While all the hunting-gathering tribes are pre-literate and hence illiterate in census terms, the Nicobarese show a literacy rate of about 31 per cent

(1981 census). They have been attending church and government schools with great interest. This percentage is quite high when compared with the situation among tribes elsewhere in India. The Nicobarese, for obvious reasons, are not considered or referred to as 'primitive', but all the same are looked upon as 'backward' by the settlers.

Besides, the six scheduled tribes mentioned above, there is a huge migrant population from India (189,000 according to the 1981 census) that has settled here since 1858 when the penal settlement was established at Port Blair by the British. The bulk of them (158,000) are concentrated in the Andaman islands. In the Nicobars there are only about 6,000 settlers, and most of them are on the Great Nicobar island, the largest and the southern-most island in the Nicobars.

Prior to 1947 most of the people were brought here as individual prisoners or as groups (e.g. Mopla, Bhatu and Karen, etc.) by way of punishment or otherwise and some came here as government officials, traders, workers, etc. Many of them settled here for good. These are the 'old settlers'.

After 1947 the first people brought here by the Government of India as free settlers were Bengali-speaking Bangladeshi (erstwhile East Pakistan) refugees. They kept on coming here, even on their own, through the 1970s. Besides, large groups kept coming here from Kerala, Tamil Nadu and Andhra Pradesh in search of white-collar jobs or to work as labourers, artisans, and fishermen and small traders.

Since 15 August 1947 (when India achieved independence from British rule) the Bay Islands have constituted a Union Territory that is directly administered by the through an administrator designated as the Lieutenant-Governor (earlier called the Chief Commissioner). There is an indirectly elected Pradesh Council whose role is advisory. The Lieutenant-Governor nominates a tribal leader from among the five small tribes to represent their interests, while the Nicobarese are able to elect their own on the basis of their numerical strength. The Andamans and Nicobars are districts of the territory each administered by a Deputy Commissioner. The islands elect one member to the Lok Sabha (lower house of Indian Parliament).

History

The existence of the Bay Islands has been known to travellers, explorers and geographers during the last 2000 years, as references in various reports show. But in place of authentic accounts there have been many myths, weird tales and lots of mystery about them. The more reliable information has come only after European missionaries and explorers started visiting the islands from the fifteenth century onwards. Colonisation efforts started from the eighteenth century onwards on behalf of the European powers. By all accounts, the Negrito hunter-gatherers and the Mongoloid Nicobarese are the oldest known inhabitants of these islands. The probability is that the Negrito people held sway in large areas of the South-East Asian mainland and migrated to these islands several millennia ago, perhaps under pressure from migrant Mongoloid hordes from mainland China. At a later stage Mongoloid people also migrated to these islands and they confined themselves to the Nicobar islands. This story remains yet in the realm of speculation.

However, the hunter-gatherers apparently found these islands very suitable and seemed to flourish here except for the occasional visits of Malaysian pirates who would try to collect birds' nests (a great delicacy) and also try to capture the Andamanese negritos to be sold as slaves in South-East Asian markets. But in return the Andamanese would try to kill foreigners and destroy their vessels whenever they could. The islands thus acquired a fearsome reputation. In any case, the Andamanese and the Nicobarese were not seriously disturbed by any outside elements.

Penal Settlement

The situation changed drastically and decisively when the European colonial powers started exploring these areas with a view to establishing permanent settlements. In 1788 the islands were surveyed by Lt. Archibald Blair and Lt. Colebrook of the British navy, and a year later the first penal settlement was established by the British East India Company on South Andaman. The settlement was shifted to North Andaman in 1794 and abandoned in 1796 due to heavy casualties.

In 1858 the British came back, following the great Indian Mutiny of 1857, and established a second and more permanent settlement. In the mean time the Nicobar islands had passed under the control of the Danish East Indian Company, but Denmark ceded the area to Britain in 1869 through a treaty.

The Andamanese, who were the sole inhabitants, thus came into direct conflict with the British administration over the occupation of their lands and forests and coastal areas (their resource areas). The conflict and skirmishes lasted several years in various areas, but the Andamanese had to give in eventually to superior technology and might at the cost of hundreds of lives. Subsequently, when peace and friendship were established on most of the islands, the Andamanese came into closer and more intimate contact with the local administration, the British soldiery and the convict supervisors. This close contact led to the spread of new diseases in epidemic form that caused a sharp demographic decline among the negritos. An estimated population of 5,000 in 1858 was reduced to less than 2,000 by

1900, and by 1931 to a mere few hundred.

Today the total population of these tribes has stabilised around a few hundred, though estimates for individual tribes vary (see Table I). In the case of the Shompen the 1981 census figure is 214, but Rizvi in 1984 reported a population of only 134 (1990).

TABLE I

Estimated/actual population of Andaman tribes from 1901 to 1990

<table>
<tr><th>TRIBE \ YEAR</th><th>1901</th><th>1911</th><th>1921</th><th>1931</th><th>1951</th><th>1961</th><th>1978</th><th>1980</th><th>1990</th></tr>
<tr><td>GREAT ANDA-MANESE</td><td>625</td><td>455</td><td>209</td><td>90</td><td>23</td><td>19</td><td>24</td><td>25</td><td>29</td></tr>
<tr><td>ONGE</td><td>672</td><td>631</td><td>346</td><td>250</td><td>150</td><td>129</td><td>106</td><td>97</td><td>98</td></tr>
<tr><td>JARAWA</td><td rowspan="2">585</td><td>114</td><td>114</td><td>70</td><td>50</td><td>300</td><td>250</td><td>250</td><td>200</td></tr>
<tr><td>SENTINELESE</td><td>117</td><td>117</td><td>50</td><td>50</td><td>100</td><td>100</td><td>100</td><td>80</td></tr>
</table>

Sources: Census reports (1901-61) and Anthropological Survey reports. Figures below the dotted line are only estimates. Estimates of total populations in 1858 (start of the penal settlement) was about 5,000 (3,500 Great Andamanese and 1,500 Onge-Jarawa-Sentinelese).

TABLE II

Populations of Shompen and Nicobarese

TRIBE \ YEAR	1901	1911	1921	1931	1951	1961	1971	1981
SHOMPEN	342	375	375	200	20	71	92	214
NICOBARESE	6501	8818	9272	10240	12009	14563	17874	21172

Source: Census of India

The stark fact that emerges from the above two tables is that the most serious problem being faced by the five small tribes of the A&N islands has been their sharp demographic decline following their close contact with outsiders. The worst sufferers have been the ten original Great Andamanese tribes (described by Man 1883 and Radcliffe-Brown 1922). From an estimated 3,000 to 3,500 in 1858 they have come down to a group of a mere 28 souls today (descended from five tribes). The fate of the Onge-Jarawa-Sentinelese group has been relatively less calamitous, as an estimated 400 survive against an estimated 1,500-2,000 population in 1858. The reason is not far to seek. The former have been in the longest and most intimate contact with the settlement and bore the brunt of the ill effects of long drawn out conflicts and skirmishes and new diseases. In the case of the latter, less contact must have helped. Let us summarise the situation obtaining today among the hunting-gathering tribes.

A HUNTER-GATHERERS

The Great Andamanese: Their total population is only 28 souls. They have been settled on a small island called Strait island (off the eastern coast of South and Middle Andaman islands) since 1970. The settlement was built by the A&N administration. and is being maintained at government cost. Each small family has a wooden house and they get monthly their requirements of food, a cash allowance plus other periodical needs. Those members who work in specific jobs (like those of teacher, medical assistant, plantation worker) are paid for their work. The leader of the group gets an extra cash allowance. The government also meets the entire expenditure on their medical care, including special treatment in mainland hospitals. A plantation has also been established in Strait island. Efforts at having a piggery have not been very successful. The social worker who stays there permanently is required to take general care of the people and the settlement. Also the idea was to encourage the Great Andamanese to do useful work for their own benefit instead of idling away their time. Besides, the habits of opium addiction and drunkenness are discouraged and medically treated wherever necessary. It was also hoped that over a period the members of the community would develop a sense of belonging and greater social cohesion. This has happened, but to a partial degree. One has to remember, of course, that the present community has come into being by bringing together the surviving members of the disorganised original ten Great Andamanese tribes. These tribes had ceased to be viable communities due to the trauma of demographic destruction caused mainly by new diseases and the upheavals resulting from their uprooting by the British administration.

In the last two decades opium addiction has been controlled to a large extent but drunkenness remains a problem not yet solved. Attention is also being paid to the serious question of outside people trying to exploit the tribals. Their young women have been physically exploited or have willingly developed liaisons with outside people, which has even led to the birth of children. There is also a case of a non-tribal woman marrying an Andamanese man and bearing him a child. The couple are now separated. But this woman's sister is in love with another young Andamanese man and wants to marry him.

All told, the 28 members of the Great Andamanese community have been pulled out of an abyss into which they had been driven due to total neglect by all concerned and their own loss of nerve and social will due to overwhelming destructive factors beyond their control. But for the intervention of anthropologists and the A&N administration since 1968, there would have been only a small fraction of this population living today, or they might have disappeared altogether.

The Onge: Friendly contact with the Onge was made in 1885 (110 years ago). But prior to that there had been several violent and hostile encounters with British ships and their crews. Sometimes the latter got killed and on other occasions the Onge had to retreat, leaving heavy casualties. The population on the island of Little Andaman and the nearby smaller islands could have been around 1,000 in the mid-nineteenth century. But by 1931 the estimates had come down to 250, in 1951 it was 150 and in 1961 the census head count was 129. In the 1971 census they were 112, in 1980 they were 97, and today they are 98. The Onge were left more or less alone by the British administration except for occasional visits by the administrators and occasional visits by Onge groups to Port Blair (quite often in their own canoes). This situation continued till the late 1960s. In 1953 a coconut plantation was built by the Agricultural Department at the Dugang Creek Onge settlement, though coconut is not a traditional food item of the Onge or other Andaman tribes.

In 1967 a big change occurred when the island of Little Andaman was opened for resettlement of outside people and with the starting of a red oil palm plantation by the Forest Development Corporation. Today the Onge share the island with several thousand settlers in several big villages. These include the Nicobarese (near the South Bay Onge settlement) and Bengali and South Indian migrants. A big jetty and breakwater have been built near Hut Bay (once an Onge settlement area). This has been a major new development, as for the first time the Onge have had to live face to face in their once exclusive habitat with an alien population (3000 or so) which is 30 times their own number and likely to increase. During the 1970s and 1980s the two major Onge settlements were redesigned with new huts of an altogether new design being built, with consequences which have not been too happy. This has gone on with parallel efforts to sedentarise them to enable the official agencies to take welfare aid to them more easily. A social worker, a doctor and a nurse, a plantation worker, etc., have been posted there. A teacher was also there for several years, but this did not lead to any literacy among them. Among the Great Andamanese only some adults and children can read and write a little Hindi. Several health surveys were done among the Onge, starting with an ICMR team which visited them in March 1969. Health records are brought to Port Blair whenever required or possible. But this kind of help during the last 20 years has not helped check the decline in their population, though it has remained steady at the level of about 97 to 49.

The closer contact with the settlers and the supply of rice, flour, etc., has led to a change in food habits. Tea and tobacco they had taken to since British days, but now they eat and cook like other Indians, using salt, sugar, oil and condiments and similar cooking techniques (as against the traditional boiling and roasting methods). Some Onge speak Hindi quite well. They have access to money paid as wages for work done in various welfare projects in their own community, some of which seem hardly relevant to their urgent daily or long-term needs (e.g. collecting resin for the contractor, working in their gardens under supervision, working on the electric generator, etc.) as per their own perceptions.

The Onge life-style has undergone certain important changes but these have not necessarily or always improved the quality of their life. It has actually led to a certain confusion in their minds regarding the direction of their own life, as they are unable to take their own decisions about what and how to do whatever they may like to do. Most of the time decisions, however good they may be (but that is not the case always), are imposed on them. Because of demographic problems some boys and men are unable to have marriage mates. Further, the ill effects of the inbreeding of a small population of less than 100 are not yet visible, but sooner or later they will appear.

However, socially the Onge society is still viable and well-knit in spite of the changes that have taken place during the twentieth century. There is hope yet that it will be able to cope with the unwise and presumptuous interference with its functioning.

The Jarawa: During the nineteenth century, while the British succeeded in bringing around the ten Great Andamanese after several years' efforts (involving the use of force and blandishment), the eleventh tribe in the Great Andaman area (South Andaman to be precise) continued to remain highly suspicious of the settlement and the settlers. They were what are known as the Jarawa. There were numerous hostile contacts and encounters with them during the late nineteenth and the first half of the twentieth century. In fact during the 1920s and 1930s the British were obliged to send many armed punitive expeditions to the Jarawa areas in the deep forests on the western coast of South Andaman. The Jarawa themselves found it expedient to spread out to the western coast of Middle Andaman under these pressures.

A special Bush police force was also created to deal with the Jarawa. After 1947 this policy underwent a basic change as the new Indian government, influenced by Nehru's philosophy, (Pandit 1989:83-92) did not subscribe to the principle of punitive expeditions against tribes except under conditions of overt and conscious violent political rebellions against the legally established government. The situation here is altogether different, as the Jarawa are still not consciously aware of being citizens of the Indian Republic. However various 'Jarawa incidents' continued from the 1950s to the 1970s, and they occur even today though to a much lesser extent. These incidents are mostly caused by the fact that the Jarawa feel disturbed by movements and certain activities of outside people in their territory and wish to discourage these by attacking the 'culprits' if very much provoked. Since 1968 much thought has been given to this matter by anthropologists and the A&N administration and certain useful measures have been taken to remove prejudice on either side. In early 1974 we succeeded in establishing friendly contact with the Jarawa in Middle Andaman. The author was among the first people and the first anthropologist to spend some time with the Jarawa in their own settlement. Since then (over 21 years) many visits have been paid to the Jarawa by official contact parties and friendship has been extended to various groups in South Andaman as well. These visits are made about once a month.

Being under considerable pressure from politically vocal sections of the people, the A&N administration appointed an Expert Committee under Dr S.C. Sinha (anthropologist) to make recommendations regarding the extension of the Andaman Trunk Road alongside Jarawa territory in the South and Middle Andaman. The committee gave conditional approval for constructing the road. But while the road has been made the conditions important for safeguarding Jarawa interests remain mostly unfulfilled due to difficulties faced by the administration and lack of will. This road remains a big hazard for the survival of the Jarawa. Their population of about 200 has an area of 600 sq km of reserved forest and tribal area. But they are surrounded by more than 105,000 (1981 census figures) settlers. Their territory could be overrun in the coming decades unless very sensible and effective measures are taken to avoid such an eventuality.

The Sentinelese: They are estimated to be about 80 to 100 and are the sole inhabitants of North Sentinel island (area about 50 sq km). They are the most isolated of all the tribal communities in India and perhaps in the world. Except for occasional visits by official parties since the British days (and perhaps poachers) nobody goes there nobody else lives there. Because of the sea, where they can get turtles and a whole variety of fish and molluscs as food, they can live comfortably even as hunter-gatherers (Pandit 1990). However, their suspicion of outsiders did not encourage them till January 1991 to have any face-to-face or handshaking contacts with us. But they do not mind gifts of coconuts, bananas, some simple iron implements or iron pieces. They let us put these things ashore while they watch from a distance. What they do not like they throw into the sea. They also come out in their dugout canoes to pick up coconuts thrown into the sea close to the beach. Since January-February 1991 the Sentinelese have relented and have had closer and more friendly contacts with us. It was then that they accepted gifts of coconuts, bananas, etc., from the hands of the members of the gift party (Pandit 1989: 92). A number of visits have been paid since and lots of gifts have been passed on to them. It is our observation and opinion that the Sentinelese population appears to have reduced since 1974, when many more people were encountered on the shore and even photographed.

The situation cannot be corrected by any means at our disposal. In any case the administration does not seem to have much idea about what might be done next. There are cases of the Jarawa and the Onge with whom friendly contacts were made in 1974 and 1885 respectively. Where have we come since then?

The Shompen: Contact of the Shompen with the outside world, directly and through the coastal Nicobarese of Great Nicobar, has existed since the early nineteenth century. It has become closer since the first half of the twentieth century. One saving grace for the Shompen has been the vast forest area that has been at their disposal. In the late 1960s and 1970s it was decided to open the Great Nicobar island for development and rehabilitation of ex-servicemen. Circular and diagonal roads were built to join the east and west coasts in the southern part of the island (403 sq miles in area). This causes very serious disturbances for the Shompen. It also seems that probably disease and intra-group hostilities among the Shompen had earlier caused the dwindling of their population. Their camps are very small and scattered over vast areas. Hence any welfare measures are difficult to take to them. In 1983-84 a Shompen complex was built to attract them so that medical aid, food supplies and some elementary educational facilities could be extended to them through a social worker and medical staff. Besides, on many occasions clothes, utensils, rice, etc., have been distributed among them. But the Shompen complex has not proved as efficacious as was expected in the absence of truly dedicated social workers and proper supervision. The welfare programme remains mostly on paper.

Welfare and Development

Work on the measures described is governed on these islands by popular notions of their meaning. The ultimate objective is understood to be to bring such communities into the 'mainstream' as they can find meaning only in merging with it. In the popular mind this means the broad merging of cultural and social identities of the smaller or weaker communities with that of the dominant culture, society or people. Quite often it starts with copying the use of externals, material objects such as clothes, domestic articles, food materials and the visible life-style. Learning of the dominant language helps greatly in achieving the goal set by the dominant people. They are satisfied if this process is effected, but neither they nor the official agencies show any sensitivity to the thought processes, the mental tensions, the humiliations and the deprivations that a relatively small 'primitive' community might undergo in the process.

There are also the popular but very subjective and unscientific notions of what is civilised'. Joining the mainstream also means that the smaller community is hopeful of getting the benefits of modern science and civilisation. In actual practice this may not happen. By these ideas the down-and-out Great Andamanese could qualify as a more civilised mainstream community, but the Jarawa would not. Left to themselves, the Jarawa life-style is qualitatively far superior to that of the Great Andamanese and the Onge. What a travesty of perceptions!

Anthropologists (like some environmentalists) have often been blamed for advocating 'protectionist', 'human zoo' concepts for tribals. There is no doubt that the five small tribes of the A&N islands are among the beleaguered human communities. They need to be protected and looked after by responsible official agencies under proper scientific supervision and guidance so that they not only survive but live as self-respecting communities. Also, they must not be hustled into getting hopelessly embroiled in the 'mainstream' conceptual monstrosity. They have to change, but the change must not be forced and thoughtlessly harsh in its implications or its speed nor entirely imposed by half-baked social workers or ignorant and unsympathetic administrators or politicians voicing the concerns and extreme selfishness of the dominant groups.

In 1986 the Government of India appointed a high-powered committee of experts to recommend special measures for these small tribes. The committee, headed by Dr S.C. Sinha, met several times, visited these tribes and made several recommendations to prepare them for change while giving them sufficient time. The idea was to appoint a team of well-chosen specialists which would actually involve itself in researching, planning and monitoring all new measures involving the people at all stages and treating their values, views and opinion with respect so that highly sensitive programmes could be evolved and implemented over a period of 10 or 15 years. But these recommendation are now in cold storage both at Port Blair and in New Delhi. And we are back at square one!

Herders and Horticulturists

The Nicobarese have followed their traditional occupations of keeping large herds of pigs and cultivating large plantations of coconut, areca nut, yams, bananas, pandanus, etc. The pigs are reared with loving care and piglets are paid special attention till they grow strong enough to take care of themselves. And adult pig, besides its normal food, may be given 5 or 6 fresh coconuts a day. The Nicobarese live in settled villages, mostly near the coast. The plantations are grown not far from their homesteads. In fact the impression one gets in Nicobar is that houses are built amidst coconut groves. Coconut trees and fruit are of great economic importance. The nut is eaten, its water drunk, its oil used for cooking, etc. The tree is used for the construction of houses, its branches as fuel and leaves for sundry purposes. The pandanus fruit and yams are important sources of food. Fishing is a most enjoyable activity and is carried out by day and by night using various techniques. The daily catch is an important source of protein. These days the Nicobarese keep some poultry also.

While the coastal areas are used for settlement and plantations, the core areas of the islands are maintained as forest land. Here pigs are taken for pasturing and to provide shady areas for rest. The forest area also provides privacy and for romantic interludes to young boys and girls. The forest serves many other needs also in day-to-day life.

The Nicobarese are seafaring people and have been travelling from one island to another in their dugout canoes for barter, trade and social visits. The Nicobarese keep their own calendar by reading the movements of the moon, the stars and the sun. They also have deep faith in various kinds of benign and evil spirits and the souls of dead ancestors. All these have to be propitiated periodically according to customary rites, rituals and sacrifices.

Pigs are eaten mainly on festive occasions. Their herds are not looked upon primarily as a source of food but as wealth bringing prestige, as precious items of barter, as symbols of general well-being and celebration of life. The blood of a pig is also a medicine and is rubbed on the body to relieve pain.

The Nicobarese enjoy sports like canoe racing and man-pig wrestling, and are very fond of dancing and singing. The coconut tree also provides them with freshly brewed toddy, which is a very popular drink among them. Grated coconut provides coconut milk in which rice is cooked. It is a delicacy. There is no provision for individual and private ownership of land among them. All land belongs to the kin group and the produce is shared among the members. Each kin group has a head and the village has a council and head (also called captain). There is also an island council and chief captain on each island.

Until 1945 the Nicobarese followed their own traditional religion and customs. But from then onwards there have been large-scale conversions to Christianity mainly through the efforts of their own Bishop Richardson, a resident and early convert to this faith in Car Nicobar.

The entry of traders and the growth of the cooperative movement under government patronage has helped the Nicobarese to sell their surplus produce of coconut and arecanut. The traders also introduced new consumer items of all kinds. This has led to some degree of consumerism. Over the decades this has also helped develop, in the midst of a traditional egalitarian economic system, an incipient class system. Some Nicobarese have acquired a lot of wealth in money terms, which has given them access to new goods and services. These have become the new symbols of status and social prestige. There are others who can only watch and envy. However, even today no member of Nicobarese society can die of starvation. The community takes care of all those who are unable to take care of themselves for reasons of health, physical disability or lack of work.

As per the 1981 census the literacy rate among the Nicobarese was about 31 per cent. In 1992 it was reported to have risen to 39 per cent (informal sources). The people are making fair use of the facilities provided by the government. Quite a few boys and girls have passed out from secondary and senior secondary schools or acquired university degrees in arts, sciences, medicine and engineering. Nicobarese youth have thus been able to occupy white-collar and technical posts, including the administrative services, to some extent. This trend will continue and more and more Nicobarese are likely to move away from their traditional moorings in terms of occupation. But as yet there are no signs of any serious conflict within their society between ordinary people and 'modernists'. The church and the adaptive processes within their cultural tradition are helping to mediate the situation of potential conflict!

Agriculturists

Agriculture, animal husbandry and fishing and a whole lot of sundry urban-oriented trades and occupations are followed by the settlers from mainland India who were brought here by the British (1858-1945) and later under various schemes of the Government of India. But hundreds and thousands have been coming here on their own, especially from Tamil Nadu, Andhra Pradesh, Kerala, Bengal, Bihar, etc. This composite group goes in for jobs of all kinds both in the public and private sectors. These include thousands of jobs provided by various state and central government departments and related institutions. In 1961 their population was about 45,000 but in 1991 they numbered about 250,000, which is an almost sixfold increase in three decades. The bulk of this population lives in the Andaman islands and some in the Nicobars.

The ecological conditions of the Bay islands are rather fragile. The topography is uneven and hilly and the soil rocky and porous with a very thin topsoil. The heavy rains that two monsoons bring simply flow down to the sea. The soil has little capacity for retaining water. In cleared spaces thousands of tons of topsoil are washed down to the sea every year. Only in two islands, North Andaman and Great Nicobar, are there perennial sources of sweet water in the shape of big streams. All over the settlement areas there is a terrible shortage of drinking water and water for daily needs and agricultural purposes. The only saving grace is that large areas are still covered by forest and vegetation. But it is not so in the large settlement areas, where there are constant demands on forest resources. With the influx of increasing numbers of people from the mainland there are heavy encroachments on forest land and a demand for other natural resources. Because of this, and in absence of effective regulatory and corrective measures, even the vast mangrove forests and coral reefs are getting damaged.

This demographically, socially, politically and economically dominant population is all-pervasive in its hunger for resources, without a thought for the immediate or distant future. The people who have come here to settle either as individuals or as fragmentary groups are culturally uprooted entities. Hence their minds, their psyches and their cultural visions and world-views remain mutilated and blind. Their experience and wisdom made sense in their native environment. Here they do not recognise even by name most of the fauna and flora. There is no idea nor any anxiety on their part to relate in any significant way to the local environment. There is, therefore, no sense of restraint or doubt in their interaction with it. The outlook is: take what you need or want and do not worry unduly about anything that comes in the way, including human beings such as the indigenous tribal populations.

There is vast ignorance all around and a lack of effort to build informed opinion to counter it. A serious environmental and human problem is gaining momentum in the Andaman and Nicobar islands which has to be dealt with in a scientific and human way. The situation in the islands in ecological terms has not yet reached a stage of desperation and can be amenable to a well-thought-out constructive, corrective and preventive policy. Much of the responsibility lies with the Government of India and the Andaman & Nicobar Administration. The policy of 'benign neglect' will not do. The island environment — the land, the sea and the air — is lovely and can be kept so if we educate ourselves and learn our lessons from the indigenous people who have taken care of it for thousands of years without harming it. These indigenous people, their culture and life-styles enrich and provide depth and a beautiful dimension to the composite society and culture of the islands. We have to show special sensitivity in ensuring their survival with dignity and honour. That way we shall show ourselves to be the true inheritors of the great culture and civilisation that is India.

14

Moral Education for Environmental Protection
The Sarvodaya Model

H.M.D.R. Herath

*Your village may boast of having a post office, telephones, electricity . . . but that is not what constitutes being developed. Development is in your head, your mind.**

— JOANNA MACY

ECOLOGY is becoming a more and more important subject today because it scientifically studies the relation of nature and living organisms with each other as well as with their surroundings. Further, this subject investigates the unique interactions in our environment. Compared with the past it is becoming a subject much referred to due to the destruction of the natural resource base through deforestation, destroying fauna and flora, and disturbing the natural environment for various development activities. Air pollution has an adverse effect on the ozone layer.

These factors need very serious attention today. If not solved they may lead us towards various unending questions. Will man senselessly destroy the ecosystems that support life on this planet? Will he be able to maintain a sustainable earth and eventually build a new humanity?

The Sarvodaya model of 'Moral education for environmental protection' is based on traditional Asian cultural values and differs from isolated, unilineal, material-oriented development models. It is unique, since it is developed through people-centred activities and for people-centred activities. Thus this model is directly associated with both an individual

*In *Dhamma and Development*.

morality and a social morality within the central value system of society. It is imperative that the development process in a community is compatible with its environment as well as with the particular culture of that community.

Human beings define their natural environment in terms of its own endowments and natural resources, and in accordance with their perceptions and interrelationships. This pattern suggests that man is a cultural animal. This research covers activities in more than 5,000 villages (out of 25,000 villages in Sri Lanka) where the Sarvodaya model has been applied to achieve environmental protection through moral education. Sarvodaya is defined as the awakening or liberation of one and all, and it follows the Gandhian concept of human advancement. The pioneer of the Sarvodaya movement in Sri Lanka is Dr A.T. Ariyarathna. He says that the Sanskrit word '*sarva*' means all-embracing, integrating everything pertaining to man, society and nature. '*Vdaya*' means awakening, unfolding or well-being. Thus the literal meaning of '*Sarvodaya*' is the awakening of one and all in the society in every respect. Mahatma Gandhi had coined the two words to signify the kind of society he desired for Independent India. The Sri Lankan Sarvodaya movement was inspired and strengthened by Gandhian thoughts as well as the teachings of Lord Buddha.

In the Sarvodaya movement moral education is totally focused on individuals' personality development to ultimate accomplish universal personality development. It is not merely an ideological model. It is certainly pragmatic in addition to being a practical model applicable through village-level educational programmes.

Individual Morality, Social Morality and Culture

In Sri Lanka society the majority (70 per cent) are Buddhists and their central value system comprises Buddhist values, norms, beliefs and morals. This value system and its chain of thought can be represented through appropriate codes of conduct. Foreign invasions and colonial occupation and accompanying influences had a negative impact and paved the way for the various conflicts, deviations and undesirable consequences that exist at present. Even in this disturbed and unsettled situation, Sarvodaya forges ahead, its moral education system expecting to achieve a society governed by Buddhist ethics.

The Sarvodaya model of moral education for environmental protection is a process that has six distinct stages. They include spiritual, moral, cultural, social, economic and political aspects.

1. *Purna paurushodaya* (Personality awakening)
2. *Kutumbodaya* (Family awakening)

3. *Gramodaya* (Village community awakening)
4. *Nagarodaya* (Urban community awakening)
5. *Deshodaya* (National awakening)
6. *Vishvodaya* (Global awakening)

The achievement of these six levels of awakening leads to universal awakening. To reach this state, moral education can contribute very effectively. To facilitate fulfilment of moral education goals there are ten basic human needs to be satisfied. Among those needs the environment should be considered one of most important.

Matrix of the Ten Basic Human Needs

BASIC HUMAN NEED	ENVIRO-NMENT	WATER	CLOTH-ING	FOOD	HEALTH	HOUS-ING	COMMU-NICA-TION	ENER-GY	EDUCA-TION	CULTURE
HUMAN GROUP										
Being										
Family										
Village										
Small Town										
Group of Villages										

These ten basic human needs are universal. They are essential and indispensable to maintain human life according to Lord Buddha. Therefore the Buddhist central value system provides teachings to protect the environment using indigenous knowledge. *Maha Mangala Sutta* states that 'living in a suitable environment is a blessing'.

Also according to the principles of Sarvodaya, complete human personality development is achievable within a suitable environment. The word 'environment' is used here to mean the physical, social, emotional and mental environment in which humans live. The physical environment includes the house, kitchen, latrine, well, sources of water (such as tanks, ponds, streams), garden, soil, land, vegetation, pathways leading to and from the house, neighbourhood, roads in the village, the main roads, air and all other things of physical character.

Social and emotional environment refers to the surroundings, neighbours, intellectual and spiritual development, concentration as well as factors such as noise, which may influence or lead to mental disturbances.

A clean and beautiful environment is one with unpolluted air, healthy soil and uncontaminated water suitable for human survival and devoid of unfavourable influences that make growing children go astray, and which provide them with physical and mental security while giving satisfaction and happiness in addition to a morally sound life-style.

Buddhism and the Central Value System

This doctrine is in perfect harmony with the Buddhist central value system. Prince Siddhartha (later Lord Buddha) was born under a *sal* tree in full bloom; he attained enlightenment under a Bo-tree and his *parinibbana* took place in a grove of *sal* trees in full bloom. This suggests that even the supreme events take place in a natural setting.

Furthermore, Lord Buddha had once said:

> A tree is unique. It has unlimited tolerance, patience, and generosity. It provides a congenial atmosphere for many living organisms to survive. It also keeps on providing shade (as long as it stands) even to the man who attempts to destroy the tree with his axe.

This statement signifies the paramount importance and value of trees, and the environment so necessary to sustain life including that of man. The trees and nature assume so great an importance that even the noblest had illustrated their value.

Lord Buddha has stated that man possesses *nama, rupa* (form and mind), energy and a consciousness unified within a physical and social environment. Although one physical object of the external world stimulates his senses and generates mental activity and provides motivation to his behaviour, it does not necessarily determine his behaviour. A person has an element of freedom or sense of choice that can be exercised with understanding.

Furthermore, from a careful study of Lord Buddha's concept of 'Sath Sathi' (seven weeks) it is evident that he spent the fifth week after enlightenment under a tree with the snake Muchalinda. To visualise a tree, a snake and a human being at the same location is imagining a mutual or reciprocal relationship. The relationship between man, tree and animal is an interesting link between nature and culture. Therefore we can assume that in Sri Lankan society, environmental protection is a part of the central value system of the culture.

Almost all Buddhists in Sri Lanka after religious observances in the morning and before going to bed recite an interesting poem. This poem amply illustrates a Buddhist's value system in relation to his environment and its components.

All living entities on this world and above it (meaning the earth and space above) such as humans, non-humans, who live far and near, ants, animals, trees, acquaintances, friends, teachers, kinsman and parents should receive these merits that I offer.

This discloses the moral values related to Sri Lankan Buddhist culture and also the relationship between man and the environment. A Sarvodaya member pledges to maintain this close and friendly relationship with nature and also recognises the hierarchical social order to be observed.

Moral Education Programme and Environment Protection Systems

The Sarvodaya moral education programme has five steps:

(i) Pre-school group

(ii) Children's group

(iii) Youth group

(iv) Mothers' group

(v) Farmers' group

PRE-SCHOOL GROUP

These children may belong to different socio-economic strata but come together during the first stage of the socialisation process. The rural Sarvodaya centres try to care for these children and duly consider their nutritional state, health, education and mental well-being as well as sociability. The children have opportunities to recognise and perceive the relationship among them and between them and the environment and culture. This is achieved through structured fancy stories, legends, small dramas and other activities. They observe the streams, sky, soil, trees, sun, moon and the clouds. Their nutrition is met by a meal of porridge prepared by village mothers and the pre-school teacher using nutritious green leaves gathered from the neighbourhood. The children are assisted in personality development and in becoming environment conscious. The programme may differ from one region to another due to ecological variations.

CHILDREN'S GROUPS

Members of these groups are schooling children receiving formal education. They initiate and engage in tree planting, maintaining small home gardens, soil conservation, prevention of water pollution, repair of small irrigation systems and group savings. They are encouraged to interact with other groups (youth, mothers' and farmers'). Sometimes they join or organise *shramadana* activities. These enhance their environmental awareness. They are trained to acquire practical skills, the development of organizations, and to participate in community development programmes. Sarvodaya headquarters assist such efforts. They are encouraged to engage in self-help activities and group activities depending on the circumstances.

YOUTH GROUP

This group is relatively mature, knowledgeable and responsible. It may be more active in environment protection than previously mentioned groups. The majority of the group members have either completed their formal education (G.C.E. ordinary level), or they may integrate school subjects with Sarvodaya cultural value-related environmental protection programmes. Some of their activities may include collecting planting materials, tree planting, participatory environmental protection programmes, etc. Some of them may receive organic farming training at the Tanamalvila Centre. There they learn natural pest control methods, ecological farming techniques, sustainable farming technology, reforestation and watersheds management, etc.

MOTHERS' GROUP

At the village level the mothers' groups are dynamic and the most powerful of all Sarvodaya groups. They are trained in child care, tree planting, moral and spiritual development, family nutrition, home economics, home crafts, sustainable farming practices, post-harvest technology of food commodities, natural resource management, etc. Such training helps them to integrate newly gained knowledge with traditional knowledge and pass on their experiences to their children. They also undertake religious programmes and attend ritual functions. Usually mothers' groups actively engage in running the pre-school groups. The children's socialisation and health problems are looked after. Mothers' groups often maintain a garden to provide raw material to produce porridge for pre-school children.

FARMERS' GROUPS

The elders of the village are in these groups. They organise all Sarvodaya activities in the village and are active members of the *shramadana* society. They enhance cooperation, unity, freedom and are interested in the prosperity and socio-cultural identity of the village.

They assist youth groups and act to satisfy the basic needs of the community, including environmental conservation, water supply, food production, housing, health, communication. energy, education and the satisfaction of the spirituals needs of their members.

Group Formation, Moral Education and Environment Protection

These five groups meet separately as well as collectively according to the needs of their own villages. Their collective group formation can be introduced as a *pawul hamuwa* (family gathering). It includes all the five groups meeting at the village Sarvodaya centre daily and weekly depending on necessity. Among their activities, moral education and unity maintenance are considered main subjects. This process can be described as a secondary level socialisation.

At the *pawul hamuwa*, after normal practices in the schedule, meditation is a major item. In the educational process at every meeting discussions involve talk of the central value system, plays and other items. Among these speeches one will be on environmental protection. It is used to emphasise the main responsibilities of the younger generation in our society. Among *pawul hamuwa* speeches the researcher has observed the following topics:

- Traditional medical treatment and environmental protection.
- Chakkawarthi Seehanada Sutta and environment.
- Traditional indicator plants in the environment.
- Traditional post-harvest methods.
- Natural pest control methods that ensure harmless control over the environment.

In addition to delivering these speeches they perform traditional drama in modified forms. All these forms of education provide necessary moral discipline to the members. At the end of the *pawul hamuwa* sessions they give merit to the environment and leave the place.

Practical Side of the Environmental Protection Mechanism in the Sarvodaya Model

The Sarvodaya development model is totally compatible with the balanced development of society and the environment. On the one hand it is related to sustainable development and on the other it is associated with the development of the human mind or moral development. Particularly four positive Buddhist virtues of loving kindness (*metta*), compassion (*karuna*), sympathetic joy (*muditha*), and equanimity (*upekkha*) are stressed. They analyse not only human resources but also non-human resources that can be influenced by the four positive virtues.

The Sarvodaya model precisely and certainly emphasises balanced sustainable agriculture based on eco-friendly farming practices; further, it promotes practices conducive to sustainable natural resource management. The following case studies depict the nature and effectiveness of the Sarvodaya model in the Sri Lankan context.

CASE STUDY 1 MORAL EDUCATION FOR ENVIRONMENTAL PROTECTION: THE PRE-SCHOOL GROUP (SINGITHI HAWULA, 0-6 YEARS)

All Sarvodaya villages have a *singithi hawula*, which is a primary moral education group of children up to 6 years of age. The main purpose of this gathering is to enable children to acquire awareness about self-protection, self-confidence and self-reliance. Normally they are the pre-school children in the village. The pre-school teacher does the primary socialisation, providing understanding fancy tales, legends, *jathaka* stories and small dramas, and tries to introduce the relationship between nature and culture. Those are the first lessons about environmental protection and those devices are complementary to moral values from the central value system. At the same time the children try to internalise nature through observation.

At the second stage the child himself has to bring a seed from home and plant it in the pre-school common home garden. He has to water the plants; he has to touch the soil with his fingers. Before the daily physical exercises the child goes to the common home garden and treats the small plants. This way he learns the interaction between humans and nature. Later on, small children prepare and plant a number of important vegetable plots collectively.

At the third stage of environmental education the pre-school teacher and mother encourage children to think about trees and their importance to human beings. Everyday selected edible green leaves are collected from their home gardens used to prepare porridge. Sometimes they collect leafy vegetables from the surroundings to make porridge. After its preparation children are exposed to sharing behaviour. Each child serves a cup of porridge to another as a daily practice. It gives an equal opportunity to share as an activity that paves the way for collective consciousness.

At the next step the pre-school children themselves organise *malperehera* (a flower parade) four times a month, particularly on *poya* days. The adult villagers have their own conflicts and problems with neighbours. But regardless of such things, every *poya* day one pre-school child carries a flower plate (*malwattiya*) to the neighbouring house. Then members of that family join the child with their own plate of flowers. This is repeated till each and every family gets together and walks, forming a *perehare* that moves towards the village temple. There they collectively make an offering. This sensitises villagers, establishes harmonious relationships among children, and leads to the development of a collective conscience among them. It paves the way for unity and solidarity. Trivial mistakes are forgotten and forgiven and harmonious relations among the participants are renewed.

The next stage of the moral education process for the village pre-school group is organising a *singithi pola* (babies' fair) at the village Sarvodaya centre. The children collect vegetables, fruits, nuts and other materials and take them to this small fair; mothers come to the fair to buy things from their own kids. This gives them training to earn and save money. In some villages pre-school children engage in rice collection, sugar collection, etc. These practices provide experience in collectivity, united earning and saving as a moral obligation.

At the end of the pre-school stage children participate in organising visits or trips, or educational contests about environmental protection or *shramadana* activities. The final outcome is that a small child learns about his role within the environmental system, and personality development is supported within this primary moral educational model. In addition, the pre-school teacher and the mothers of the village have to look after the nutrition, health, education and mental well-being and sociability of children. At the end of the pre-school stage they form a *singithi hawula* to assist other small formal organisations of Sarvodaya.

CASE STUDY 2 ENVIRONMENTALLY SUSTAINABLE GRAVITY-BASED VILLAGE WATER SUPPLY SCHEME ORGANISED BY THE ELDERS' GROUP

This case study aims to explain the secondary level socialisation process and how the implementation of a moral education programme through practical experience is attempted. The location of this included 10 communities, 36 schemes and their gravity-based water supply schemes in Kandy, Badulla, Matara and Nuwaraeliya districts. These programmes were completed in 1985 and evaluation was done in 1987. This second evaluation was done in 1995.

The main objectives of the case study were

- To identify whether the communities had achieved environmentally sustainable gravity-based village water supply schemes.
- To examine how this construction had changed values and fulfilment of the water needs of the area.
- To see whether they had achieved the moral values in the Sarvodaya value systemin practice through different *hawulas* such as youth *hawula*, mothers' *hawula*, and farmers' and elders' *hawulas*.

In the Sarvodaya model of moral education, activities are practically demonstrated to prove their value to youths, mothers and elders, so that they can all perform them in their everyday lives.

For the water supply project, Sarvodaya provided technical cooperation from its Rural Technical Services (RTS) unit. In addition it provided the necessary materials which had to be purchased. In line with the Sarvodaya philosophy of normal education the following decisions were made. In the hilly areas water projects should be gravity-based ones and people should not pollute or destroy the environment. There is no use of chemicals or toxic substances. At the initial stage different groups in the village got together and collectively decided on the necessity of a water scheme, then they carefully searched for a water spring within the village. After getting consent they cleaned around the spring and dug properly to conduct further investigations, such as the quantity of water available. After gaining collective approval the selected place was taken over by the Sarvodaya village centre and converted legally into common property.

Environment Protection and Naturalisation of the Process

After these initial steps the Sarvodaya technical team visited and measured the water level, power of gravity, annual fluctuations in water availability and the capacity of the water spring. Following this the village *shramadana* society got together and started infrastructural work to develop the water spring without excessively disturbing the location. Further, they collected gravel, stones, sand and other necessary materials on a *shramadana* basis and constructed a protective tank, while taking remedial environmental measures. After having started the process the *pawul hamuwa* often got together at night to discuss developments or review the progress of the gravity-based water scheme. The management group of the Sarvodaya *pawul hamuwa* had given necessary guidelines in relation to resource management and environmental protection. After their common decision the *shramadana* society permitted the spring area protective scheme. First the land area was protected by a wire fence. Then trees were established around the catchment area and associated with the water spring. Attempts have been taken to protect the spring from soil degradation and contamination by human and non-human elements.

After development of the water spring, the Sarvodaya society constructed a stock tank at the highest suitable location below the spring. The water collected by the tank was to be purified. The process of purification was completely managed by local experts. They used stones, gravel, sand and other suitable materials to filter the spring water. The collected water in the stock tank was distributed by gravity-based pump lines. This was done to avoid disturbing the natural soil. Natural purification methods were used.

The researchers studied 36 gravity-based water projects providing water for thousands of people all over the hilly regions. In all of them the whole concept was found to be compatible with conservation of the natural environment, and the sustainability of the projects was high. The operations of the water project were done voluntarily by the villagers. Their collective consciences and internal peace and love had helped to smoothly conduct the activities. Basic values related to moral education had been internalised. The social and individual morality developed with team spirit from childhood enabled the individuals to establish and maintain harmonious relationships in later life. The Sarvodaya model of moral education was both socially effective and environmentally valuable.

Conclusion

Environmental protection concerns within the Sarvodaya moral education model are dealt with by appropriate organisation of the community followed by appropriate orientation, awareness sessions and training. The Sarvodaya model focuses on the integration of cultural values with environmental concerns through a harmonious, synchronised and friendly approach. The aim is to implement the most appropriate programmes to achieve well-defined objectives. The progress made so far suggests that this model enables the achievement of sustainable and adequate development in village settings.

References

Ariyarathna, A.T., 1985, *Development from below.*

———, 1988, *Sarvodaya concept of development and its applicability to building up an Asian regional network including Japan.*

———, 1990, 'Managing by values and vision', lecture series 1.

———, *Cakkavattisihananda Sutta.*

Kantowsky, Detlef, 1980, *Sarvodaya*, New Delhi: Vikas.

Macy, Joanna, 1983, *Dhamma and development.* Connecticut: Kumarian Press.

Palmer, M., 1995, 'Ecology prophetic or pathetic'. *Expository Times*, January.

15

African Modes of Transmission of Traditional Knowledge

Charles S. Makari

FIRST, it should be pointed out that foreigners to the African way of living often find difficulties in comprehending the values and beliefs of African culture, and as a result often conclude that the African is primitive, uncivilised, barbaric, unreligious, etc. Yet, when one closely examines the African way of life, one finds that its culture is full of values even richer than the modern world-view which purports to be superior to traditional world-views.

In this paper I shall highlight the traditional African way of imparting knowledge from generation to generation, with special emphasis on the Zimbabwean context. At the very outset, it is important to mention that the people of the Republic of Zimbabwe are made up of several clans or tribal groups which branched from the so-called Bantu people during their immigration from the north to the southern regions of Africa. It is believed that the Zimbabweans finally settled in this central part of Africa around the tenth century. Since then, these clans have practised their traditions inherited from their ancestors. Tradition, which is always understood to reflect both man's past and present, is transmitted through oral history, folklore dances, drama, etc. In the traditional context, the chief is the custodian of his people's cultural heritage and owns the land which is distributed to his subjects. The chief is viewed as the head of his clan while men are considered heads of their respective families.

We will also note that culture enables man to comprehend his existence in his perplexing cosmology and total environment. It should as well be observed that the traditional Zimbabwean culture is imbued with myths and beliefs transmitted from generation to generation by the 'Masvikiro' spirit mediums who are recognised by society as the African fraternity, believed to be the repository of African history. Indeed, oral history plays an important role in Zimbabwean culture, yet its opponents view it as unreliable and go on to say that it is subject to variations through passage of time, and in the process, loses its essence and reliability. Fortune seems to disagree with these opponents when he stresses that oral history is a means that draws 'great memories' of the past from faithful repositories of human knowledge and experience, which he sees as a prerequisite to the study of the culture, art and history of the people.

Indeed, the importance of oral history should not be minimised in any way, as it is equally true that throughout the world, it is known that before the advent of written records, oral traditions were used as source materials, for example by early writers in the Mediterranean, India and China. Jan Vansina concurs with the idea when he says that oral traditions have a crucial role to play in the reconstruction of the past, as it must always be understood as a reflection of both the present and the past in a single breath.

I now want to briefly touch on the traditional Zimbabwean marriage process and discuss how new life enters our world through childbirth and trace its life span through adult life to death, the end of the journey. In the process, we will examine the African man's beliefs and observe how he interacts with his environment, ritual arts, family and society at large. We shall also analyse the roles he plays towards the living, towards his ancestral spirits as well as towards his creator, *Mwari*, God.

In the Zimbabwean traditional context, marriage is viewed as something that involves the entire families of the two parties. When a boy and girl fall in love, they follow a certain protocol where each part has to inform family members from the most junior to the nucleus parents. This is done so that every member of each family is fully aware of the engagement and possible marriage. In the process, members give their recommendations or disapprovals. In case the parties meet with disapproval, they give up their plans without contesting their elders. In the traditional way, arguing with elders' decision is viewed as being impolite since elders are considered to have seen it all throughout their long lives. On the other hand, if elders approve of the engagement, then protocol is again followed and the prospective husband is expected to pay a dowry in form of money and animals. This is considered a token of appreciation, not by any means buying a wife, as it is often interpreted by those who do not fully understand African culture. Apart from paying the dowry, the bridegroom goes through counselling by elders on how to behave as a husband and, in the same vein, the bride also prepares articles to use as a wife, i.e., baskets, pots, cooking sticks, etc. Before the bride finally goes to her new home, she undergoes special training on how to handle her husband and manage a house. This task is administered by the bride's father's sisters (aunts). It is also the aunts whose duty it is to accompany the bride to her new home and hand her over to the new family, where she is expected to behave as a trusted dignified wife who sticks to one partner.

When the bride has her first pregnancy, the preparations for delivery include lessons on how to handle the new baby; and certain herbal medicines are administered to facilitate normal delivery (without operation).

When the couple is blessed with the first baby, the wife stays with her parents for a couple of months while the family makes sure that the baby and mother are fit to be taken back to their home. The traditional care of the child is that after weaning, the child is given back to the parents of the wife to be taken care of until the age of six to ten years. The child is taught how to behave with members of the family and the public. S/he also does the chores of the community, i.e., herding goats and cattle, fetching water and firewood, hunting, grinding corn, cooking, rituals, preparing herbal medicines, etc. Indeed, this training makes the child a disciplined and a fully balanced citizen who comprehends his hereditary taboos and the rituals which go with them. When the child finally goes to settle with his parents, s/he would have understood the link between the two families and will eventually transmit this knowledge to his/her own offspring. In this way, knowledge is acquired in various ways, i.e., observation, folk tales, association, instruction, imitation of the peer group, etc. The child gradually adapts and fits in his environment as he becomes aware of his relationship to society at large. In the African tradition, all elders deserve respect and one is expected to behave cordially towards all the members of the community.

It should be pointed out that in the traditional Zimbabwean culture divorces were very rare, but in situations which warranted divorce, this was regarded as a serious matter which went through several protocols even up to the chief of the land. In most cases minor issues were settled at lower levels. All in all, divorces were minimal in our society.

However, going back to how traditional knowledge is transmitted from generation to generation, it should be pointed out that from childhood, the child is made aware of the taboos and his relationship with his family, community and society. He is also taught how to observe certain norms of his tribe. He is made aware of his earthly existence and his connection with his ancestral spirits and of worship of the Almighty God (*Mwari*), the creator of heaven and earth. As s/he grows up, s/he is expected to participate in performing roles of appeasing ancestral spirits, how to worship *Mwari*, the creator of the human race and all living and non-living things. He also acquires knowledge on how to use herbal medicines to treat and cure certain diseases or illnesses. In traditional Zimbabwean culture, the transmission of knowledge is carried out orally from generation to generation. This is done through instructions, stories, folklore, drama, poems, praise songs, etc. It should, however, be reiterated that in Zimbabwe there are several ethnic or clan groupings with different languages and dialects, which observe different customs and rituals: for example, while most of the tribes do not circumcise their people, the Fingos and Rembas have for centuries been circumcising their children using traditional methods.

There are also other groups which identify themselves by cutting permanent marks on parts of their bodies. And various tribal groupings have different dances, beliefs, ways of living, etc.

It should be further noted that traditional Zimbabwean people are connected to their tribesmen by their totems (*mutupo*). They are of the monkey, zebra, fish, lion, elephant, etc., clans. As such, they are expected to treat these totems with unquestionable respect. They are not allowed to eat their totems. According to the tradition, if one eats his totem, something evil will befall him. And people of the same totem cannot marry one another: they are to be treated as relatives even if it means distance relationships. Homosexuality of either sex is unheard of in the traditional Zimbabwean culture. However, if a misdemeanour such as having a sexual relationship with someone's wife or daughter is discovered, the tribal courts would try the case and make the culprit pay a heavy fine in money or animals. The penalty varies with the gravity of the crime. For instance, if you behave badly towards your parents you would be asked to take a retreat far away from your village after being stripped off almost all your clothes and dressed in tattered rags. Then you would be jeered at by any person who meets you, a process called 'Kutamba botso'. After a period, the punishment would have served its purpose and you would be accepted back into the community as a reformed person. Such treatment was effective and deterred people from misbehaviour towards their community and society. As a result, misconduct was minimised and peace prevailed.

So far, in our general discussion we have noted various methods of disseminating knowledge in the traditional way in Zimbabwe. It should also be observed that once the African child enters the world he is bound by his tradition from birth to death and even up to life after death. In fact, when he goes sick all herbal medicines are applied with the help of traditional ceremonies administered in order to request his ancestral spirits to intervene. In case s/he dies a certain burial ceremony is administered where the elders request the deceased's ancestral spirits to guide and present his spirit to God.

If, on the other hand, the sick man gets well, because of the treatment or the intervention of ancestral spirits or both, he is expected to brew some beer, kill some cattle or goats and call friends and family members to come and perform some ceremonies as thanksgiving to the spirits and Mwari. The African person grows knowing the existence of good and bad spirits and God the Almighty.

Ruth Finnegan seems to lament the opponents of oral tradition when she says the current significance of oral tradition is being 'played down', if not overlooked completely by those societies whose assumption is that written literature is the highest form of knowledge. After all, no meaningful literature can be produced without inputs from oral history.

All in all, this paper attempts to portray how the traditional Zimbabwean culture is passed from father to son and mother to daughter. It has also demonstrated that generally, traditional African culture is complete in its own context and that by no means should it be viewed as inferior to other cultures of the world.

List of Contributors

Sunderlal Bahuguna	Chipko Information Centre P.O. Silyara - 249 155 Via Ghansali, Tehri Garhwal (U.P.)
A.K. Das	Professer of Museology National Museum Institute Janpath New Delhi - 110 011
Ajay Vishwas Dandekar	C/o Shri R.K. Parachure B - 3, NIA - Baner Road Balewadi, Pune - 411 045 (Maha.)
H.M.D.R. Herath	Department of Sociology University of Peradeniya Peradenia (Sri Lanka)
Rajiv Ranjan Jha	Badlao Founation Mihijam, Dumka - 815 354 (Bihar)
Molly Kaushal	Research Officer Indira Gandhi National Centre for the Arts Central Vista, Janpath New Delhi - 110 001
Rakesh Khanduri	Assistant Curator International Roerich Memorial Trust Hall Estate P.O. Naggar - 175 130 Kullu Dist. (H.P.)

John V. Kingston	Regional Director UNESCO 8, Poorvi Marg, Vasant Vihar New Delhi - 110 067
R.P. Lama	Sammelan Bhavan 15, Sonam Wangdi Road Darjeeling - 734 101 (West Bengal)
Charles Samson Makari	Director National Arts Council of Zimbabwe Kufara House 101 Robert Mugabe Road, Box UA 463, Union Avenue, Harare, Zimbabwe
B.L. Malla	Research Associate Indira Gandhi National Centre for the Arts Central Vista, Janpath New Delhi - 110 001
A.S. Mishra	Central Soil and Water Conservation Research and Training Institute, 218, Kaulagarh Road, Dehradun - 248 195 (U.P.)
R.S. Negi	29-A Circular Road Dehradun - 248 001 (U.P.)
T.N. Pandit	C/36 Pamposh Enclave New Delhi - 110 048
Ramakar Pant	Research Associate Indira Gandhi National Centre for the Arts Central Vista, Janpath New Delhi - 110 001
P.S. Ramakrishnan	School of Environmental Sciences Jawaharlal Nehru University

	New Delhi - 110 067
D.S. Rasaily	Woodland Villa Above DRC Godown 622, Hill Cart Road, Darjeeling - 734 101 (West Bengal)
Sachchidananda	157, Kadam Kuan, New Area Patna - 800 003 (Bihar)
Baidyanath Saraswati	Unesco Professor Indira Gandhi National Centre for the Arts Central Vista, Janpath, New Delhi - 110 001
Kapila Vatsyayan	Academic Director Indira Gandhi National Centre for the Arts Central Vista, Janpath, New Delhi - 110 001
Virginius Xaxa.	Department of Sociology Delhi School of Economics University of Delhi Delhi - 110 007

Plate 4.1: Damaged girder bridge at Ganeshpur near Uttarkashi town after the earthquake.

Plate 4.2: Damaged house as a result of earthquake of Jamak village in Uttarkashi.

Plate 4.3: Deforestation has resulted in the failure of slope, which has given rise to landslide.

Plate 4.4: Garbage left by tourist at Gangotri.

Plate 4.5: Landslide at village Ongi, Uttarkashi continues threat to travellers and pilgrims.

↑ Plate 4.6
Patch after the forest fire
near Budhakedar village, Tehri.

→
Plate 6.1
Gaddi couple in
traditional Gaddi dress.

↑
Plate 6.2
A view of
Chauṛasi temple complex.

↑
Plate 6.3
Gaddi shephered and his folk on move.

Plate 6.4
Gaddi samans in Chaurasi,
on Pilgrimage to mount Mani Mahesh
↓

Plate 6.5
A view of Mani Mahesh.
↓

Plate 6.6: A view of Bharmour village

Plate 13.1; An Onge couple.

Plate 13.2
Jarwa boy
bearing a
bark sheath
→

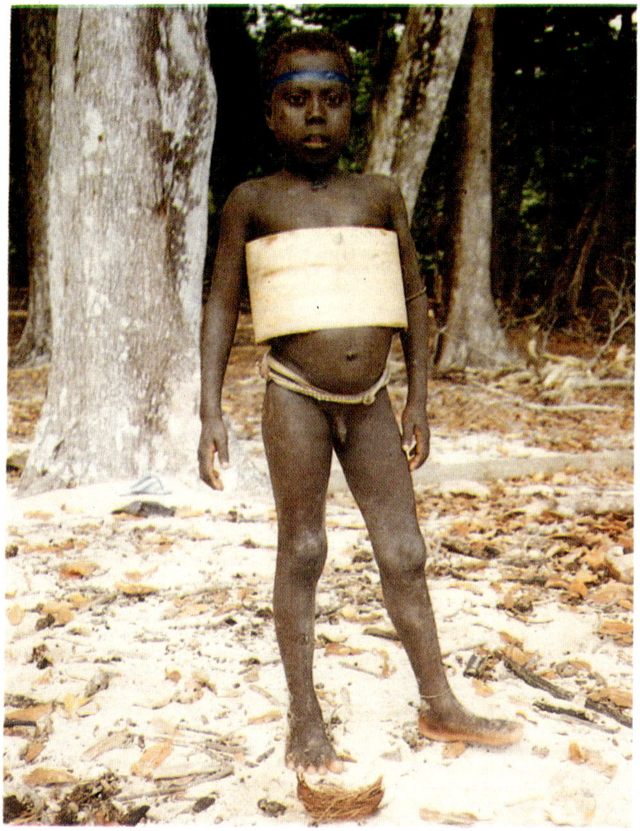

↓ Plate 13.3
Jarwa couple
with their baby

Plate 13.4
Jarwa women and children on the beach
with a fishing net.

↑ Plate 13.5
Jarwa collecting gifts.

↑ Plate 13.6
A Nicobarese hut
in a Car-Nicobar village.

Plate 13.7: Nicobarese boys dancing in their village in Car-Nicobar.

Plate 13.8: Sentinelese men using their adze for retreiving coconuts from the sea.